T0388285

Field Studies in Environmental Criminology

This book includes fieldwork from five continents and demonstrates the breadth of techniques used by environmental criminologists to understand crime.

Environmental criminologists seek to understand crime within the physical, and even digital, contexts where it occurs – believing that crime occurs when people converge in time and space and that the environment impacts the opportunity for crime. Understanding the environment aids the researcher in answering an essential question: what can be done to alter the place to prevent or reduce crime? However, to understand complex environmental influences, researchers need to engage in fieldwork. Fieldwork involves researchers entering the environment they are studying to observe, listen, and experience the surroundings in a way that influences their understanding of the place and people in the environment.

This book highlights the broad array of crime types – from package theft in the suburbs to poaching in the Nile basin – that environmental criminology is well suited to address. Finally, it advances methods and techniques, tests established protocols, and offers reflections on experiences during fieldwork, demonstrating the value of the techniques for environmental criminology and offering solutions to crime problems.

The chapters in this book were originally published in special issues of *Criminal Justice Studies*.

Ben Stickle is Associate Professor of Criminal Justice at Middle Tennessee State University. With nearly twenty years of practitioner experience, his research interests include policing, crime prevention, and property crime (e.g., metal theft and package theft). He has published widely in scholarly journals, books, and other outlets.

Field Studies in Environmental Criminology

Edited by
Ben Stickle

LONDON AND NEW YORK

First published 2022
by Routledge
4 Park Square, Milton Park, Abingdon, Oxon OX14 4RN

and by Routledge
605 Third Avenue, New York, NY 10158

Routledge is an imprint of the Taylor & Francis Group, an informa business

British Library Cataloguing in Publication Data
A catalogue record for this book is available from the British Library

ISBN: 978-1-032-14633-1 (hbk)
ISBN: 978-1-032-14634-8 (pbk)
ISBN: 978-1-003-24028-0 (ebk)

DOI: 10.4324/9781003240280

Typeset in Myriad Pro
by Newgen Publishing UK

Publisher's Note
The publisher accepts responsibility for any inconsistencies that may have arisen during the conversion of this book from journal articles to book chapters, namely the inclusion of journal terminology.

Contents

Citation Information

The following chapters, except chapter 6, were originally published in *Criminal Justice Studies*, volume 32, issue 2 (2019). Chapter 6 was originally published in volume 33, issue 2 (2020) of the same journal. When citing this material, please use the original page numbering for each article, as follows:

Chapter 1
Provoked poachers? Applying a situational precipitator framework to examine the nexus between human-wildlife conflict, retaliatory killings, and poaching
William D. Moreto
Criminal Justice Studies, volume 32, issue 2 (2019), pp. 63–80

Chapter 2
When a loved one is on community supervision: the crime controller strategies used by 'PoPPs' (parents/partners/peers of probationers and parolees)
Lacey Schaefer, Emily Moir and Gemma C. Williams
Criminal Justice Studies, volume 32, issue 2 (2019), pp. 81–98

Chapter 3
Putting qualitative methodology in perspective: reflections on the relevance of fieldwork into the field of Environmental Criminology
Elenice Oliveira
Criminal Justice Studies, volume 32, issue 2 (2019), pp. 99–119

Chapter 4
Exploring the influence of daily microroutines on residential guardianship and monitoring patterns
Emily Moir, Danielle M. Reynald, Timothy C. Hart and Anna Stewart
Criminal Justice Studies, volume 32, issue 2 (2019), pp. 120–139

Chapter 5
Yelping about a good time: casino popularity and crime
Virginia Sosa, Gisela Bichler and Lianna Quintero
Criminal Justice Studies, volume 32, issue 2 (2019), pp. 140–164

Chapter 6

Porch pirates: examining unattended package theft through crime script analysis
Ben Stickle, Melody Hicks, Amy Stickle and Zachary Hutchinson
Criminal Justice Studies, volume 33, issue 2 (2020), pp. 79–95

Chapter 7

Fieldwork protocol as a safety inventory tool in public places
Vania Ceccato
Criminal Justice Studies, volume 32, issue 2 (2019), pp. 165–188

For any permission-related enquiries please visit:
www.tandfonline.com/page/help/permissions

Notes on Contributors

Gisela Bichler is Professor of Criminal Justice at California State University, San Bernardino. Her recent scholarship explores the interplay between the environment and offending behavior, with an emphasis on the influence of social networks.

Vania Ceccato is Professor at the Department of Urban Planning and Environment, School of Architecture and the Built Environment, KTH Royal Institute of Technology, Stockholm, Sweden. She coordinates the national network Safeplaces (Säkraplatser). Ceccato is interested in the relationship between the built environment and safety, in particular, the space-time dynamics of crime and people's routine activity.

Timothy C. Hart is Assistant Professor in the Department of Criminology and Criminal Justice at the University of Tampa, Florida. His areas of interest include survey research, applied statistics, geographic information systems (GIS), and victimisation. His scholarship appears in the *Journal of Quantitative Criminology*, the *Journal of Research in Crime and Delinquency*, *Criminal Justice and Behavior*, and the *British Journal of Criminology.*

Melody Hicks is a graduate teaching assistant in the Criminal Justice Administration Department at Middle Tennessee State University. Her research interests include crime analysis, situational crime prevention, corrections, and substantive criminal law.

Zachary Hutchinson holds a bachelor's degree in Criminal Justice Administration and is pursuing a degree in Computer Science from Middle Tennessee State University. His research interests involve crime data analysis and crime trend modeling.

Emily Moir is Lecturer in the School of Criminology and Criminal Justice, Griffith University and a member of the Griffith Criminology Institute in Brisbane, Australia. Her PhD examined Guardianship In Action (GIA) in the Brisbane suburbs. Her other research interests include situational crime prevention, crime prevention through environmental design, and elder abuse prevention.

William D. Moreto is Assistant Professor in the Department of Criminal Justice at the University of Central Florida. He received his PhD from the Rutgers School of Criminal Justice in 2013. His research centers on the study of wildlife crime, wildlife law enforcement, environmental criminology and crime science, situational crime prevention, policing, and conservation social science.

Elenice Oliveira is Assistant Professor in the Justice Studies Department at Montclair State University. Her research has focused on policing and crime prevention, crime opportunity and spatial analysis, and international and comparative research on crime and criminal justice.

Lianna Quintero is a research assistant in the Center for Criminal Justice Research. Her academic area of specialization is crime analysis.

Danielle M. Reynald is Senior Lecturer in the School of Criminology and Criminal Justice at Griffith University and a criminologist at the Griffith Criminology Institute in Brisbane, Australia. Her research focuses on how guardianship functions as a crime control mechanism in a variety of domains (including in residential, workplace, public, and cyber contexts), crime prevention through environmental design, and offender decision-making.

Lacey Schaefer is Senior Lecturer in the School of Criminology and Criminal Justice at Griffith University and a Research Fellow with the Griffith Criminology Institute. She holds research expertise in criminological theory and correctional ideologies and interventions.

Virginia Sosa is a research assistant in the Center for Criminal Justice Research. Her academic area of specialization is crime analysis.

Anna Stewart is Professor in the School of Criminology and Criminal Justice, Griffith University and a member of the Griffith Criminology Institute in Brisbane, Australia. She is interested in the use of government administrative data, and has examined the longitudinal contacts individuals have with child protection, youth justice, and adult criminal justice system.

Amy Stickle is Mathematics Lecturer in the University Studies Division at Middle Tennessee State University. Teaching courses in Algebra and Statistics, her research interests include math anxiety and the application of mathematical and statistical concepts in criminal justice.

Ben Stickle is Associate Professor of Criminal Justice Administration at Middle Tennessee State University. With nearly twenty years of practitioner experience, his research focus is on applying theory to practice in the areas of policing, crime prevention, and property crime.

Gemma C. Williams is a PhD student in the School of Criminology and Criminal Justice at Griffith University. Her doctoral thesis uses a matched pair longitudinal design to examine how prisoners' expectations of reentry correspond with their actual reentry experiences. Her research interests include reentry, correctional practices, and desistance.

Introduction

Ben Stickle

Field Studies in Environmental Criminology highlights the merger of theory and method to understand crime better. While not unique to this book, this merger is vital for advancing the study of crime and crime prevention techniques. Environmental criminologists seek to understand crime within the physical (and even digital) contexts where it occurs—appreciating that crime happens in a place and that the people and things in that place impact what occurs. Field studies also aid researchers in answering an essential question, what can be done to alter the environment to prevent or reduce crime? This book highlights a collection of research that answers this fundamental question through seven research chapters based on environmental criminology perspectives and fieldwork.

Environmental criminology is a group of theories that focus on the criminal event and the immediate circumstances in which they occur (see Wortley & Townsley, 2016). One of the unique aspects of these theories is that they focus on using the environment to shape and change opportunity structure rather than concern over the personality, genetic makeup, or motivation of an offender. In other words, environmental criminology argues that "criminal events must be understood as confluences of offenders, victims or criminal targets and laws in specific settings at particular times and places" (Brantingham & Brantingham 1991, p. 2). As such, research using these theories can identify, test, and evaluate techniques to reduce or even prevent crime.

This book provides important examples of how these approaches address crime, confirm or enhance research methods, and develop prevention techniques. For example, in Chapter 3 by Elenice Oliveira, the author reflected upon her experiences, challenges, and successes of conducting field studies in Brazilian Favelas (a densely populated ghetto or slum). Oliveira's fieldwork allowed her to encounter and identify aspects of Favelas that could not be captured by maps, photos, or other quantitative methods. The results include a better understanding of the environment where crimes occur and the persons involved (offenders, victims, and police officers). Further, Chapter 5 by Virginia Sosa, Gisela Bichler, and Lianna Quintero uses a novel approach of analyzing Yelp reviews of casinos and comparing those reviews to area crime rates. The findings demonstrate that publicly available data can be used to investigate the criminogenic capacity of risky facilities. Moreover, this process of digital fieldwork offers a unique example of how digital information can help understand and evaluate the physical environment.

Field studies have been a cornerstone of social science research since its inception. Field studies are the process by which researchers always enter the physical or digital environment and often the social environment of those being studied to understand the activities of people in these places. This research style passes beyond the boundaries of quantitative studies, comprised of surveys, opinions, reflections and scores, ranks, and static measures. Field studies are more qualitative and seek to understand the nuances of those being studied. However, this research style is demanding, time-consuming, full of pitfalls, and can even be dangerous. Perhaps this is why field studies have fallen out of favor over the last few decades, with fewer published studies.

However, field studies are essential for many reasons. First, field studies help establish and ground a new area of research. This grounding is critical when studying crime because without a thorough understanding of those involved in a crime (e.g., offenders, victims, witnesses), it is challenging to develop a quantitative method to understand the crime and those involved. For example, one of the first studies on package theft is included in Chapter 6 by Ben Stickle, Melody Hicks, Amy Stickle, and Zachary Hutchinson. With minimal qualitative data on this emerging crime type, the study conducted a video data analysis of surveillance footage of thieves in action. The knowledge gained from this research then served as the basis for a follow-up study that enabled researchers to define package theft and develop a survey that resulted in estimates of prevalence, costs, and fear associated with package theft (see Hicks et al., 2022).

Secondly, field studies can produce a knowledge-based experience that helps confirm previous research. On occasion, the only data available on a crime or prevention method requires evaluation through quantitative means. However, it is not easy to know how accurate these findings are until fieldwork can establish the accuracy of the data or interpretation of the data. For example, in Chapter 7, Vania Ceccato led a research team into parks, transportation facilities, and shopping areas in Stockholm, Sweeden, to study a previously established research process (Field Protocols) validity, reliability, and generalizability. Ceccato concluded that Fieldwork Protocols, which provides valuable insight to enhance date collection for future studies, are better suited in structured environments (e.g., subway stations) than less structured environments (e.g., parks). Similarly, Chapter 2 by Lacey Schaefer, Emily Moir, and Gemma C. Williams, utilized field interviews and observation of probation and parole officers who use the Triple-S: Social Supports in Supervision method to engage clients. Their research identified eight strategies commonly used by community supervision officers to successfully implement social support crime control strategies among offenders, confirming previous research and helping establish what works with this strategy.

Lastly, field studies allow us to understand how the environment impacts crime and crime prevention techniques. Crime does not occur in a vacuum, and other people and the physical environment impact crime. However, this is not always easy to capture with traditional research methods. Researchers conducted in a field study can observe, listen, and experience the surroundings in a way that impacts the researcher's understanding of the events that occur in that place. For example, in the first chapter by William D. Moreto, factors affecting human–wildlife conflict are examined after the researcher spent time in Uganda observing, interviewing, and working alongside wildlife officers. The study reveals how human–wildlife conflict can provoke individuals to engage in retaliatory killings and poaching. Understanding the complex interplay between society and their environment (including animals) allows the researcher to learn why human–wildlife conflict occurs and develop suggestions to prevent it. Similarly, Chapter 4 by Emily Moir, Danielle M. Reynald, Timothy C. Hart, and Anna Stewart expands on previous studies of guardianship and routine activities in neighborhoods. The research team visited homes in Brisbane, Australia, asking about resident's routine activities within their homes. They used this information to understand how microroutines impact neighborhood surveillance, enhancing what is known about residential guardianship.

By including field studies in environmental criminology from five continents, this book demonstrates the breadth of application in technique, crime type, and method that environmental criminology has contributed to the study of crime and crime prevention. It advances the topic through methods and techniques, testing established protocols, and reflecting on experiences that demonstrate the value of field studies and environmental criminology. Field studies in environmental criminology are helpful for researchers, policymakers, and practitioners alike to understand the complex interplay between society and the environment while enhancing what we know about crime and how to respond to it.

References

Brantingham, P. J., & Brantingham, P. L. (Eds.). (1991). Introduction to the 1991 reissue: Notes on environmental criminology. In *Environmental Criminology* (pp. 1–6). Waveland Press: Long Grove, Illinois.

Hicks, M., Stickle, B., & Harms, J. (2022). Assessing the fear of package theft. *American Journal of Criminal Justice*. https://doi.org/10.1007/s12103-020-09600-x

Wortley, R., & Townsley, M. (Eds.). (2016). *Environmental Criminology and Crime Analysis*. Taylor & Francis: Oxfordshire, United Kingdom.

Provoked poachers? Applying a situational precipitator framework to examine the nexus between human-wildlife conflict, retaliatory killings, and poaching

William D. Moreto

ABSTRACT

The poaching of wildlife has received substantial interest from criminologists in recent years. In particular, prior research has attempted to better understand the factors that drive individuals to engage in such behavior. One driver that has been acknowledged is human-wildlife conflict. To date, however, there has been little research examining the situational factors that link human-wildlife conflict, retaliatory killings, and poaching. Moreover, there are few studies that have attempted to theoretically explain such convergence. Based on fieldwork in Uganda, and drawn from data collected from formal interviews, participant observation, and informal conversations with rangers, the present study demonstrates the utility of viewing the intersection between human-wildlife conflict, retaliatory killings, and poaching from a situational precipitator framework. Findings suggest that human-wildlife conflict can prompt, pressure, permit, and provoke individuals to engage in both retaliatory killings and poaching. Additionally, it was found that human-wildlife conflict directly influences community-ranger relations in Uganda.

Implications for theory, practice, and prevention are discussed.

Introduction

It has been proposed that the world is entering its sixth mass extinction (Ceballos, García, & Ehrlich, 2010). Concerns from the scientific community and the public (see Hilton-Taylor et al., 2009) have drawn attention to the 'wicked problem' (Rittel & Webber, 1973) of declining global biodiversity and increasing extinction rates. Historically, the study of environmental issues has tended to operate from a natural sciences orientation, however, scholars have recently called for the integration of the social sciences to better account for the human dimensions of environmental matters. In an article by Bennett and colleagues (2017), the authors identified 18 distinct conservation social science orientations, including environmental sociology, human-environment geography, and environmental economics, considered to be useful in such an endeavour. Notably missing from this list, unfortunately, is the role of criminology.

Although still relatively new in criminology, the study of environment-related topics has generated considerable interest from researchers in the last two decades. Specifically, criminologists have examined a variety of topics, including illegal wildlife markets (Moreto & Lemieux, 2015a; van Uhm, 2016; Wyatt, 2009), illegal fishing (Petrossian & Clarke, 2014), climate change (White, 2018), and wildlife law enforcement (Cowan, Burton, & Moreto, 2019; Moreto, Cowan, & Burton, 2018). In addition to these areas, one line of research that has received substantial consideration from criminologists is the poaching – or the illegal taking – of wildlife species. Indeed, poaching has received a considerable amount of attention of researchers from a variety of disciplines. Prior studies on poaching have largely focused on three main areas: examining the commission of the act itself (Moreto & Lemieux, 2015b; Warchol & Harrington, 2016), the framing of such activities and the associated harms that surpass the limitations of a purely legalistic perspective (White, 2008), and the driving factors and motivations that result in individuals committing such acts (Bell, Hampshire, & Topalidou, 2007; Forsyth & Marckese, 1993; Muth & Bowe, 1998; Von Essen, Hansen, Kallstrom, Peterson, & Peterson, 2014; Wyatt, 2013).

Based on fieldwork conducted in 2014, which resulted in 89 face-to-face interviews with law enforcement and community conservation rangers, this research contributes to the criminological study of human-wildlife conflict (HWC) and wildlife crime by examining the situational factors that influence both in Uganda. Using a situational precipitator framework, the present study assesses how HWC can prompt, pressure, permit, and provoke individuals to poach or illegally kill wildlife species. Additionally, this study examines how HWC influences community-ranger relations to further understand the immediate context in which anti-poaching initiatives are designed and implemented. Implications for theory and practice of both environmental criminology and conservation science are also addressed.

Poaching and poachers: a contested designation

From a purely legal standpoint, the terms 'poacher' and 'poaching' broadly refers to hunting or harvesting practices that contravene or violate local, national, regional, and international laws. The hunting or harvesting of endangered fauna and flora species, the hunting or harvesting of wildlife in protected or private land without prior authorization, and illegal hunting practices during legal hunting seasons (i.e. 'spotlighting' or the use of high-powered lights to identify and blind wildlife at night) are examples of what would constitute as poaching based on this definition.

However, the act of poaching and the resulting label of poacher to individuals who engage in such activities is controversial (Von Essen et al., 2014). This is especially the case for traditional hunting practices that have been deemed illegal, or when laws and regulations disproportionately impact indigenous populations. The social construction of poaching as a crime also contributes to this controversy. Scholars have noted that despite the illegality of such actions, poaching may not be deviant within specific subcultures. Such actions are deemed to be relatively harmless and do not 'tarnish the identity of those who commit them' (Phillips, Mitchell, & Murrell, 2014, p. 283). For example, Forsyth and colleagues (1998) conducted interviews with both poachers and game wardens in Louisiana, USA, and found support that poaching was viewed as a folk crime that had both instrumental (i.e. for survival) and affective (i.e. traditional practices) purposes.

Given the contested conceptualization and designation of poaching, it is not surprising that prior research attempting to develop poacher typologies has led to the identification of a wide variation of individuals and their rationale for poaching. Previous scholars have found that individuals are motivated to poach due to subsistence and personal use resulting from poverty, for commercial gain and profit, for recreation or thrill seeking, and for the attainment of pets and trophies (Leberatto, 2016; Moreto & Lemieux, 2015b; Muth & Bower, 1998; Warchol, 2004; Wyatt, 2013). Other researchers have found support for broader macro-level factors influencing poaching behaviors, including political economy forces such as capitalism and colonialism (Gibson, 1999), political rebellion (Bell et al., 2007), and longstanding cultural and traditional practices, such as the use of traditional Asian medicine (Schneider, 2012) or the consumption of bushmeat (Brasheres et al., 2004).

Prior assessments have also identified HWC as a main contributor to wildlife crime. Shepherd and Magnus (2004), for instance, found that retaliatory killings – or the killing of wildlife species as a direct result of HWC – were attributed to human-tiger conflict, and that such killings contributed to the inclusion of tiger products into the illegal market. HWC is one of the central problems facing conservation today and is likely to become an enduring issue given the growth of human populations and ongoing competition over land, water, and other resources between people and wildlife (see Campbell, Gichohi, Mwangi, & Chege, 2000).

Understanding the proximal, situational elements of human-wildlife conflict: implications for poaching and its prevention

Most of the drivers described in the previous section are distal correlates of poaching. Such factors tend to be enduring, multi-faceted, and very difficult to solve. Conversely, examining proximal correlates – or factors that are more situational and are explicitly linked to specific problems in a particular time and space (Ekblom, 1994) – provides an opportunity to develop strategies, including situational crime prevention (SCP), that can have an immediate impact in preventing or reducing human-wildlife conflict (HWC) and poaching (Moreto & Pires, 2018). As will be discussed in more detail later, by explicitly investigating the situational elements of HWC, a more comprehensive and holistic assessment of the social factors that influence such conflict can also be understood (see Dickman, 2010). While broader macro-level factors will undeniably exist, the manifestation of these influences may not necessarily be clear or immediately understood. Moreover, macro-level explanations may be limited in explaining the central situational elements that may promote or hinder HWC and subsequently retaliatory killings and poaching.

Environmental criminology concepts and theories are well-suited to assess and examine the situational elements of HWC and poaching (see Moreto & Pires, 2018). Although not explicitly operating from an environmental criminology perspective, prior scholars have assessed the role of situational characteristics in influencing HWC. For example, in their study of livestock predation by endangered African wild dogs in Botswana, Gusset and colleagues (2009) found that HWC declined as distance from protected areas (PAs) increased. Moreover, poor guardianship and place management, as indicated by ineffective husbandry practices during the day, also led to HWC. Similar results were found by Ogada, Woodroffe, Oguge, and Frank (2003) in Kenya, where the lowest livestock predation rates were associated with attentive herding during the day, and enclosure in *bomas* (traditional corrals) at night.

Environmental criminology approaches have also been used to examine poaching. The routine activity approach has been used to investigate trophy poaching in the United States (Eliason, 2012) and abalone poaching in South Africa (Warchol & Harrington, 2016). In a recent study by van Doormall, Lemieux, and Ruiter (2018), the rational choice perspective was utilized to examine illegal border crossings by rhino poachers in South Africa. The authors found that poachers preferred to enter and exit reserves where there were high densities of rhino. Moreover, they determined that high road densities were associated with the odds of an illegal entry. Notably, the study of poaching has also led to the extension of established frameworks as well. In their assessment of poaching in a Ugandan PA, Moreto and Lemieux (2015b) proposed that the routine activity crime triangle needed to be adjusted to account for the influence of different poaching techniques on the intersection in space and time between offenders and targets (i.e. such intersection would differ between poachers who use snares compared to those that use firearms).

From a crime prevention standpoint, researchers have also suggested the use of SCP as an alternative to traditional anti-poaching measures (e.g. ranger patrols) to prevent and reduce poaching (Kurland, Pires, McFann, & Moreto, 2017; Lemieux, 2014; Moreto & Pires, 2018; Pires & Moreto, 2011). These strategies aim to alter the immediate built and natural environment where crime occurs to make criminal activity riskier, more difficult, and less rewarding, while also removing potential excuses or provocations. The latter is particularly relevant to the current study as it provides an explanation of the link between HWC, retaliatory killings, and poaching of wildlife. Specifically, HWC events can incite individuals to engage in, or be willing to allow poaching or illegal kills of problem wildlife.

Situational precipitators: a framework to link human-wildlife conflict, retaliatory killings, and poaching

Situational precipitators are 'any aspect of the immediate environment that creates, triggers or intensifies the motivation to commit crime' (Wortley, 2017, p. 63). The situational precipitators of crime (SPC) conceptual framework was partly developed to address two main concerns levied against SCP during the 1990s: 1) its emphasis on target hardening strategies, and 2) its reliance on the rational choice perspective (Wortley, 1996). In a series of publications, Wortley (1997, 1998, 2001) proposed that operating from solely a bounded rational choice perspective (RCP) was inadequate in sufficiently appreciating the person-situation interaction that existed during crime commission. He argued that situations themselves can actively create an environment where crime is viewed as an appropriate response. In other words, the immediate environment is not simply a backdrop for crime; it can stimulate criminal behavior.

Wortley (2017) outlines four different types of precipitators: *prompts* are elements of the immediate environment that initiate underlying thoughts, feelings, and desires. Prompts can trigger and signal criminal behavior, as well as provide models for learning and imitating problematic activities. Situational prompts can also provide information on expectancies, which can result in individuals responding or reacting to predetermined notions of particular situations. Another type of precipitator are *pressures*. Pressures refer to the coercive influence that situations may place on individuals to conform, obey, and comply or defy. The pressures provided by situations can also provide individuals with a sense of anonymity. *Permissions* are another type of precipitator and provides avenues for individuals to neutralize feelings of guilt or liability. This includes the ability to minimize rules, responsibility, consequences, and victims. The final precipitator, *provocations*, refers to situations that result in stress leading to anti-social responses, including those that involve some level of aggression.

When comparing RCP and SPC, a clear distinction can be found. SPC focused on the *antecedents* (e.g. incidents and stimuli) of contemplated criminal behavior, while the RCP focused on the *consequences* (e.g. decisions) of contemplated criminal behavior. Notably, offender motivation is viewed to be situationally dependent and can fluctuate within a SPC orientation, while RCP views motivation to be a constant. The psychological processes involved in SPC operates at a sub-cognitive level, whereas it is at a conscious level within RCP. Finally, an SPC approach considers offenders to have little control over criminal acts, while RCP views such criminal actions to be deliberative.

Despite operating from different orientations, RCP and SPC should be viewed as complementary perspectives that provide a more holistic understanding of the person-situation nexus. As Wortley (2017) states: 'The first stage of offending involves the situational forces that ready the potential offender for crime (precipitators); the second stage involves an assessment of the criminal opportunities (rational choice)' (66). For the present paper, emphasis will be placed on the first stage of offending and the situational elements that pressure, permit, and provoke individuals to poach or illegally hunt.

Further understanding the existence of situational precipitators has considerable implications for crime prevention. Indeed, the refinement and expansion of SCP was largely due to the recognition of the influential role that situational precipitators had on offender decision making (see Cornish & Clarke, 2003). Specifically, SCP was extended to include several strategies to address precipitating elements, including reducing frustration and stress, avoiding disputes, and reducing emotional arousal. Such knowledge would also prove to be useful within the scope of wildlife crime prevention. By examining the crime itself, a more tailored prevention strategy can be developed would could ultimately result in a more effective approach (Moreto & Pires, 2018). Furthermore, appreciating the existence and role of situational precipitators can lead to contextually and ethically appropriate measures minimizing counterproductive or even harmful outcomes (see von Hirsch, Garland, & Wakefield, 2000).

Current study

This research stems from a larger study that examined ranger culture and operations within the Uganda Wildlife Authority (UWA) based on frontline ranger experiences and perceptions. The topics covered ranged from occupational stress to community-ranger relations. Questions related to illegal activities and HWC were also examined, which is the basis for the current study. Given their experiences and interactions with local communities, as well as the variation in their roles and responsibilities (i.e. rangers are required to respond to problem wildlife in protected areas; see Moreto & Matusiak, 2017), it was determined that frontline rangers would be able to provide comprehensive insight necessary for study objectives.

This research examines situationally dependent elements of HWC that create and establish a context where retaliatory killings and poaching are viewed to be an appropriate alternative or response. Prior research suggesting that HWC is related to poaching has tended to be largely descriptive and atheoretical. Furthermore, previous studies have tended to assume retaliatory killings fall within the broader category of poaching. The present study contributes to the existing literature by providing a theoretical framework to better understand the nexus between HWC, retaliatory killings, and poaching. By doing so, it is suggested that situational crime prevention measures can then be developed to address minimize HWC thereby reducing retaliatory killing and poaching of wildlife. Moreover, by focusing on HWC as opposed to poaching, which is often the objective of law enforcement or anti-poaching initiatives, it is believed that community engagement and stewardship can be fostered in a more direct and collaborative manner. Thus, the research objectives for this study are two-fold: first, to examine the impact of human-wildlife conflict on the community-ranger relations in Uganda. Next, to assess the applicability of the situational precipitator framework in illuminating the nexus between human-wildlife conflict, retaliatory killings, and poaching in Uganda.

Study setting

The Republic of Uganda is a landlocked nation located in East Africa. Identified to be a key nation in wildlife trafficking, particularly the illegal ivory trade, as both a source and transit location (Rossi, 2018; Runhovde, in press), Uganda is one of the most biodiversity-rich countries in the world. The governing agency responsible for Uganda's PAs and wildlife is the Uganda Wildlife Authority (UWA). Within the UWA, there are several departments, including community conservation, law enforcement, tourism, and monitoring and research, amongst others.

Data for the present study was collected from five study sites: Kibale National Park, Lake Mburo National Park, Queen Elizabeth National Park, the UWA headquarters in Kampala, and the Entebbe International Airport/Uganda Wildlife Education Center (UWEC). The three national parks were chosen due to variability in topography, size, and organizational characteristics, while the UWA headquarters and Entebbe International Airport/UWEC provided additional insight on wildlife crime matters within the region.

Data and methods

Data collection occurred between June and August 2014. After arriving at each study site, the author met with management and command staff of the community conservation, law enforcement, and monitoring and research departments of the UWA to discuss study objectives and logistics. An administrative personnel list was provided and used as a sampling frame for interviews. A mixed, nested purposeful sampling strategy was used, specifically a utilization-focused, operational construct sampling approach (Patton, 2015). A utilization-focused sampling 'involves selecting cases that will be relevant to the issues and decisions of concern to an identifiable group of stakeholders and intended users' and is developed to examine 'factors and explanations [that] can be used to inform decision-making and support programs, practices, and/or policy improvements' (Patton, 201, p.295). Operational construct sampling requires 'selecting real-world examples' with the objective of 'deepening or verifying theory in new contexts, new time periods, or new situations' (Patton, 2015, p.289). For the present study, community conservation, law enforcement, and intelligence UWA rangers were included. Nested within this larger sampling strategy was a homogenous approach sampling approach which involved the explicit sampling of female respondents.

In total, 89 rangers were formally interviewed, representing 32 per cent of the total ranger population within the study areas. Most of study participants were male (84 per cent) and the response rate for the interviews was 98 per cent. Of the 89 respondents, 73 (82%) consented to have the interview digitally recorded. For interviews that did not involve a recording device, detailed field notes were taken by the author. All interviews were conducted in private and face-to-face. The interview guide was semi-structured and included open-ended, questions, enabling the author to inquire about similar topics throughout the interviews, while also providing space for additional probing. Interviews lasted about one hour on average. Informed consent was provided to all participants and verbal consent was acquired for confidentiality purposes. Sampling continued until theoretical sufficiency (Dey, 1999) was reached, which was determined by preliminary coding of completed interviews during data collection.

In addition to the formal interviews, the author participated in approximately 600 hours of observation, including participant observation of ranger foot patrols. Such observations were useful in informally interacting with rangers and witnessing their daily activities. Importantly, such an approach was useful in developing trust and rapport (see Moreto, 2017), while also supplementing and providing insight on how to appropriately contextualize data from interviews (Patton, 2015). Daily interactions with study participants also led to several informal conversations which were documented through detailed field notes.

Data was analyzed using ATLAS.ti 7, a computer-assisted qualitative data analysis program. As a result of the research objectives (i.e. the first exploratory, while the second was theoretically grounded), two distinct analytical processes were used. For the first research objective, and as a result of its exploratory nature, a two-prong analytical approach was used: first, data was separated into distinct sections to identify basic similarities and differences (Saldaña, 2016). For the first objective, 18 distinct codes were identified from study participants' responses. Next, pattern coding, which involves the identification of overarching themes, was then completed and is presented below (Miles & Huberman, 1994). For the second research objective, hypothesis coding, which involves the 'application of a researcher-generated, predetermined list of codes' (Saldaña, 2016, p. 171), was first completed. In total, 21 codes were identified in this first stage. Second, elaborative coding or the analysis of 'textual data in order to develop theory further' was performed (Auerbach & Silverstein, 2003, p. 104).

Findings

This research contributes to the criminological and conservation science literature by theoretically exploring the intersection between human-wildlife conflict (HWC), retaliatory killings, and the poaching of wildlife in protected areas in Uganda. Additionally, this study also examines how HWC can influence interpersonal dynamics between community members and frontline criminal justice actors, namely rangers. The findings for the latter are presented first, then the findings from a situational precipitators assessment afterward. Pseudonyms are used to protect the identity of the study participants, and their responses are presented verbatim.

'People pointing fingers at us': the impact of human-wildlife conflict on community-ranger relations

Community-ranger relations in Uganda is complex and multi-faceted. This is complicated by the varied responsibilities and roles designated to specific departments, particularly community conservation and law enforcement. Collectively, these two departments are responsible for a number of tasks, including enforcing the law, community education and outreach, and responding to HWC and problem species.

In general, study participants felt that that relationship between the community and the rangers was mixed. While respondents believed that community members generally respected rangers, and would be willing to cooperate and provide information, they also felt that there was still an issue with trust between the two parties. Respondents also felt that community members distinguished between rangers working in different departments, and viewed those working in community conservation in a more favorable light than those in law enforcement (see also Moreto, Brunson, & Braga, 2017). To some extent, this is not surprising given the mandate for the departments: law enforcement rangers are primarily tasked with enforcing the law, while community conservation rangers are responsible for sensitizing the community (i.e. educating the villagers on the benefits of local conservation efforts).

However, law enforcement is also responsible for providing a social and public service by responding to problem species before, during, and after incidences of HWC. Study participants described how this service was viewed positively by most community members and helped build community relations by providing security from potentially dangerous wildlife. As Roger stated: 'We help them protect their lives and crops from being destroyed by the wild [animals].' In his response, Simon explained:

> Yeah, they trust [us] when they have a problem [...] They call and we respond and we can help. Maybe a buffalo or any problem animal comes in [their community] [...] They feel very happy when those animals are chased back and [we] come to secure the conservation area. They feel very happy.

Despite their efforts, study participants also mentioned how incidents of HWC and the presence of problem wildlife species negatively impacted community-ranger relations. Specifically, rangers highlighted three main themes: *the lack of compensation for losses incurred, delays and related logistical challenges in efficiently responding to communities*, and *the presumption of ownership and responsibility of wildlife species.*

Currently, there are no formal programs in Uganda to compensate community members for losses resulting from HWC. Respondents considered the lack of compensation to be one of the primary issues that hindered community-ranger relations. Specifically, rangers described the challenges the organization faced during community sensitization meetings after HWC incidents occurred and how community members would lament over their losses, while expressing frustration over the lack of compensatory support.

While no formal compensation program currently exists, communities do receive revenue sharing, which is 20 per cent of all entrance fees that the PAs receive from visitors. Although respondents felt that this program was helpful in offsetting *some* of the losses resulting from HWC, the amount was not enough. Unfortunately, communities living near PAs tend to receive little of the revenue sharing funds. This is due to the allocation of the funding (i.e. starting at the district level and then trickling down), as well as potential corruption. As George said, 'We feel bad because we feel this money (revenue sharing funds) should go to the people who are living near the Park because it is [these] people whose crops are being destroyed by wild animals.' In its current structure, respondents felt that the revenue sharing program was not only ineffective in compensating communities, especially specific households that are affected, but that the current process further delegitimized local conservation efforts in the eyes of villagers.

In addition to the lack of compensation, respondents described how delays in responding quickly to community concerns negatively impacted community-ranger relations. Rangers in the present study expressed frustration over being unable to immediately respond to ongoing situations of HWC or arriving at a considerably later hour. Study participants attributed this to the lack of available resources (e.g. vehicles), being understaffed, the size and topography of the PAs, and issues with physically accessing communities (i.e. poor road networks make it difficult to reach certain communities even with a vehicle) (see also Moreto, 2016). Several respondents discussed these issues in their responses:

> The extent of us helping them has not been satisfactory. So, sometimes we go in the communities and we find all the crops have been destroyed. Sometimes the elephants come at night and they inform us in the morning. We've seen anger. [Community members] almost crying. So, it takes time for us to console them. And other people, because of anger, the reaction towards us is always bad. (Patrick)

> They can trust you to some extent [...] Because if I respond to these problems and cases [of problem wildlife], if you go today, they will have trust in you. When they call you next time and maybe you are not there, maybe you- they have called you from a far distance, it is late in the night, you don't respond, then that one, they will lose trust in you. (Isaiah)

Finally, study participants described how community members would often attribute ownership and responsibility of problem species to the rangers. Respondents explained how community members would complain about the perceived double-standard that existed. Specifically, wildlife species and PA land were protected by rangers from harm, while community members were not – at least not in the same extent as the former. For instance, Derrick recalled how community members grumbled how when their 'cows escape, [they] are arrested, but your (referring to rangers) zebras are in my land.'

Respondents also felt that villagers believed that rangers deliberately neglected their community-centered duties in favor of wildlife species. Godfrey reflected on this belief:

> We have many challenges. Like animals raiding their crops, [and] they feel like you, the ranger, has failed to control the animals [...] They feel like [the] rangers [are] pushing the elephants into the community. They do not go and scare them away [and] push them back into the protected area.

In summary, villagers would blame HWC on the rangers inability to properly manage wildlife species. This led to mistrust between the communities and rangers, as well as frustration from both parties. Rangers described how their ability to effectively, efficiently, and quickly respond to problem species was largely determined by the availability of resources and operational logistics. Study participants also remarked how broader policies and practices, particularly the lack of compensation and the distribution of revenue sharing, also negatively impacted community-ranger relations.

Precipitating poaching? the prompts, pressures, permissions, and provocations resulting from human-wildlife conflict

The second research objective centered on assessing the applicability of using a situational precipitator framework to examine and understand HWC in Uganda, and its relationship to retaliatory killings and poaching. Before discussing how HWC can create a situation where retaliatory killing and poaching is viewed to be appropriate or even desired, the HWC situation in Uganda needs to be described. To obtain this information, respondents were asked to provide insight on drivers that influenced poaching in Ugandan protected areas (PAs). A number of factors were identified by study participants similar to prior research, including subsistence, commercial purposes, cultural beliefs and customary practices, family traditions, and ignorance of the law. Problem species and the resulting HWC was also viewed to be a significant factor in the poaching of wildlife in PAs as well.

While more details will be provided shortly on the nuances related to specific factors that result in HWC, it is worth noting here that respondents largely centered their attention on crop raiding and livestock depredation committed by problem wildlife when discussing HWC. When referring to wildlife species, Harriett, for instance, described how 'they're destroying their [villagers'] crops.' Study participants also described how HWC could result in the injury or death of villagers, which prompted community anger and tension towards the PAs, the wildlife, and the Park staff. Notably, respondents believed that HWC was likely to continue as communities grow and scarcity in resources result in contested shared space between people and wildlife, as well as the potential for the spread of disease. Indeed, disease transmission was another aspect of HWC that respondents alluded to. Moses, for example, described how wildlife can 'be mixed up with [villagers'] cows' and that 'the wild animal brings the ticks to kill the cows.'

The situational precipitators of poaching and retaliatory killings in Uganda will now be presented. As a reminder, *prompts* can trigger and signal criminal behavior; *pressures* compel people to conform, obey, comply, or deny; *permissions* enable individuals to neutralize feelings of accountability or culpability; and *provocations* create a stressful situation resulting in an anti-social response. It is important to note that the following themes are not mutually exclusive and there is some overlap between the different precipitating elements.

Prompts and provocations

While distinct, *prompts* and *provocations* appear to operate in joint fashion in the present study. In particular, recent instances of crop raiding, livestock depredation, and injury or harm to community members by wildlife can prompt or provoke community members to engage in retaliatory killings or poaching. Incidents whereby community members incur sudden loss – monetarily or otherwise – can result in frustration and even anger leading to favorable reaction towards retaliation. George described how, 'when they poach, it is like they are avenging [their crops]. When they see animals come to destroy their crops, sometimes, they also feel like the animal should be killed', while Kenneth described how villagers 'want animals to disappear from a particular area because of problem animals and vermin.' Hamilton also commented on how some communities are 'convinced these groups [of problem wildlife] are coming to destroy them' and how community members felt the need to 'kill the animals' and Howard simply commented how, 'it's all about revenge.'

Respondents also described how the mere presence of wildlife in communities may create a situation where criminal behavior is prompted despite there being no harm done. Rangers believed that such actions may be simply be a preemptive form of retaliation due to villagers' past experiences (i.e. prior cases of HWC within the community) pointing to the reinforcing and cumulative nature of HWC incidences. Respondents also believed that such preemptive actions on the part of the community may point to vicarious experiences as well (i.e. community members hearing about other HWC in other nearby communities) or expected attributes of particular species (i.e. lions targeting livestock).

Pressures and permissions

Respondents described how the agricultural harm due to problem species would create a situation where community members were *pressured* to poach in order to replace lost food sources. In other words, as a result of HWC and its impact on agricultural practices, villagers would deny the regulations and laws meant to protect wildlife in Uganda. Beyond personal consumption and use, the economic loss resulting from problem wildlife placed added strain on community members, especially in being able to provide for the health and education of their children. For example, the following rangers commented on the impact that HWC had on personal consumption and the ability of individuals to provide for their children, which would ultimately result in poaching:

> Others poach because of the problem animals they face, 'cause when the animals go out of the Park, they destroy their crops. So, you know that the communities have nothing to eat. So they revenge. Revenge for meat [...] You find people have planted their gardens and whatever, tomorrow within no time you find that it is all cleared. And their children, they're starving. They've lost school fees. So, you find [community members saying], "Ah! I have no other option. I'll go for poaching." (Gabriel)

> You find somebody who has land [and] he is expecting to have cornfields for the child and have food for his personal availability. And they (crops) are all destroyed. That means it will force him to go and start poaching. To look for what? For income to take care of the children. (Ambrose)

The detrimental impact of problem species on the personal and economic well-being of villagers and their families living on the boundary of PAs can be considerable. It is therefore not surprising that respondents believed that community members were able to deny personal responsibility, deny the wildlife victims, and condemn condemners (i.e. Park officials) to neutralize feelings of guilt (Sykes & Matza, 1957; see also Eliason & Dodder, 1999; Rytterstedt, 2016). Study participants explained how community members would often argue how they were the actual victims in cases of HWC, and not the wildlife. Moreover, any retaliatory actions could be attributed to the inability of Park officials to adequately and appropriately respond to the concerns and needs of those affected by problem species. Respondents believed that such attitudes permitted villagers to engage in retaliatory or even preemptive killing of wildlife. In his explanation, Barnabas offered:

> If a Buffalo has gone out of the Park and into the communities, even if someone doesn't have that feeling of poaching, [they can think], "Some of these [Buffalo] have come [back]. Why don't we poach? Again they come and they destroy our crops." Now also the communities organize and come and destroy what? Animals.

In essence, prior instances of HWC provided sufficient justification for community members to illegally kill wildlife species *prior* to any potential future cases of HWC. As mentioned previously, one area of contention between community members and rangers is the lack of compensation provided after cases of HWC. Not surprisingly, the absence of monetary compensation for crops, livestock, and lives harmed or loss enables villagers to further vindicate retaliatory acts against wildlife. Okello explained:

> Animals kill the community [members] on their land. There is no compensation. Hmm? When they (wildlife) destroy their crops, no compensation. So, these elements within community, they (villagers) just keep them in their minds. That's why animals are being killed. Because animals are going to destroy their crops, no compensation, eh? Animals are killing their people, no compensation.

Finally, another way that HWC can nullify villagers' liability or remorse is by permitting them to hire poachers from outside of the community. Not only does this remove the perception of direct involvement in the hunting and killing of wildlife, but also reduces any guilt that may be felt. Moses, for example, recalled: 'Sometime back, when the big land owners outside of the Park, don't want the animals on their lands. So now, they hire poachers from outsider there to come.' He added, how these individuals were specifically 'hired to poach the animals in that land.' David also described how villagers would 'look for people to poach so they (wildlife) can decrease in number.'

Discussion

The present study contributes to the criminological and conservation science literature by demonstrating the applicability of utilizing a situational precipitator framework in understanding the link between human-wildlife conflict (HWC), retaliatory killing, and poaching. Findings suggest that the existence of HWC in Uganda can prompt, pressure, permit, and provoke community members to engage in retaliatory killings and poaching. Additionally, it was found that HWC complicates community-ranger relations. Importantly, the study highlights the role that criminology, as a social science, can have in examining and understanding the human dimensions of conservation science and practice.

This research points to the importance of focusing on the proximal, situational characteristics that can result in illegal activities in protected areas (PAs). By doing so, researchers and policymakers can gain a better grasp of the unique problems that particular communities situated near PA boundaries face. Furthermore, a more nuanced understanding of the convergence or the intersection of poaching with other phenomenon, including HWC, can provide guidance on developing effective and ethically appropriate responses (see von Hirsch et al., 2000). In other words, by recognizing that individuals who poach are not all driven by the same factors can lead to the important realization that a single, one-size fits all response will not be effective, nor is the framing or stigmatizing of such individuals appropriate.

This research highlights how more traditional forms of crime prevention, such as law enforcement patrols, may be ineffective in addressing poaching that is a direct result of HWC. Such strategies may be counter-productive as they may be viewed as unfair by community members who are directly impacted by HWC broadening the gap between villagers and rangers. These findings highlight the potential role of further embedding a community problem-solving policing model for protected area management and monitoring (Moreto & Pires, 2018). Operating from a problem-oriented policing, which functions well with SCP (see Braga, 2009), can be used to develop problem-specific responses tailored to particular places within communities. By addressing recurring problems that plague communities, it may be possible that unwanted outcomes – like retaliatory killings or poaching of wildlife – can be avoided.

The current study exhibits the potential utility of situational crime prevention (SCP) in preventing poaching by addressing reoccurring problems that create an environment where poaching may be welcomed. As mentioned earlier, the realization that situational precipitators can result in crime led to the extension of SCP techniques to include 'softer' approaches to complement strategies focused more on target hardening, increasing risks, and reward reduction. The findings presented here support this proposition by highlighting how particular SCP techniques may be especially useful in addressing HWC, and therefore, may have a direct impact on poaching. The digging of trenches, for example, was viewed useful in avoiding human and wildlife disputes by physically making it difficult for wildlife to cross into community lands (see Figure 1). Daniel described how 'we make trenches in the communities for reinforcements. Trenches where animals enter' and Barnabas commented on how 'we are trying to protect them (villagers) against the problem animals by digging a trench around the Park boundary.'

The use of physical barriers also points to the utility of crime prevention through environmental design (CPTED) concepts within the scope of poaching prevention (cf. Moreto & Pires, 2018). In addition to the use of trenches, for example, the development of buffer corridors or zones were also suggested by study participants to be a potentially useful approach in reducing HWC. As explained by Joseph:

Figure 1. A photograph of a trench in Uganda made to reduce human-wildlife conflict.

> If we are managing a Park as an ecosystem, then the standard design should be that the Park should have a buffer area, a buffer zone where the animals can disperse [...] And at the same time, it will buffer the Park from other human actions [...] [If] you have areas of the Parks where there are no buffer zones, no effective corridors, when the animals want to disperse into [community] areas, they find human beings, they find crops, you know? So, you find human and wildlife conflict increases. The animals want to move out and there is no corridor, so they must go through people's crop fields. That increases the human wildlife conflict. So to me, the design is the biggest problem [...] If you mitigate that conflict, you find that the communities can tolerate wildlife and are willing to live alongside wildlife

While this paper focused primarily on proximal correlates, the influence of distal factors cannot be ignored. For instance, the lack of compensation for agricultural losses or for injury resulting from HWC (distal) mentioned earlier was believed to exacerbate instances of livestock predation (proximal). This points to the importance of understanding the role of controllers and super controllers in conservation matters. Controllers refer to individuals who are considered responsible for places (manager), targets (guardian), and offenders (handler), while super controllers 'control the controllers' by creating 'incentives for controllers to prevent or facilitate crime' (Sampson, Eck, & Dunham, 2010, p. 40). An example of a controller would be rangers (guardian), while a super controller would be the organization responsible for the rangers. Whether the organization adequately supports, encourages, and rewards rangers in crime prevention efforts will impact ranger investment and success. One example of the role of both controllers and super controllers is exhibited by efforts to reduce (distal) emotional arousal through community conservation meetings. To solidify the critical role of community conservation and to ensure that the community had outlets to voice their concerns and reduce some of the emotional tension resulting from HWC, the UWA formally established the community conservation department. Future studies should further examine the role of controllers and super controllers in addressing HWC and poaching.

Geographical and ecological differences and nuances should also be further explored. Throughout the interviews, there was some indication that the proximity of communities, location of agricultural practice (e.g. livestock rearing), landscape and topography, and wildlife species distribution can have an impact on HWC and poaching opportunities. Combining interviews with spatial data on HWC and poaching incidents would not only further inform policy decisions (i.e. developing tailored responses to targeting problem areas), but can contribute to further testing concepts found within the environmental criminology literature (e.g. journey-to-crime).

Considerable effort was made to reduce the limitations of the research presented here, however, it is expected that the credibility and transferability of the study can be questioned (Lincoln & Guba, 1985). To minimize potential threats to the data and subsequent findings, a multi-method approach (formal interviews, participant observation, and informal conversations) was used to triangulate the data collected. Engaging in fieldwork also enabled the author to perform 'member checks' with study participants throughout data collection and during analysis, helping confirm or refute initial interpretation of the data. The involvement of a trusted gatekeeper (see Moreto, 2017), and constant interaction with study participants, was helpful in developing trust and rapport as well. Finally, while the findings of the current study are not suitable for statistical generalizability, the findings are 'generalizable to theoretical propositions' (Yin, 2009, p. 15) by contributing to the situational precipitator framework.

As shown in this study, the intersection between HWC, retaliatory killings, and poaching is complicated and is situationally dependent. This research displayed the utility of examining wildlife crime from an environmental criminology perspective, and showed how such an approach can unravel distinct idiosyncrasies related to the nexus between these distinct topics. Specifically, by using a situational precipitator framework, a better understanding of the link between HWC, retaliatory killings, and poaching can be established. Such insight is vital in developing specifically-tailored strategies to address problems which may ultimately result in the retaliatory killing or poaching of wildlife species.

Disclosure statement

No potential conflict of interest was reported by the author.

References

Auerbach, C., & Silverstein, L.B. (2003). *Qualitative data: An introduction to coding and analysis.* New York, NY: NYU Press.

Bell, S., Hampshire, K., & Topalidou, S. (2007). The political culture of poaching: A case study from Northern Greece. *Biodiversity and Conservation, 16*, 399–418.

Bennett, N.J., Roth, R., Klain, S.C., Chan, K., Christie, P., Clark, D.A., Wyborn, C. (2017). Conservation social science: Understanding and integrating human dimensions to improve conservation. *Biological Conservation, 205*, 93–108.

Braga, A.A. (2009). *Problem-oriented policing and crime prevention* (2nd ed.). Monsey, NY: Criminal Justice Press.

Brashares, J.S., Arcese, P., Sam, M.K., Coppolillo, P.B., Sinclair, A.R.E., & Balmford, A. (2004). Bushmeat hunting, wildlife declines, and fish supply in West Africa. *Science, 306*, 1180–1183.

Campbell, D.J., Gichohi, H., Mwangi, A., & Chege, L. (2000). Land use conflict in Kajiado District, Kenya. *Land Use Policy, 17*, 337–348.

Ceballos, G., García, A., & Ehrlich, P.R. (2010). The sixth extinction crisis: Loss of animal populations and species. *Journal of Cosmology, 8*, 1821–1831.

Cornish, D.B., & Clarke, R.V. (2003). Opportunities, precipitators and criminal decisions: A reply to Wortley's critique of situational crime prevention. *Crime Prevention Studies, 16*, 41–96. Monsey, NY: Criminal Justice Press.

Cowan, D., Burton, C., & Moreto, W.D. (2019). Conservation-based intelligence-led policing: An intra-organizational interpersonal examination. *Policing: An International Journal, 42*, 108–122.

Dey, I. (1999). *Grounding grounded theory*. San Diego, CA: Academic Press.

Dickman, A.J. (2010). Complexities of conflict: The importance of considering social factors for effectively resolving human-wildlife conflict. *Animal Conservation, 13*, 458–466.

Ekblom, P. (1994). Proximal circumstances: A mechanism-based classification of crime prevention. In R.V. Clarke (Ed.), *Crime prevention studies* (2nd ed., pp. 185–232). Monsey, NY: Criminal Justice Press.

Eliason, S.L. (2012). Trophy poaching: A routine activities perspective. *Deviant Behavior, 33*, 72–87.

Eliason, S.L., & Dodder, R.A. (1999). Techniques of neutralization used by deer poachers in the western United States: A research note. *Deviant Behavior, 20*, 233–252.

Forsyth, C.J., Gramling, R., & Wooddell, G. (1998). The game of poaching: Folk crimes in Southwest Louisiana. *Society & Natural Resources, 11*, 25–38.

Forsyth, C.J., & Marckese, T.A. (1993). Thrills and skills: *A* sociological analysis of poaching, *Deviant Behavior, 14*, 157–172.

Gibson, C.C. (1999). *Politicians and poachers: The political economy of wildlife policy in Africa*. New York, NY: Cambridge University Press.

Gusset, M., Swarner, M.J., Mponwane, L., Keletile, K., & McNutt, J.W. (2009). Human-wildlife conflict in northern Botswana: Livestock predation by Endangered African wild dog *Lycaon pictus* and other carnivores. *Oryx, 43*, 67–72.

Hilton-Taylor, C., Pollock, C.M., Chanson, J.S., Butchart, S.H.M., Oldfield, T.T., & Katariya, V. (2009). State of the world's species. In J.-C. Vié, C. Hilton-Taylor, & S.N. Stuart (Eds.), *Wildlife in a changing world – An analysis of the 2008 IUCN red list of threatened species* (pp. 15–41). Gland: IUCN.

Kurland, J., Pires, S.F., McFann, S., & Moreto, W.D. (2017). Wildlife crime: A conceptual integration, literature review, and methodological critique. *Crime Science, 6*. doi:10.1186/s40163-017-0066-0

Leberatto, A. (2016). Understanding the illegal trade of live wildlife species in Peru. *Trends in Organized Crime, 19*, 42–66.

Lemieux, A.M. (Ed). (2014). *Situational prevention of poaching*. New York, NY: Routledge.

Lincoln, Y.S., & Guba, E.G. (1985). *Naturalistic inquiry*. Beverly Hills, CA: Sage Publications, Inc.

Miles, M., & Huberman, A. (1994). *Qualitative data analysis* (2nd ed.). Thousand Oaks, CA:Sage Publications, Inc.

Moreto, W.D. (2016). Occupational stress among law enforcement rangers: Insights from Uganda. *Oryx: the International Journal of Conservation, 50*, 646–654.

Moreto, W.D. (2017). Avoiding the tragedy of (un)common knowledge: Reflections on conducting qualitative criminological research in conservation science. *Qualitative Research, 17*, 440–456.

Moreto, W.D., Brunson, R.K., & Braga, A.A. (2017). "Anything we do, we have to include the communities": Law enforcement rangers' attitudes towards and experiences of community-ranger relations in wildlife protected areas in Uganda. *British Journal of Criminology*, 57, 924–944.

Moreto, W.D., Cowan, D., & Burton, C. (2018). Towards an Intelligence-led Approach to Address Wildlife Crime in Uganda. *Policing: A Journal of Policy and Practice, 12*, 344–357.

Moreto, W.D., & Lemieux, A.M. (2015a). From CRAVED to CAPTURED: Introducing a product-based framework to examine illegal wildlife markets. *European Journal on Criminal Policy and Research, 21*, 303–320.

Moreto, W.D., & Lemieux, A.M. (2015b). Poaching in Uganda: Perspectives from law enforcement rangers. *Deviant Behavior, 36*(11), 853–873.

Moreto, W.D., & Matusiak, M.C. (2017). "We fight wrong doers": Law enforcement rangers' roles, responsibilities, and patrol operations in Uganda. Deviant Behavior, *4*, 426–447.

Moreto, W.D., & Pires, S.F. (2018). *Wildlife Crime: An Environmental Criminology and Crime Science Perspective*. Durham, NC: Carolina Academic Press.

Muth, R.M., & Bower, J.F., Jr. (1998). Illegal harvest of renewable natural resources in North America: Toward a typology of the motivations for poaching. *Society & Natural Resources: An International Journal, 11*, 9–24.

Ogada, M.O., Woodroffe, R., Oguge, N.O., & Frank, L.G. (2003). Limiting depredation by African carnivores: The role of livestock husbandry. *Conservation Biology, 17*, 1521–1530.

Patton, M.Q. (2015). *Qualitative research & evaluation methods*. Thousand Oaks, CA: SAGE Publications, Inc.

Petrossian, G.A., & Clarke, R.V. (2014). Explaining and controlling illegal commercial fishing: An application of the CRAVED theft model. *British Journal of Criminology, 54*, 73–90.

Phillips, D.W., Mitchell, L.B., & Murrell, C.M. (2014). Folk crime. In C.J. Forsyth & H. Copes (Eds.), *Encyclopedia of social deviance* (pp. 282–283). Thousand Oaks, CA: SAGE Publications, Inc.

Pires, S.F., & Moreto, W.D. (2011). Preventing wildlife crimes: Solutions that can overcome the 'Tragedy of the Commons'. *European Journal on Criminal Policy and Research, 17*, 101–123.

Rittel, H.W.J, & Webber, M.M. (1973). Dilemmas in a general theory of planning. *Policy Sciences, 4*, 155–169.

Rossi, A. (2018). *Uganda Wildlife Trafficking Assessment*. TRAFFIC Report, TRAFFIC International. Cambridge: UK.

Runhovde, S. (in press). Merely a transit country? Examining the role of Uganda in the transnational illegal ivory trade. *Trends in Organized Crime*, Online First. https://link.springer.com/article/10.1007%2Fs12117-016-9299-7

Rytterstedt, E. (2016). 'I don't see myself as a criminal': Motivation and neutralization of illegal hunting by Swedish Norrland Hunters. In G.R. Potter., A. Nurse., & M. Hall (Eds.), *The geography of environmental crime: Conservation, wildlife crime, and environmental activism* (pp. 217–239). UK: Palgrave Macmillan.

Saldaña, J. (2016). *The coding manual for qualitative researchers* (3rd ed.). Thousand Oaks, CA: SAGE Publications Inc.

Sampson, R., Eck, J.E., & Dunham, J. (2010). Super controllers and crime prevention: A routine activity explanation of crime prevention success and failure. *Security Journal, 23*(1), 37–51.

Schneider, J.L. (2012). *Sold into extinction: The global trade in endangered species*. Santa Barbara, CA: Praeger.

Shepherd, C.R., & Magnus, N. (2004). *Nowhere to hide: The trade in Sumatran Tiger*. TRAFFIC Southeast Asia.

Sykes, G.M., & Matza, D. (1957). Techniques of neutralization: A theory of delinquency. *American Sociological Review, 22*, 664–670.

van Doormaal, N., Lemieux, A.M., & Ruiter, S. (2018). Understanding site selection of illegal border crossings into a fenced protected area: A rational choice perspective. *Crime Science, 7(7)*. doi: 10.1186/s40163-018-0081-9

van Uhm, D.P. (2016). *The illegal wildlife trade: Inside the world of poachers, smugglers, and traders*. Switzerland: Springer International Publishing.

Von Essen, E., Hansen, P.H., Kallstrom, H.N., Peterson, M.N., & Peterson, T.R. (2014). Deconstructing the poaching phenomenon: A review of typologies for understanding illegal hunting. *The British Journal of Criminology, 54*, 632–651.

von Hirsch, A., Garland, D., & Wakefield, A. (eds.). (2000). *Ethical and social perspectives on situational crime prevention*. Portland, OR: Hart Publishing.

Warchol, G., & Harrington, M. (2016). Exploring the dynamics of South Africa's illegal abalone trade via routine activities theory. *Trends in Organized Crime, 19*, 21–41.

Warchol, G.L. (2004). The transnational illegal wildlife trade. *Criminal Justice Studies, 17*, 57–74.

White, R. (2008). *Crimes against nature: Environmental criminology and ecological justice*. Portland, OR: Willan Publishing.

White, R. (2018). *Climate change criminology*. Chicago, IL: Bristol University Press.

Wortley, R. (1996). Guilt, shame and situational crime prevention. In R. Homel (Ed.), *The Politics and Practice of Situational Crime Prevention, Crime Prevention Series*, (Vol. 5, pp. 115–132). Monsey, NY: Criminal Justice Press.

Wortley, R. (1997). Reconsidering the role of opportunity in situational crime prevention. In G. Newman. & S.G. Shohan (Eds.), *Rational choice and situational crime prevention* (pp. 65–81). Aldershot, UK: Ashgate.

Wortley, R. (1998). A two-stage model of situational crime prevention. *Studies on Crime and Crime Prevention, 7*, 173–188.

Wortley, R. (2001). A classification of techniques for controlling situational precipitators of crime. *Security Journal, 14*, 63–82.

Wortley, R. (2017). Situational precipitators of crime. In R. Wortley. & M. Townsley (Eds.), *Environmental criminology and crime analysis* (2nd ed., pp. 62–86). New York, NY: Routledge.

Wyatt, T. (2009). Exploring the organization of Russia Far East's illegal wildlife trade: Two case studies of the illegal fur and illegal falcon trades. *Global Crime, 10*, 144–154.

Wyatt, T. (2013). *Wildlife trafficking: A Deconstruction of the crime, the victims and the offenders*. New York, NY: Palgrave Macmillan.

Yin, R.K. (2009). *Case study research: Design and methods* (4th ed.). Thousand Oaks, CA: SAGE Publications, Inc.

When a loved one is on community supervision: the crime controller strategies used by 'PoPPs' (parents/partners/peers of probationers and parolees)

Lacey Schaefer, Emily Moir and Gemma C. Williams

ABSTRACT

Scholars have called for the incorporation of informal social control agents into the community supervision of offenders, although systematic efforts to do so have been slow to come. This project reports on an initial trial of such a practice. In *Triple-S: Social Supports in Supervision*, probation and parole staff engage in opportunity-reduction tactics by, in part, recruiting and training members of their clients' social networks who may serve as offender handlers, target guardians, and place managers. The current study analysed interview data from a sample of these *PoPPs* (parents/partners/peers of probationers and parolees) to uncover the strategies they use in preventing their loved one from reoffending. A thematic analysis revealed eight categories of actions taken by PoPPs: (1) social support, (2) instrumental support, (3) moulding routines and altering environments, (4) reshaping social circles, (5) trigger identification and avoidance, (6) threats, (7) monitoring and intervention, and (8) co-desistance. We further describe the impact of closeness, willingness to intervene, opportunity, and knowledge on the crime control (in)actions of the interview participants, calling for further research on the nature of handling, guarding, and managing behaviours when the relationship between the crime controller and the offender is pre-existing.

Introduction and literature review

The overarching philosophies that guide the community supervision of offenders have remained largely unaltered for more than a century. The ideologies that frame probation and parole practices focus mainly on offender motivation; practices aim to reduce criminal propensity through treatment efforts (in the form of correctional interventions or service brokerage) or generic uses of deterrence theory (such as threats of punishment for non-compliance with supervision conditions). Yet these practices ignore the other ingredient necessary for a crime to occur: opportunity. This state of affairs has led to speculation that 'the current practice of community supervision could be improved, perhaps dramatically, by adopting a new paradigm – a new way of thinking – about how best to supervise offenders on probation and parole' (Cullen, Eck, & Lowenkamp, 2002, p. 28). One form of reinvention has called for probation and parole practices that focus less on controlling offender propensity, but more on reducing opportunities for reoffending. Through the application of environmental criminological theories to community corrections practices, *Environmental Corrections* prevents reoffending by reducing chances to commit crime, and by teaching offenders to recognise, avoid, and resist these opportunities for relapse (Schaefer, Cullen, & Eck, 2016). One strategy for accomplishing this objective is through the recruitment of agents of informal social control, in which probation and parole staff operate as super controllers who identify and train members of their clients' social network to act as offender handlers, target guardians, and place managers. This paper describes the results of such an effort, detailing a trial of a model of opportunity-reduction supervision. Following interviews with the informal social control agents, we identify the strategies they used to prevent reoffending by their loved one. First, we describe the research evidence-bases regarding opportunity-reduction supervision and crime controllers that guided the trial.

Opportunity-reduction supervision

Environmental criminology has revolutionised our understanding of the ingredients of a crime event and how to reduce opportunities for offences. Unfortunately, however, many correctional interventions neglect these demonstrably effective crime prevention strategies, instead monitoring offenders' compliance with generic supervision conditions and brokering services through external providers. In response to the high rates of failure in probation and parole, there has been a growing call to systematically incorporate opportunity-reduction principles in community corrections (Miller, 2012; Schaefer et al., 2016; Schaefer, Cullen, & Manchak, 2017; Schaefer & Williamson, 2017). One such model, *Environmental Corrections*, seeks to redesign the routine activities of community-supervised offenders so criminogenic risks are avoided or effectively controlled. A pilot test of this approach was recently conducted (Schaefer, 2018a), where officers were provided training in the fundamentals of crime prevention, teaching them to develop supervision conditions that reduce opportunities for reoffending and to incorporate brief interventions that alter how the supervisee interprets and exploits remaining crime opportunities. An evaluation of this pilot test of *Environmental Corrections* demonstrated a 28% reduction in police-recorded reoffending six months post-intervention (Schaefer & Little, under review).

A subsequent field trial sought to expand these opportunity-reducing elements beyond the probation and parole office where the bulk of supervision takes place. Deemed *Triple-S: Social Supports in Supervision*, the trial trained probation and parole staff as super controllers who engage additional crime controllers, pursuing the recommendation that supervision ought to draw on the offender's natural support systems to stimulate, support, and stabilise change (Denney, Tewskbury, & Jones, 2014; Taxman, 2011). As community-supervised offenders spend a miniscule proportion of their time actively engaged with probation and parole authorities, the control that community corrections agencies have over their clients must be extended in some way. As such, scholars have called for agencies to move away from 'fortress supervision' towards a more community-integrated approach (Pew Center on the States, 2008; Schaefer et al., 2017; Western & Schiraldi, 2017). In addition to a focus on the real criminogenic risks within each community, such an approach would foster relationships with stakeholders, resource providers, and neighbourhood residents who know the offenders and can form part of the solution to crime problems (Solomon et al., 2008). Accordingly, probation and parole staff should incorporate offenders' social networks into community supervision (Denney et al., 2014; Pew Center on the States, 2008), as these social supports can encourage desistance and aid in re-entry and desistance processes which are known to be difficult (Petersilia, 2003; Travis, 2005; Urban Institute, 2006). Social networks can be useful in this process by helping with accommodation, employment, social inclusion and other types of personal and emotional support. The loved ones of probationers and parolees are arguably more effective crime controllers than supervising officers, as these informal social control agents know the individual (and their risks and routines) better, have greater capacity for monitoring, have a stake in preventing reoffending, and are more influential in swaying the offender's behaviour (National Research Council of the National Academies, 2008; Piquero, 2003; Taxman, Young, & Byrne, 2004). The *Triple-S* model thus seeks to incorporate the loved ones of community-supervised offenders who can serve a critical crime prevention role.

Crime controllers

The roots of opportunity-reduction supervision are drawn from Cohen and Felson's (1979) routine activity theory, which stipulates that crime occurs when three conditions converge in time and space: a motivated offender, a suitable target, and the lack of a capable guardian. Crime prevention scholars have further added crime controllers that influence the opportunities for crime: a handler prevents an individual from committing an offence, a guardian makes targets less vulnerable to victimisation, and a manger makes a place less attractive for crime and influences the behaviours of people that occupy that space (Eck, 2003). Crime can be prevented when these controllers are present and effective in their roles.

Some theorists have suggested that the offender-handler relationship and its impact on effectiveness is monotonic, whereby familiarity or intimacy is linearly related to prevention. Felson (1995) speculated that people who are personally related to the offender are more likely to be effective handlers compared to strangers. Tillyer and Eck highlight how 'handling can be a highly intimate act between two people who have an existing relationship' (2011, p. 190). Indeed, this degree of familiarity can allow controllers to engage in crime preventive efforts that are unique to the circumstances of that individual offender and environment. The difficulty, however, is that this existing relationship may also *prevent* prevention. Some research has found that crime controllers are *less likely* to intervene when they have a personal relationship to the perpetrator of the offence (Nicksa, 2014). Individuals report less favourable reactions to the intervention, both perceived (Bennett & Banyard, 2016) and real (Moschella, Bennett, & Banyard, 2018), when the individual knows the offender compared to stranger bystander intervention. These findings infer that crime prevention tactics aimed at encouraging intervention must consider the relationship between the crime controller and the perpetrator (Bennett, Banyard, & Edwards, 2017). Some crime prevention strategies cannot, therefore, be purely situational, focusing on the amalgamation and disruption of the ingredients of a crime event at a key moment in time; rather, research must address how crime controllers exert their influence when relationships are pre-existing.

PoPPs: parents/partners/peers of probationers and parolees

While social networks of offenders are often thought to be part of the problem, they may also play an important part of the solution. Simply put, 'the behaviour of individuals under community supervision occurs in the context of, and is influenced by, family systems' (Executive Session on Community Corrections, 2017, p. 6). Drawing on the desistance and re-entry evidence-bases, we suggest that supervision will be more effective when community corrections agencies incorporate the informal social controls in offenders' lives. Within the *Triple-S: Social Supports in Supervision* project, we sought to integrate *PoPPs: parents/partners/peers of probationers and parolees*. The model leverages probation and parole officers as super controllers (Sampson, Eck, & Dunham, 2010) who identify, recruit, and train people in the offender's life who could fulfil the functions of handling, guardianship, and managing. Felson (1986) articulates that offenders are rarely actually 'unhandled'; most people have handles (social bonds that tie people together and encourage prosocial behaviour), but life must be organised such that handles can be grasped (Felson, 1995). Thus, the Triple-S model gives probation and parole staff the skills required to teach PoPPs how to be more effective crime controllers. In this paper, we explore the strategies used by these PoPPs to prevent reoffending by their loved one that is on a community corrections order.

Method

The current project is drawn from a larger trial of a novel model of probation and parole performed in a large metropolitan area in Australia.[1] The *Triple-S: Social Supports in Supervision* framework is underpinned by the research evidence-bases of offender interventions, re-entry, and desistance, in addition to environmental criminology. In this study we are focused on probation and parole officers acting as super controllers to recruit members of the client's social network (PoPPs) to serve as offender handlers, target guardians, and place managers. Probation and parole staff were provided training in opportunity-reduction strategies and taught how to coach relevant behaviours in PoPPs, supported through supplementary project materials (for an example, see, Schaefer, 2018b). Interviews were conducted with a sample of these PoPPs to uncover the crime control strategies that they use to dissuade their loved one from reoffending. Our methods for collecting and analysing these data are detailed below.

Procedure

For two weeks the research team attended the probation and parole office where the Triple-S trial was being performed (approximately four months after the trial started). A convenience sampling scheme was used: when a probationer or parolee (i.e. client) would report to the office for his or her routine case management meeting, if a PoPP accompanied the client, the case manager extended an invitation to participate in an interview with the research team upon completion of that meeting. A member of the research team then met with the participant in a private interview room. The research project was explained in greater depth and informed consent was obtained. Each participant was given a unique identification number to promote confidentiality and anonymity, and participants were ensured that their individual responses would not be reported back to the supervising agent or agency. All interviews were audio recorded and transcribed. Upon completion of the interview, the participant was provided with a $20 grocery voucher. Each participant received a debrief, which included a list of agencies and resources that were available for support if needed. Interviews ranged in length from 10 to 55 minutes, averaging 30 minutes (*SD* = 12 minutes).

Participants

Across the two weeks of data collection, a total of 218 clients reported to the probation and parole office. Of those clients, 48 brought a loved one with them to the meeting (22.02%). Of the 48 PoPPs that received an invitation to participate, 29 individuals accepted and completed the interview – a response rate of 60.41%. Summary information about the PoPPs that participated and the client that they serve as a support person for is displayed in Table 1. The PoPPs interviewed largely included the parents of clients (seven mothers and four fathers) and partners (11 girlfriends, one boyfriend, and one husband); other relationships included two brothers, one daughter, one cousin, and one roommate. Twenty interviewed PoPPS were female (68.97%).

The clients whose PoPPs were interviewed were serving probation orders (*n* = 10, 34.48%), board-ordered parole orders (*n* = 10, 34.48%), and court-ordered parole orders (*n* = 9, 31.03%). Sentence lengths ranged from 5 months to 8 years (*M* = 20.55 months, *SD* = 19.14 months). The orders resulted from violent offences (*n* = 9, 31.03%, including one sex offence), property offences (*n* = 12, 41.38%), drug offences (*n* = 3, 10.34%), driving offences (*n* = 2, 6.90%), and justice offences (*n* = 3, 10.34%). The clients on community corrections orders were aged between 18 and 48 (*M* = 31.70, *SD* = .78), and were predominantly male (86.21%) and Australian (89.66%; the remaining three clients are Aboriginal or Torres Strait Islander). The clients' risk categorisations (as assessed by the agency's standardised instrument for risk of reoffending) determine their level of service. Our sample of PoPPs corresponded to clients with service levels of low (*n* = 4, 13.79%), standard (*n* = 7, 24.14%), enhanced (*n* = 8, 27.59%), and intensive (*n* = 10, 34.48%), with corresponding reporting frequencies of weekly (*n* = 7, 24.14%), fortnightly (*n* = 12, 41.38%), and monthly (*n* = 10, 34.48%). There was considerable variation in the extent of the clients' correctional history; six of the clients were on their first corrective order while all others had served a probation or parole order previously (*Max* = 9, *M* = 3.14, *SD* = 2.13).

Materials

The interviews were semi-structured, loosely following an interview guide of 30 questions across eight domains: relationship with the client, overall experiences with corrective services, current (and if any past) experiences with probation and parole, involvement with the client's supervision order, role in the client's life, the client's involvement in crime, the client's efforts to stay out of trouble, and hopes for the future. This study focuses on data produced by those prompts within each interview that specifically relate to the actions taken by PoPPs that may serve crime preventative ends; these include: How do you support your loved one? Has probation and parole helped you to help [client] better? Have

Table 1. Participant and client characteristics.

Participant identification	Relationship to client	Length of relationship	Client sex, age	Order type, length	Most serious offence	Order number	Level of service	Reporting frequency
701	Brother	Life (25 years)	Male, 25	Court-ordered parole, 6 months	Property damage	4	Intensive	Fortnightly
702	Mother	Life (24 years)	Male, 24	Board-ordered parole, 5 months	Burglary	2	Intensive	Fortnightly
703	Father	Life (35 years)	Female, 35	Probation, 1 year	Possession of stolen goods	2	Standard	Monthly
704	Father	Life (33 years)	Male, 33	Court-ordered parole, 1 year and 4 months	Burglary	1	Standard	Fortnightly
705	Girlfriend	1 year	Male, 37	Board-ordered parole, 1 year and 3 months	Wounding	2	Low	Weekly
706	Father	Life (42 years)	Male, 42	Probation, 2 years	Assaulting police	5	Standard	Weekly
707	Daughter	Life (27 years)	Male, 48	Board-ordered parole, 3 years and 4 months	Burglary	4	Enhanced	Monthly
708	Mother	Life (35 years)	Male, 35	Board-ordered parole, 1 year and 10 months	Sexual assault	2	Low	Weekly
709	Girlfriend	5 years	Male, 31	Probation, 9 months	Drug possession	3	Enhanced	Fortnightly
710	Girlfriend	6 months	Male, 40	Court-ordered parole, 2 years	Armed robbery	9	Enhanced	Monthly
711	Girlfriend	2 years	Male, 36	Court-ordered parole, 1 year and 6 months	Drug manufacturing	1	Low	Monthly
712	Girlfriend	5 years	Male, 30	Board-ordered parole, 2 years	Drug trafficking	1	Standard	Fortnightly
713	Girlfriend	15 years	Male, 29	Board-ordered parole, 5 years and 6 months	Assault (grievous bodily harm)	4	Intensive	Weekly
714	Roommate	5 years	Male, 21	Probation, 1 year	Breach of bail	3	Standard	Weekly
715	Mother	Life (18 years)	Male, 18	Probation, 1 year	Stalking	1	Low	Fortnightly
716	Mother	Life (36 years)	Male, 36	Board-ordered parole, 1 year	Breach of bail	6	Enhanced	Weekly
717	Husband	2 years	Female, 27	Probation, 1 year	Breaking and entering	1	Enhanced	Monthly
718	Father	Life (36 years)	Male, 36	Court-ordered parole, 11 months	Weapons possession	7	Enhanced	Weekly
719	Cousin	Life (30 years)	Male, 38	Board-ordered parole, 9 months	Domestic violence	4	Intensive	Fortnightly
720	Girlfriend	1 year	Male, 43	Court-ordered parole, 2 years	Dangerous driving	2	Standard	Monthly
721	Girlfriend	7 years	Male, 35	Board-ordered parole, 8 years and 1 months	Burglary	3	Intensive	Monthly
722	Mother	Life (21 years)	Male, 21	Probation, 1 year	Property damage	2	Enhanced	Monthly
723	Girlfriend	2 years	Male, 21	Probation, 1 year	Property damage	2	Enhanced	Monthly
724	Boyfriend	3 years	Female, 22	Board-ordered parole, 5 months	Wounding	2	Intensive	Monthly
725	Girlfriend	1 year	Male, 20	Probation, 1 year	Stalking	1	Standard	Fortnightly
726	Brother	Life (34 years)	Female, 34	Court-ordered parole, 6 months	Burglary	3	Intensive	Fortnightly
727	Mother	Life (33 years)	Male, 33	Court-ordered parole, 6 months	Theft	8	Intensive	Fortnightly
728	Mother	Life (25 years)	Male, 25	Court-ordered parole, 6 months	Property damage	4	Intensive	Fortnightly
729	Girlfriend	3 years	Male, 32	Probation, 1 year	Driving under disqualification	2	Intensive	Fortnightly

you learned anything from [client's] case manager about how you can help [client]? Has your behaviour changed as a result of [client] being on a probation/parole order (and how so)? What could you do to help [client] steer clear of trouble? What have you tried before (and has it worked, why or why not)?

Analyses

The semi-structured interview data drawn from the questions above were entered into a database. The research team filtered the data so that only those statements that contained some form of action were retained for analysis. Inclusion criteria included those statements where the action referenced was (1) performed *by* the PoPP, (2) *toward* the client on probation/parole, (3) with the *intention of aiding the client* in some way. Where a compound statement contained multiple ideas, elements of the statement were separated. The data were approached inductively through a thematic analysis. The researchers read through the interview excerpts multiple times to generate a list of dominant themes. The data were then coded against those themes, which evolved (combining themes, altering inclusion definitions, disaggregating subthemes, etc.) as the coding progressed.

Results

Interviews were conducted with 29 *PoPPs* (parents/partners/peers of probationers and parolees) as part of a trial of *Triple-S: Social Supports in Supervision*, a model of community corrections which has officers work as super controllers who recruit members of the offenders' social networks to serve as handlers, guardians, and managers. Here we report the results of our analyses of a subset of data drawn from questions about the crime control strategies PoPPs use with their loved one that is on a community corrections order. We analysed 341 excerpts about the specific actions taken by PoPPs toward the probationer/parolee. The number of action-oriented statements per interview participant ranged from three to 31 ($M = 11.76$, $SD = 6.70$). Upon completion of our thematic analysis, each statement was coded into one of eight categories of strategies used by PoPPs: (1) *social support* (34.31%), (2) *instrumental support* (20.23%), (3) *moulding routines and altering environments* (12.02%), (4) *reshaping social circles* (10.26%), (5) *trigger identification and avoidance* (7.62%), (6) *threats* (7.33%), (7) *monitoring and intervention* (6.74%), and (8) *co-desistance* (1.47%). An overview of these themes is provided in Table 2. We describe each of these eight categories below, providing interview excerpts to highlight the forms, strategic aim, impetus, and perceived impact of each action as communicated by the participant.

Social support

More than one-third ($n = 117$, 34.31%) of all of the action-oriented statements provided by the PoPPs related to the *social support* they provide to their loved one serving a community corrections order. Many of these statements related to a subtheme of *presence*, whereby the participant described themselves figuratively available (*'As long as he knows that we're all behind him, he'll keep making those good choices.'* – #702), incorporating the client into the family or friendship fold (*'I always make sure there's an extra seat for him.'* – #707), as a steady force in the client's life (*'I'm just there all the time. It's sort of like a stable thing. He says to me,*

Table 2. Crime control strategies used by PoPPs (parents/partners/peers of probationers and parolees).

Theme	Prevalence in Data [n (%)]	Features
Social support	117 (34.31%)	Being figuratively available, giving advice and encouragement, providing positive reinforcement, being a sounding board, de-escalating heightened emotions
Instrumental support	69 (20.23%)	Provision of concrete life needs (accommodation, food, transport, finances, etc.), ensuring the client's accountability to supervision conditions, arranging the delivery of rehabilitative interventions and social services
Moulding routines and altering environments	41 (12.02%)	Relocating residence to avoid criminogenic risks or to increase exposure to prosocial influences, changing routines to steer clear of known crime opportunities, avoiding boredom by staying busy
Reshaping social circles	35 (10.26%)	Expanding prosocial networks, severing criminogenic relationships
Trigger identification and avoidance	26 (7.62%)	Learning provocations of misbehaviour, redirecting behaviour when triggers arise
Threats	25 (7.33%)	Warning of consequences, gentle cautions, strict ultimatums, reporting noncompliance to corrections officers, using aggression
Monitoring and intervention	23 (6.74%)	Observing behaviour and acting when needed, asking the client for information
Co-desistance	5 (1.47%)	PoPP is an ex-offender, working with the client toward a shared crime-free future

"You're my rock."' – #704), or as unconditionally supporting the client (*'He can talk to me…even though sometimes I don't like it and we argue about it. But he knows at the end of the day I'm here.'* – #729). Compared to some of these more passive actions, another subtheme emerged that took the form of *coaching*; here, the PoPP would supply their own advice or motivation specific to the client's situation (*'I said, "At the moment, you're crawling – you've got to crawl to walk. Don't take big steps, but look towards the future."'* – #728), or to encourage the client to make better choices (*'Because sometimes when he gets angry, he just says shit he shouldn't say. I try and teach him to think before he speaks.'* – #701). Some participants described how probationers and parolees also require positive reactions when prosocial changes are seen, forming a subtheme of *cheerleading* (*'I'm supporting him, encouraging him in his choices… letting him know how proud I am for him, the way he's thinking and progressing.'* – #712).

Although many of the statements in the category of *social support* seem non-directive on the surface, this can be misleading. Within their broader narratives, several of the PoPPs described how this tactic serves more goal-oriented purposes. Some explained how being a seemingly passive ear allows their loved one to vent (*'He can talk to me and let out all of his anger and drama.'* – #729), such that allowing their loved one to have escalated emotions achieved the aim of de-escalation (*'Just listen to him; just let him have his little blah. Then that calms him down.'* – #721). Some of the participants described that they had to learn specialised communication techniques to more effectively manage their loved one's behaviour, particularly in the face of mental illness or substance abuse; this led to a confidence in their ability to reliably *'talk her down'* (#719), *'keep her sane'* (#717), and *'calm him down if he's ready to lose it'* (#721).

Instrumental support

The second largest theme, categorising one-fifth of the statements ($n = 69$, 20.23%), was *instrumental support*. More than fifty statements related to the PoPPs' provision of concrete life needs to the client, such as accommodation, food, transport, and finances. While some described these acts as something that they feel obliged to do (due to allegiance to family) or compelled to do (out of guilt or fear of what may happen to the client or how the client may retaliate if they do not), many described their delivery of material resources as a form of social support; doing things to help a loved one demonstrates dependability (*'I'm always there for him. He rings me up and says, 'this is happening and that's happening' and I either go pick him up or go and give him money or whatever he wants.'* – #704) and unconditional love (*'Anything I've got to do for him, I do it. My life is theirs basically. I think that's what any mum would say.'* – #715).

Just as with the subthemes within *social support*, however, many of the statements within this theme are deeper than what first appearance may suggest. Indeed, while many of the comments relate to the logistics of re-entry (*'I've got to take him different places today to help him out, get him all settled back in.'* – #704), the broader narratives reveal more strategic aims. Some acts of *instrumental support* aimed to help the client to be accountable to their supervision conditions (*'Making sure he gets to parole, making sure he gets to work and he gets home, making sure he goes to his drug and alcohol meetings; it's the only way we can support him.'* – #702), particularly those that are cumbersome (*'I know that you've got to let them go and be themselves but, if they've got restrictions and things like that, well then you've got to be there to help them.'* – #715). Some expressed how they used their *instrumental support* as a way of ensuring that the client successfully completed the correctional order (*'I try and keep on top of his appointments and stuff like that. I'd have a funny feeling they'd miss parole, and then they'd get in trouble, and then they go back into the system and through the rolling doors again.'* – #726). Other PoPPs described how they took steps to arrange for interventions (*'We'd booked in to go for a Gambler's Anonymous meeting. And I booked him in to see the doctor, to get a referral for counselling.'* – #712) or using their own capital to obtain treatment for their loved one (*'I arranged to get her into rehab.'* – #703). Even more explicit was the belief that the provision of material support would help the client to avoid a breach of supervision conditions (*'He even saw her* (the aggrieved in a restraining order) *somewhere and he said, "Can you come and get me? I can't get on the train. She's on the train"...I said, "Yeah, I'll come and get you."'* – #714) or directly prevent an offence (*'I've bought him everything so there's no need for him to go and steal things.'* – #704).

Moulding routines and altering environments

Consistent with many crime prevention theories, some PoPPs reasoned that the chances of a reoffence could be diminished by *moulding routines and altering environments* (n = 41, 12.02%). Relocation was the most drastic action taken by some, seen to eliminate many of the opportunities for offending that old settings provided (*'I've even moved out here to try and get him away from the stuff.'* – #704), or to increase engagement with prosocial opportunities (*'Out there there's not much you could do. Being such a small town, you really can't go anywhere without going past a pub. Down here you've got the beaches, you've got shopping centres; it's a bit easier, I think.'* – #717). Others described how, since they remain in the same neighbourhood, they have altered their routines to avoid risks for relapse (*'Stay at home, do your courses, do your work, don't go out at night.'* – #705). Beyond environments that may be criminogenic, many participants within this theme cited how boredom is the catalyst to the client seeking out those risky places (*'Idle hands means they're going to get up to no good.'* – #711). Consequently, some PoPPs feared free time and sought to fill the client's day with activities (*'When he gets really bored and has nothing to do, he will go and do whatever he damn well pleases. So we've been keeping that at bay.'* – #707); this seemed to ring true particularly when the client was battling addiction (*'Yeah, plan things. Because if you've got nothing planned, you're going to be like, "Fuck, this is boring, I've got nothing to do, we're doing nothing today, let's go get on."'* – #713). Others described how filling their day either distracted the client from misbehaviour (*'How do I control him? Take his mind away from it. Go up the coast or take him to some place.'* – #713) or left no time remaining to engage in risky behaviours (*'Well we don't really do nothing...by the time we do house cleaning and the jobs that adults get, it's time to pick [daughter] up.'* – #720).

Reshaping social circles

While some of the statements in the above theme referenced antisocial peers, those efforts described the avoidance of environments that *contain* undesirable contacts (*'We don't shop at the shops where all the dickheads and the drug dealers used to go.'* – #705). Although related, this theme contains statements where the PoPP describes efforts that are aimed explicitly at *reshaping social circles* (n = 35, 10.26%). Some actions were made to expand the prosocial network of the probationer or parolee (*'Well, I got him into church...I took him down there and I introduced him to some people...because [client's] got a bad habit of finding the bad people and then he gets easily led astray. So to try and get him around the right sort of people.'* – #701). Other times, the PoPP described how criminogenic relationships were severed (*'We don't see the people that we usually see....everyone we know is in the drug scene or crime-based... we need to make new friends, really.'* – #709), minimising the opportunity for further trouble (*'We've cut all contact...if there's people who are stirring shit, they're wiped.'* – #710). A few participants in the sample admitted to attempts to independently alter their loved one's social network (*'We bought him a mobile phone with a new number to keep away from these people.'* – #719), sometimes without the client's knowledge (*'It's just who he associates with and the people he hangs around...I tried to delete all his numbers.'* – #713).

Trigger identification and avoidance

In addition to the more general categories of crime-conducive places and peers, PoPPs described other factors unique to their loved one that would generate relapses. Here participants described tactics of *trigger identification and avoidance* that were explicitly aimed at crime control (n = 26, 7.62%). Some PoPPs explained that they could identify some triggers as the client's behaviour changed in that moment (*'I can sort of read when he's starting to get upset and stuff. So we'll just go and get the football or something and go down to the beach and kick the footy and have a chat.'* – #701), while others cropped up unexpectedly (*'You take him out and he might see somebody and you don't want him to see that person...I say to him, "Do you want to go somewhere else?" We'll go and do something else.'* – #704). Some of the clients' triggers related to the PoPPs' behaviours; participants learned when they were the provocation for the misbehaviour (*'I've worked out when to keep my mouth shut.'* – #718), effectively teaching them what not to do (*'Not yell at him because if you yell at him, you just lose him. He gets worse and god help you if you're on the receiving end.'* – #722). One participant disclosed that she helps her boyfriend to administer his drugs to avoid the consequences of a bad trip (*'It just saves arguments; just do it up so he didn't hit a nerve or waste it, missed his vein, didn't feel the hit.'* – #713), sometimes even giving him drugs without his knowledge to avoid the aggressive behaviour that accompanies detox (*'just for my safety when he's coming down off it.'* – #713). Although an extreme example, the sentiment was the same: that triggers for undesirable behaviours could be pinpointed and avoided.

Threats

Some participants described how they tried to prevent reoffences by their loved ones through *threats* (*n* = 25, 7.33%). Some of these statements served as a beneficent warning of the consequences that may come should misbehaviours appear (*'As long as he lives by the rules and doesn't have friends over and doesn't do drugs at the house, he's fine to stay here.'* – #727). Other times, the PoPP tried to encourage positive behaviour through gentle cautions (*'He'll say to me, "what do you think I should do, mum?" It's like, "Well, I don't think you should do this, I can't support you if you do this, but I can support you if you go the other way."'* – #702) or strict ultimatums (*'I said, "Look, if you're going to do drugs, fuck off...I don't want it in my life." I'm not putting up with it. I said, "You use: See you!"'* – #710). Indeed, one PoPP felt so strongly about the importance of choice-consequence contingencies, that she would tell her father that she would report any noncompliance to his parole officer (*'I said, "If you do anything I will be ringing them (parole)." I said, "I don't care if it's going to dob you in. If it puts you back on the line, I don't care."'* – #707). While sometimes the participant acknowledged that they backed down, other times PoPPs affirmed that it was the follow-through of the threatened outcome that produced positive behaviour (*'He's slipped up a couple of times but I've just stood my ground and he's like, "Oh, okay, well she's not going to let me get away with that one," so he's just turned it all around again.'* – #707). While some interviewees reported using aggression to combat unwanted behaviours (*'Yelling and growling at him...good smack on the backside.'* – #722), or physical consequences for misbehaviours (*'I used to smack him around the head...chase him with sticks.'* – #713), they generally concluded that these approaches were ineffective (*'Tried dragging him away a couple of times, but that didn't work; he's just strong-headed.'* – #723).

Monitoring and intervention

Some of the participants indicated that they did not have the knowledge of how to help their loved one or did not want to overreach the boundaries of their relationship, instead opting to observe the client's behaviour and then act if a specific situation called for it. This theme of *monitoring and intervention* (*n* = 23, 6.74%) contained many references to target guardianship and place management strategies. Some PoPPs tracked how their loved one was progressing (*'Make sure he's making the right decisions.'* – #701) or kept watch for regressions (*'Making sure that we keep an eye on his condition to see that he is not reverting in any way. There's definite signs that show if he's going to revert.'* – #706). Some of the PoPPs described how they would attempt to get information from their loved one through seemingly innocent prompts (*'I keep an eye on him a bit more and just sneakily ask a few questions.'* – #714), other times digging for information directly relevant to supervision conditions (*'I said, "You're on Facebook, who are you talking to? What are you doing?" He said, "Oh, I'd like to meet someone." We discussed that. "That's fine," I said, "but you have to be careful."'* – #708). When risky situations emerged, some of the PoPPs were not hesitant about intervening (*'I did the only thing I could do: stand between my boys, because I know for a fact neither one would've ever put a hand on me.'* – #702). In other situations, continual monitoring of the situation was deemed more appropriate (*'I just step back and observe, and if anything does come of his outburst I will then step in before the police are called.'* – #722).

Co-desistance

A small but unique subset of statements emerged from the dataset. Some of the PoPPs, recruited by the probation and parole officers to serve as prosocial influences for the clients, had extensive criminal and correctional histories themselves. All the PoPPs within this category were the partners of clients. The dynamics of their co-offending seemed to at times facilitate positive *co-desistance* behaviours ($n = 5$, 1.47%). Here, participants described a partnership between themselves and the client, oriented around the expectation of a shared future (*'I think we're back on that same page again with our goals…I'll be looking into a lot of things that I can help him to…or help us both to do what we need to do.'* – #712). One PoPP described how both herself and her boyfriend were trying to stay clean (*'I'm a bad enabler at times…the biggest way that I do support him is not using. We've made the decision to make a good go of this so I've stopped.'* – #709) and regain custody of their children (*'There's too much riding on it now – getting our kids back…we're doing it together…if we don't do it together and accept responsibility because we both – we're the reason why we are at where we're at.'* – #709). Dual correctional orders proved to be mutually beneficial for one pair (*'It's worked out in both ways, that we've both got to behave in a way.'* – #723), while another PoPP described that she felt obliged to behave for her partner (*'Yeah, I stuffed up a little bit…but since he's been on, I'm too scared if I was to get in trouble for something, it would stuff him up.'* – #721).

Discussion

Many scholars have called for the incorporation of informal social control agents into the community supervision of offenders (Executive Session on Community Corrections, 2017; Pew Center on the States, 2008; Schaefer et al., 2016), but systematic efforts to do so have been slow to come. This project reports on an initial trial of such an approach to probation and parole practices. In *Triple-S: Social Supports in Supervision*, probation and parole staff engage in opportunity-reduction tactics by, in part, recruiting and training members of their clients' social networks who may serve as offender handlers, target guardians, and place managers. The current study analysed interview data from a sample of these PoPPs (parents/partners/peers of probationers and parolees) to uncover the strategies that they use in preventing reoffending by their loved one. Results indicated that these informal social control agents engage in several crime preventative behaviours, some as passive forms emotional support, but many of them with the explicit aims of handling, guardianship, and managing.

While the results of this study demonstrate that the loved ones of probationers and parolees take many crime control actions, these efforts, and their impacts, varied both between and within participants. We thus wish to caution readers from drawing the firm conclusion that the inclusion of an offenders' loved ones in community supervision will be unequivocally effective. Our findings showcase just how nuanced these relationships between PoPPs and offenders can be, helping to unpack the function and efficacy of offender handling. There seems to be an assumption that a close relationship between handler and offender will produce more effective crime control than through stranger bystander intervention (e.g. Felson, 1995), forming one impetus for the recommendation that probation and parole practices incorporate the offender's social network into supervision (National Research Council of the National Academies, 2008; Pew Center on the States, 2008). Yet the association between offender-handler closeness and handling effectiveness was not linear or exponential in our data. Rather, consistent with some recent studies on the willingness to intervene, we find that existing relationships may *discourage* action (Bennett & Banyard, 2016; Moschella et al., 2018; Nicksa, 2014). Tillyer and Eck (2011) articulated a model of effectiveness for offender handling, comprised of four key ingredients: (1) the degree of closeness between the handler and the offender, (2) the handler's willingness to intervene, (3) opportunities for intervention, and (4) the handler's knowledge of situations that allow or provoke offending. In this algorithm, these factors are multiplicative; this critical formulation means that if willingness, opportunity, or knowledge are set to zero (that is, if they are absent or defunct), then the effectiveness of handling will be diminished even if the weight for the variable of closeness is quite high. The participants in our sample, while clearly close with the offender in some way, provided support for the contingencies in Tillyer and Eck (2011) equation.

Most notably, the association between closeness and willingness was not monotonic. Some of our interviewees expressed that they were hesitant to intervene with their loved one, even when relapse seemed probable, out of concern that the intervention would damage their relationship (particularly when prior intervention had indeed hurt their closeness); that is, willingness and closeness were inversely related. This problem was particularly exacerbated in parent-child relationships, with some PoPPs expressing unease about defying the traditional dynamics of parent-child relationships, feeling as though a parent cannot instruct their adult child how to behave (*'He's not a kid now and I can't forcefully drag him to counselling or doctor's appointments or anything.'* – #727), or how uncomfortable it is for an adult offspring to provide instruction to their parent (*'I'm your daughter so technically you should be the one being a parent to me and telling me about the road I should be going on. Not the other way around.'* – #707). Although their designation as a PoPP demonstrates some degree of closeness and of willingness, their reflections demonstrate that this relationship is not straightforward.

Closeness also reduced the element of knowledge at times. Some interviewees communicated an unease in thinking of their loved one as an 'offender', which at times led them to avoid monitoring or to interpret misbehaviours in an optimistic way (*'I like to see the good in everybody...I don't ask questions. Maybe I stick my head in the sand a bit too much. I probably know what's going on, but don't want to know.'* – #712). In this way, their closeness tinted their knowledge in ways that prevent prevention. Some of our participants described how closeness does not ensure knowledge (*'I don't know what we can do. As a mother, I don't know what I can do to help him.'* – #716). Such comments indicate that more work is needed to train these informal social control agents to be effective in their roles to stop and reduce recidivism of those on community corrections orders. We think such approaches would be especially useful for PoPPs who viewed previous efforts as futile or when their loved one had extensive criminal histories.

Closeness could also hamper opportunity. When the PoPP lived with the client, this physical closeness enabled opportunities for vigilance and intervention; our participants provided ample illustrations of actions they took that were facilitated by their co-habitation, thus showcasing how closeness can lead to opportunity. Yet the link between closeness and opportunity was not ubiquitous. While it may be the case that a PoPP spends more time with a community-supervised offender than a case manager does, their presence is still variable and their efforts can be tenuous. As Felson (1986) indicates, offenders may have handles but can flee their handlers. This certainly occurred within our sample, with many PoPPs describing how their loved one would work to evade crime control efforts (*'He'll start staying out and not coming home and he'll start turning the phone off so you can't ring him.'* – #704). Critically, it was the closeness that led to the offender removing the opportunity for intervention (*'He says to me, "I don't want you to see me like that."'* – #704).

Among those PoPPs that described their *inaction*, participants expressed that reduced reoffending can only result from the will of the offender. Others believed that crime prevention is best left to formal social control, particularly the criminal justice system. This sentiment aligns with previous research that shows how crime controller action can be inhibited when responsibility is believed to be rested in others (Moir, Hart, Reynald, & Stewart, 2018; Schaefer, Mazerolle, & Kapnoulla, 2017). Yet we know that effective crime controlling behaviour *does* prevent crime (Eck & Madensen, 2018; Hollis-Peel, Reynald, van Bavel, Elffers, & Welsh, 2011), even without altering the motivation of the prospective offender (Schaefer et al., 2016). This may suggest that future efforts to incorporate informal social control in probation and parole should educate handlers not only on actions that they can take, but also on the positive effects that those behaviours can have. In other words, PoPPs may need to be convinced that their actions will have an impact for them to act.

Yet, beyond the overall goal of preventing crime, it is worthwhile to note the other important intermediate impacts that have been observed as the result of incorporating probationers and parolees' loved ones into the supervision process. Several PoPPs described how alone they have traditionally felt while trying to support their loved one through a correctional order (*'The only person I'm not helping is myself...I can't because I'm helping out every Tom, Dick, and Harry, and it's not helping me...everyone's got everyone to help, except I haven't got anyone to help me.'* – #726). Many of the interview participants cited the support they now felt from the agency and the supervising officer (*'I really don't think parole could do anything better than what they are doing. [Case manager] is very supportive, not just of [client], but of me, as well. If I need to talk to her about anything, I can just ring her and just speak to her.'* – #702). Families and friends of criminal justice-involved persons frequently describe how they are victims in the process, often feeling chastised and judged for 'allowing' the offence to happen; irrespective of whether these efforts are 'effective' in the crime prevention space, programs that provide support for the networks of ex-offenders serve important humanitarian purposes (*'As soon as people know that you've got a child been in jail, they sort of give you a wide berth...[case manager] talks to me. There's no judgement.'* – #727).

Overall, our study demonstrates that the informal social control provided by the networks of community-supervised offenders can be beneficial, yet the presumed causal association is not straightforward. This project is an important first step toward unpacking how the loved ones of probationers and parolees help (and hinder) crime prevention efforts. Importantly, however, our study also reveals how much is unknown, thus providing a prompt for further research. Indeed, this project has a number of shortcomings which produce more questions than answers. First, the *Triple-S* trial trained probation and parole staff to identify prosocial associates of their clients, which skews the results toward positive effects. Moreover, our sampling strategy relied on volunteers. Our data are thus representative of offenders' social supports that are invested and motivated, and we are unable to comment on the crime control efforts of the innumerable potential crime control actors who were not involved in *Triple-S* or our data collection for this study. Next, it is important to note that this study does not examine the effectiveness of the strategies used by our participants. We are thus unable to comment on efficacy or on moderation effects. While a pilot project of *Environmental Corrections* showed promise in reducing re-offending (Schaefer & Little, under review), future research should explore the impact of these strategies, but should also investigate whether the inclusion of social supports in probation and parole is more or less effective for particular groups. Finally, although community corrections practices in Australia are quite similar to those in the United States, the United Kingdom, and elsewhere, it is important that replications of our study occur in other contexts to ensure generalisability of our findings. This recommendation includes the need to explore the utility of *Environmental Corrections, Triple-S,* and other comparable probation and parole frameworks at other locations within Australia, as well, as our results may not extend beyond the one office where this field trial occurred.

Yet, even considering all of the nuanced conditions described above, our results demonstrate that the inclusion of members of the social networks of probationers and parolees can be useful, as they report a number of crime control behaviours. The PoPPs articulated many actions that they take to prevent reoffending by their loved one, some of which were learned from probation and parole authorities, and some of which we would anticipate to be effective. Our findings lend foundational support to the suggestion that probation and parole staff can serve as super controllers that work collaboratively with offenders' social networks to reduce reoffending of those on community supervision orders. Additional studies are required to evaluate the overall impact of *Triple-S* and of the PoPPs' actions, yet we believe that this study provides an initial step toward unpacking just how the loved ones of probationers and parolees discourage reoffending. More broadly, we encourage further research that dissects the modes and motivations of offender handling, particularly in relationships where the degree of closeness between offender and handler is high.

Note

1. Readers may enquire about the generalisability of our study to other countries if they are unfamiliar with Australian criminal justice populations and practices. While some differences exist, overarchingly, probation and parole practices in Australia are virtually identical to those used in the United States or the United Kingdom.

Disclosure statement

No potential conflict of interest was reported by the authors.

ORCID

Lacey Schaefer http://orcid.org/0000-0002-2981-2542
Emily Moir http://orcid.org/0000-0001-6943-4788

References

Bennett, S., & Banyard, V.L. (2016). Do friends really help friends? The effect of relational factors and perceived severity on bystander perception of sexual violence. *Psychology of Violence*, *6*, 64–72.

Bennett, S., Banyard, V.L., & Edwards, K.M. (2017). The impact of the bystander's relationship with the victim and the perpetrator on intent to help in situations involving sexual violence. *Journal of Interpersonal Violence*, *32*, 682–702.

Cohen, L.E., & Felson, M. (1979). Social change and crime rate trends: A routine activity approach. *American Sociological Review*, *44*, 588–608.

Cullen, F.T., Eck, J.E., & Lowenkamp, C.T. (2002). Environmental corrections: A new paradigm for effective probation and parole supervision. *Federal Probation*, *66*(2), 28–37.

Denney, A.S., Tewskbury, R., & Jones, R.S. (2014). Beyond basic needs: Social support and structure for successful offender reentry. *Journal of Qualitative Criminal Justice and Criminology*, *2*, 39–67.

Eck, J.E. (2003). Police problems: The complexity of problem theory, research and evaluation. *Crime Prevention Studies*, *15*, 67–102.

Eck, J.E., & Madensen, T.D. (2018). Place management. In G.J.N. Bruinsma & S.D. Johnson (Eds.), *The Oxford handbook of environmental criminology* (pp. 629–663). New York, NY: Oxford University Press.

Executive Session on Community Corrections. (2017). *Toward an approach to community corrections for the 21st century*. Cambridge, MA: Harvard Kennedy School.

Felson, M. (1986). Linking criminal choices, routine activities, informal control, and criminal outcomes. In D.B. Cornish & R.V. Clarke (Eds.), *The reasoning criminal: Rational choice perspectives on offending* (pp. 119–128). New York, NY: Springer-Verlag.

Felson, M. (1995). Those who discourage crime. In J.E. Eck & D. Weisburd (Eds.), *Crime and place* (pp. 149–167). Monsey, NY: Criminal Justice Press.

Hollis-Peel, M.E., Reynald, D.M., van Bavel, M., Elffers, H., & Welsh, B. (2011). Guardianship for crime prevention: A critical review of the literature. *Crime, Law and Social Change, 56*, 53–70.

Miller, J. (2012). Probation supervision and the control of crime opportunities: An empirical assessment. *Crime and Delinquency, 60*, 1235–1257.

Moir, E., Hart, T.C., Reynald, D.M., & Stewart, A. (2018). Typologies of suburban guardians: Understanding the role of responsibility, opportunities, and routine activities in facilitating surveillance. *Crime Prevention and Community Safety*. doi:10.1057/s41300-018-0057-4

Moschella, E.A., Bennett, S., & Banyard, V.L. (2018). Beyond the situational model: Bystander action consequences to intervening in situations involving sexual violence. *Journal of Interpersonal Violence, 33*, 3211–3231.

National Research Council of the National Academies. (2008). *Parole, desistance from crime, and community integration*. Washington, DC: National Academies Press.

Nicksa, S.C. (2014). Bystanders' willingness to report theft, physical assault, and sexual assault: The impact of gender, anonymity, and relationship with the offender. *Journal of Interpersonal Violence, 29*, 217–236.

Petersilia, J. (2003). *When prisoners come home: Parole and prisoner reentry*. New York, NY: Oxford University Press.

Pew Center on the States. (2008). *Putting public safety first: 13 strategies for successful supervision and reentry*. Washington, DC: The Pew Charitable Trusts.

Piquero, N. (2003). A recidivism analysis of Maryland's community probation program. *Journal of Criminal Justice, 31*, 295–307.

Sampson, R., Eck, J.E., & Dunham, J. (2010). Super controllers and crime prevention: A routine activity explanation of crime prevention success and failure. *Security Journal, 23*, 37–51.

Schaefer, L. (2018a). Environmental corrections: An application of environmental criminological theories to community corrections practices. *Advancing Corrections, 5*, 22–33.

Schaefer, L. (2018b). *When a loved one is on a probation or parole order*. Brisbane, AUS: Griffith Criminology Institute. Retrieved from https://www.docdroid.net/9YIJi8G/when-a-loved-one-is-on-a-probation-or-parole-order.pdf

Schaefer, L., Cullen, F.T., & Eck, J.E. (2016). *Environmental corrections: A new paradigm0020for supervising offenders in the community*. Los Angeles: Sage.

Schaefer, L., Cullen, F.T., & Manchak, S.M. (2017). The role of place in probation and parole. In J. E. Eck & D. Weisburd Eds., *Unraveling the crime-place connection: New directions in theory and policy* (Advances in Criminological Theory series, Vol. 22, pp. 191–215). New York, NY: Routledge.

Schaefer, L., & Little, S. (under review). A quantitative evaluation of the environmental corrections model of probation and parole. *Revised and Resubmitted to Journal of Experimental Criminology*.

Schaefer, L., Mazerolle, L., & Kapnoulla, M. (2017). Different actions for different crimes: Explaining individual action in local crime problems. *Journal of Community Psychology, 45*(7), 922–939.

Schaefer, L., & Williamson, H. (2017). Probation and parole case management as opportunity-reduction supervision. *Journal of Offender Rehabilitation, 56*(7), 452–472.

Solomon, A.L., Osborne, J., Winterfield, L., Elderbroom, B., Burke, P., Stroker, R., ... Burrell, W. (2008). *Putting public safety first: 13 parole supervision strategies to enhance reentry outcomes*. Washington, DC: Urban Institute.

Taxman, F.S. (2011). Parole: Moving the field forward through a new model of behavioral management. In L. Gideon & H.-E. Sung (Eds.), *Rethinking corrections: Rehabilitation, reentry, and reintegration* (pp. 307–328). Thousand Oaks, CA: Sage.

Taxman, F.S., Young, D., & Byrne, J.M. (2004). With eyes wide open: Formalizing community and social control intervention in offender reintegration programmes. In S. Maruna & R. Immarigeon (Eds.), *After crime and punishment: Pathways to offender reintegration* (pp. 233–260). Portland, OR: Willan.

Tillyer, M.S., & Eck, J.E. (2011). Getting a handle on crime: A further extension of routine activities theory. *Security Journal, 24*, 179–193.

Travis, J. (2005). *But they all come back: Facing the challenges of prisoner reentry*. Washington, D.C.: Urban Institute Press.

Urban Institute. (2006). *Understanding the challenges of prisoner reentry: Research findings from the Urban Institute's prisoner reentry portfolio*. Washington, D.C.: Author.

Western, B., & Schiraldi, V. (2017, July 20). Want to shrink our prisons? Fix probation and parole. Retrieved from https://thecrimereport.org/2017/07/20/ want-to-end-mass-incarceration-fix-probation-and-parole/.

Putting qualitative methodology in perspective: reflections on the relevance of fieldwork into the field of Environmental Criminology

Elenice Oliveira

ABSTRACT

This study reflects upon ethical issues and methodological lessons learned by the researcher in conducting fieldwork involving 'hang-outs' with law enforcement and gang members in a dangerous favela in Brazil. This paper also emphasizes the relevance of integrating fieldwork into the field of environmental criminological research, especially today when the in-person observation of crime settings has been challenged by the more cost-effective as well as time-effective use of cutting-edge mapping technology, particularly Google Street View. Finally, it discusses the advantages and constraints experienced by the researcher who is an insider to Brazil but is also nonetheless an outsider to the favela, and how occupying such a liminal space impacted the progress of any fieldwork regarding access to information, creating a rapport with both the police and the gang members, and dealing with the problem of conflicting information provided by both parties.

Quantitative research has traditionally dominated the field of criminology (Meuser & Löschper, 2002; Tewksbury, Dabney, & Copes, 2010), particularly in Environmental Criminology, which attempts to explain the dynamics and variations of crimes, their convergence, and their absence in specific times and places (Weisburd, Bushway, Lum, & Yang, 2004). According to Wortley and Townsley (2017) this field of research has evolved tremendously since the 1990s with the advancement of cutting-edge mapping technology and the Geographic Information System (GIS). Indeed, crime mapping techniques have become just as essential a tool for researchers as statistics (Clarke, 2004). Additionally, mapping technologies like as Google Street View (GSV), besides being more cost-and-time effective, have produced significant progress in gathering environmental data to help explain crime patterns and boost the reliability of research findings (Vandeviver, 2014). This, in turn, has contributed to expanding the influence of Environmental Criminology in crime analysis, policing, and crime prevention policies (Ratcliffe, 2010).

However, this paper asserts that in order to enhance researchers' attempts to understand crime patterns, quantitative analysis driven by official data and mapping technology should be supplemented by qualitative information. There are many places in which computer technological tools falls short, making complete reliance on them a stumbling block. This issue becomes especially relevant when researchers study crime in diverse cultural and social settings that are not only unfamiliar to them, but also may be dangerous. For instance, the low quality of images captured by mapping technology such as GSV can leave a researcher unprepared for the reality of the environment he or she is going to encounter. Oliveira and Hsu (2018) demonstrated that environmental features are not always easily captured by technological tools and are rarely included in quantitative data analysis. Visibility is often limited, and images captured by GSV might not be taken from an angle that would better represent the environmental features that is specific for the researcher. Additionally, the significance of environmental features may be subject to cultural and social contexts that qualitative methods would overlook, particularly in the field of international research (Oliveira & Hsu, 2018; Vandeviver, 2014).

Another problem arises when crime mapping analysis relies on police data containing inaccuracies regarding, for instance, the exact location and time that a crime occurred. This is a crucial issue if researchers are studying crime in impoverished communities such as 'favelas' (De Souza, 2010). The favela, which in Portuguese refers to a densely-populated ghetto, shantytown, or slum, typically located within large Brazilian cities, is important to this specific study as well as to the wider field because it can be considered a fairly accurate representation of similar environments in other developing Latin American countries. Compared with impoverished neighborhoods in more developed countries, Brazilian favelas possess distinct features such as hilly terrain, a chaotic maze of alleyways, a cluttered building landscape, and disorderly numbered addresses. Such a setting has helped create obstacles for investigative police work and has affected the accuracy of official crime data in these areas. Aside from that, there is also the methodological issue caused by the pervasiveness of crime: the literature on violence in favelas (De Souza, 2010; Zaluar, 1994) indicates, for instance, that favelas' residents are often reluctant to report crime to the police. On one hand, this is explained by the fact that drug lords, having been born and continuing to live in the favela, have established closed ties to the community, giving them the status of family members and acquaintances of its other inhabitants. On the other hand, they exercise a ruthless dominance over the community and drive out anyone who tries to interfere with their criminal activities. Residents are keenly aware that drug dealers are establishing ties with political leaders and corrupt police agents in order to expand their own control over the favela, which makes its inhabitants feel helpless or endangered should they speak out.

Finally, the increased reliance on technological tools has also inhibited researchers from exploring different sources of primary data and a variety of productive qualitative methods, specifically in fieldwork, such as interviews with offenders and community residents, as well as direct observation of hotspots. With all of this in mind, empirical research on crime patterns should be supplemented by qualitative fieldwork, especially when researchers intend to explore and understand the association between crime and environment in unfamiliar settings – above all those existing within developing countries, such as the Brazilian favela. In such a context, qualitative fieldwork becomes crucial, offering insights on the researcher's firsthand experience and illuminating the environmental mechanisms and opportunities for crime that are unique to settings that are foreign to outside researchers .

This paper argues that qualitative methods – the human element of a researcher making observations in the actual field – remain crucial for examining issues relating to crime, achieving truly accurate results, and developing productive solutions for real-world problems. Qualitative methods provide researchers with the opportunity to explore how environmental mechanisms are interpreted by criminals as well as local police, acquiring specific meanings within a diverse cultural and social context. In demonstrating the validity of this argument, this paper not only contributes to comparative Environmental Criminology research and theories on an international level, but also advances design crime-prevention policies that take into account the socio-cultural and geographic environment.

This study

In order to explore and analyze the crime and policing in a particular violence-ridden favela in Belo Horizonte, the sixth largest city in Brazil, this study employed Environmental Criminology, which assumes that crime patterns are influenced by the immediate environment and opportunities presented. While not all favelas are hotbeds of crime, they have a reputation of being dangerous places where illegal drug trade and violence thrive with impunity. In line with Environmental Criminology, this aspect of study poses the following research question: how do geographical and environmental mechanisms influence the perception and behaviors of the police and violence-prone individuals in terms of safeguarding the community effectively or committing crime, respectively. The study explores the premise that criminals commit murders with impunity when and where surveillance is limited, where access is easy, and where escape routes are available.

The study also reflects on the methodological leanings and challenges faced by a female researcher in her firsthand experience of conducting fieldwork in the favela. It evaluates how the intersectionality of the researcher's various social identities affects the process of creating the necessary rapport and acquiring trust, particularly during interviews with male subjects. For instance, this author is a female police researcher who is a Brazilian native, but is nevertheless an outsider to the favela, and her acceptance within the local police force benefitted her in many ways, but also presented an obstacle in gaining the acceptance of gang members. The particular research question that emerges from this aspect of the study concerns how the intersectionality of the researcher's social identities affect the fieldwork process, especially when involving two opposing male-dominant groups – law enforcement officers and gang members.

Mixed methods were employed in conducting the research, including the use of secondary police data on gang-related homicides from the period 2006 to 2011 as well as primary data based on regular visits to a local precinct, outings with police officers, and interviews with law enforcement personnel and gang members. Due to safety issues, the field work was conducted during two separate periods: from June to November 2005 – when I conducted my observations at the police precinct, and from February to April 2006 – when I conducted the interviews with gang members. The whole process of data collection and fieldwork was completed in a total period of 7 months.

Qualitative fieldwork within the unique context of a Brazilian favela demands the attentiveness that is also common in the traditional fieldwork employed by ethnographers of crime and deviance, especially when researchers decide to relocate to the place of study. These ethnographers tend to apply a vast array of strategies in order to understand and interpret the meaning of criminal behavior and deviance from the viewpoint of their subjects (Ferrell & Hamm, 1998). As a result, they can establish an in-depth experience and full-time interaction with participants in the study, usually over an unlimited period of time (Maanen, 2011; Spradley, 2016). However, in doing so field researchers often expose themselves to physical harm and unpredictable situations (Arrigo, 1998; Jacobs, 1998; Weisheit, 1998), which has in turn made them the subjects of potential legal, professional, and disciplinary disapproval (Ferrell & Hamm, 1998). Therefore, as is the case with any fieldwork researcher, the examination of the favela in this study required the ability to choose the best strategy, based on the researcher's own judgment and ethics, to solve practical problems and ethical issues *ad hoc* (Hammersley & Atkinson, 2007). Lessons learned from this study contribute to enhancing the variety of methods useful for researchers examining the correlation between environmental mechanisms and crime, as well as resolving ethical issues in dangerous settings.

This current study starts with a reflection on the benefits and constraints unique to being a female researcher, an insider to Brazil, an 'insider-outsider' to the police, and an outsider to the favela, and how occupying such a liminal space affected the progress of the fieldwork. The paper goes on to describe the uniqueness of the environment and the reasons behind the escalation of violence in the favela being studied. The fieldwork with law enforcement is described and subjected to analysis. The paper also reflects on how the geography of the favela affects crime and policing operations, and on the main challenges faced by the researcher regarding gaining access to the favela, including acquiring an informant and contacting gang members. Finally, the study stresses how, in order to understand the violence in the favela, the accounts of the police and gang members as well as the field observation of the favela were crucial, since otherwise the researcher would have been limited to simply reviewing and analyzing homicide statistics and using computer mapping technology.

The intersectionaliy of the researcher's social identities and the field

The intersectionality of my social identities, including my status as 'outside-insider' to the police, my social identity as an 'insider to Brazil, but outsider to *favela*', my gender, and my status as a researcher contributed to create different dynamics with the subjects, including two male dominant opposing groups – police officers and gang members, and strategies to deal with safety issues. While this study is primarily concentrated within a specific geographical area in Brazil, the issues discussed and confronted by the researcher translate across fields and can be applied universally.

The academic debate on the challenges faced by researchers in the fieldwork is not new. However, as the influence of Environmental Criminology in crime analysis abroad expands, it is paramount to generate a more robust discourse on the main methodological challenges faced by researchers exploring crime in settings that not only are unfamiliar, but also potentially dangerous, such as Brazilian favelas. While attempting to gain permission and access to the subjects at hand, it becomes clear that one of the main issues lies in the researcher's unique characteristics and the way in which they are received by the subjects. Along the same lines, the process of creating rapport and acquiring trust is neither neutral nor objective, but is essentially a power negotiation at different degrees and in different contexts between the researcher and the participants (Belur, 2014; Manderson, Bennett, & Andajani-Sutjahjo, 2006). Accordingly, the researcher must be aware of the many ways in which his or her social identities interact with variables in the field. By opening up a discourse on this key issue for researchers, this paper aims to contribute to the advancement of qualitative methodological strategies as well as to guide future fieldwork researchers interested in exploring and comparing crime patterns at the international level.

'Outside-insider' to the police

Studies show the importance of the researcher's perceived status in studying police organizations, as the police readily accept those who are of the same position or are legitimate insiders (Belur, 2014; Huggins & Glebbeek, 2003; Reiner, 2000). Brown (1996) created four categories which classifies the status of a police researcher: a researcher who is civilian and works for a police organization is an insider-outsider; a police officer conducting research on policing is an insider; a researcher from outside the police organization is an outsider; and a former police officer conducting police research is an outsider-insider.

Although my status does not formally fit into Brown's classification statuses, my past experience as an instructor at the police academy in Belo Horizonte, as well as my work as a police researcher at a local university, allowed me to classify myself as a 'legitimate insider' or as a quasi 'outsider-insider.' Added to this is the element of luck, which no doubt is one of the most influential 'strategies' used in facilitating the process of collecting data. This is illustrated by my having discovered old acquaintances now in top-ranking positions in law enforcement, including top commanders of the Military Police, responsible for crime prevention and control, and the commander of the military precinct where I conducted the fieldwork. These fortunate connections contributed to speeding up the process of acquiring official approval when complying with the police's bureaucratic system, and made it easier to carry out the required scientific procedures when conducting field observations at the police station, which has jurisdiction over the particular favela in this study. Additionally, my connections allowed me to be more easily accepted by those in command, which also facilitated the establishment of good rapport with low ranking officers. Finally, I was presented with certain opportunities that pure 'outsiders' could not enjoy – one could say I was given *carte blanche*.

Insider to Brazil and outsider to the favela

In establishing myself as an insider to Brazil, I refer to the fact that I was born and raised in Belo Horizonte and am familiar with the culture and crime that has prevailed throughout the country over many years. This could be considered a disadvantage, as my complete immersion in Brazilian culture may cause me to appear biased. However, being trained as a researcher and having lived in the United States for many years afford me a vastly different viewpoint and open mind. I have achieved a unique balance, which in fact has helped me exercise the anthropological skill of self-detachment from my familiarity with Brazil's culture and its fabric of violence, thus being able to employ a more objective and unbiased perspective. This enabled me to play both sides of the fence and to bring to my research the essence of ethnographic work – making the strange familiar, and the familiar strange (Maanen, 1995).

On the other hand, my being an outsider to the favela also had an important impact on the fieldwork. Superficially, my familiarity with the language and my mixed complexion opened certain doors to me, as I may be perceived as someone 'familiar' to the inhabitants of favelas. It is a fact that most residents in favelas are of Afro-Brazilian descent (Ferrari, 2013), and my skin color easily allowed me to blend in with the residents whose complexions range from light brown to black. Despite being a Brazilian native and Portuguese-speaker with 'mixed' skin tone, it was impossible to conceal the fact that I was not an insider to the favela, particularly in the suspicious eyes of gang members. My middle class manners, educated speech, and my very gestures – all indicated that I was obviously 'different.' This would become a huge obstacle I had to surmount. I was trying to insinuate myself into a community where residents, including drug dealers and other criminals, represent a part of the population that is marginalized by conventional society and constantly under police surveillance (Zaluar & Alvito, 1998). As part of living in the underground of illicit activities, drug dealers and users are constantly discriminated against as a result of their race and their lack of self-worth, and therefore, the majority of them distrust representatives of the mainstream society, as indicated by Bourgois (1995). As a result, I would have to remove the barrier between 'Them' and 'Me' if I had any hope of establishing rapport and trust with various gang members.

Moreover, during my fieldwork I was consistently shocked by what I learned. Despite my secondhand knowledge of favelas as a Brazilian insider, my firsthand experience of exploring their terrain, dangers, and social dynamics shattered any preconceived ideas I may have previously had. Furthermore, during in-person meetings and interviews with criminals, I, as an outsider, was often astonished by what I discovered upon engaging with the participants' perspective. This sense of wonderment that of is, course, central to fieldwork (Maanen, 1995).

Status as female and a researcher

Despite the fact that all researchers working in dangerous settings may potentially be subjected to criminal victimization, regardless of their gender (Howell, 1990; Sluka 1990; William et al. 1992), it is noteworthy that female researchers have additional issues to contend with which emerging solely from their status as women (Williams et al. 1992). They are at risk for sexual harassment, sexual assault, or rape, as well as other types of sexual demands from their male participants. Some female researchers have had their work constrained and even discontinued as result of these problems (Adler and Adler 1987; Horowitz 1986; Howell 1990; Warren 1989). Another factor to consider is the gender inequality, which tends to be inherent in male-dominant groups such as gangs (Miller & Brunson, 2000), with women being seen as 'sexual objects' or 'possessions' (Miller, 1998a) rather than as people. However, my status was elevated in the minds of the gang members partly due to my being constantly accompanied by my informant (which will be elaborated on below), who was familiar to the gang members, and partly because my position as a researcher (I was introduced to the gang members in this fashion) gave me an aura of accomplishment. These mitigating factors compensated for any previous imbalance of power existing in my relationship with the gang members due to my gender or my status as an outsider to favela. Neverthless, in navigating the in-between space I occupied as a female researcher, a Brazilian native, and an outsider to the favela, it was necessary to create a variety of well-crafted strategies in order to access information, recruit participants, foster rapport and trust with both the police and gang members, and deal with the issue of conflicting information provided by both parties.

The particulars of the field: revealing the uniqueness of the favela

The formation of Brazilian favelas began as a social process resulting from the struggle of the economically disadvantaged part of the population to find homes to live in. Similar to shantytowns in other developing countries, favelas are densely populated and built up in a very disorganized and informal manner, without basic urban infrastructure and no social services (De Souza, 2010). Despite the urbanization of Brazilian favelas, the geography and environment of these settlements, usually comprised of a maze of alleys located on hilly terrain, not only poses challenges to policing but also provides a complex environment in which crime can flourish. Although not all favelas are hotbeds of violence, homicides related to local drug trafficking are highly concentrated in few Brazilian favelas and are particularly concentrated in specific locations (De Souza, 2010; De Souza & Miller, 2012). This spatial concentration of violence in favelas makes them a promising field to study in order to understand the influence of environments on crime.

General reasons behind crime in favelas

As previously mentioned, though favelas in Brazil have a common reputation as being dangerous places saturated with drugs and violence, not all favelas are hotbeds of crime. The incidence of violence in favelas can be explained by the explosion of the transnational trafficking of illegal drugs in the 1980s – particularly, with the emergence of cocaine, the rearrangement of local drug dealing groups in favelas, and the increased availability of weapons to local youths involved in gangs (Misse, 2007). This, together with the failure of the government to provide social services and other mechanisms of social control to empower local institutions and the community to restore the quality of life and fight against crime, has caused favelas to become an ideal playground for drug distributors and weapons smugglers to establish their networks with local drug dealers (Misse, 1997). In fact, the marginalization of favelas contributed to the police's well-attested corruption and misuse of force, which in turn has led to the continuous growth of violence (Zaluar & Alvito, 1984). Young armed drug lords challenge state and public authorities, expanding and protecting their criminal interests, and consequently, illegal drug trafficking invades public spaces and becomes a visible activity in the daily life of favelas (Zaluar & Alvito, 1984).

Additionally, a variety of other factors contribute to the proliferation of violence in favelas, such as the fact that a lack of strong gang leadership in local drug trafficking precipitated increased friction among less established drug dealers; conflicts frequently arise motivated by drug debts, revenge, and the dispute of territory with outside gangs. Many young men have been shot dead by other gang members as a result of being involved in local drug trafficking, their bodies left to litter the streets and alleyways. Furthermore, rival gang wars in drug-dealing areas have sparked deadly confrontation between dealers and the police. The police are at a disadvantage here: the disorderly urban landscape of a favela and its labyrinthine geography favors armed drug dealers' attempts to increase their domain over that territory. The pervasiveness of *bocas de fumo* ('smoked mouth' or drug selling spots) at strategic locations exerts informal control over residents, making violence an ordinary event there. No doubt, these factors generate not only an atmosphere of suspicion and uncertainty regarding safety in the community, but also feelings of animosity, intimidation, and fear from local inhabitants.

The favela under examination and its particular reasons for becoming a hotbed of crime

The favela in this study is located in the city of Belo Horizonte, the sixth largest city in Brazil, located southeast of the country. This particular favela occupies an area of 0.83 square kilometers with an estimated 21,499 inhabitants. In the early 2000s, the favela was identified as one of the six hot-spots of violence out of a total of 226 favelas within Belo Horizonte (Instituto Brasileiro de Geografia e Estatisica [Brazilian Institute of Geography and Statistics], 2010).

From 2000 to 2006, official data recorded 112 murders in the favela, with a peak of 27 deaths in 2005. Similar to other Brazilian favelas, the cycle of violence here can be traced to its drug culture. According to officers' accounts, a woman dubbed the 'Drug Queen' – the widow of a drug lord, had dominated local drug trafficking in the middle of 1980s. Despite the presence of other small-time drug dealers and independent vendors, she was the sole distributor of cocaine and marijuana in this particular favela in the 1990s. At this time, the favela was considered the center of distribution and dealing in Belo Horizonte, and while there was local demand for marijuana, the highest demand was from outside buyers attracted to the high quality of the cocaine.

In 1998, to combat this illegal market, law enforcement executed a large police operation known as '*Cavalo de Troia*' (Trojan Horse). In this operation, trucks inconspicuously carrying police officers infiltrated the favela. Once inside and having successfully evaded lookouts, these police officers were able to arrest active drug dealers, including the 'Drug Queen' and her associates. The arrest of the 'Drug Queen' meant the loss of a centralized power in the drug-dealing community, which led to eight gang rival turfs springing up and taking root among local criminals in an effort to seize control of drug sales. These gangs became known for their penchant to kill and maim. In the 2000s, one of the largest of these gangs, located northeast of the favela, became the major cocaine and marijuana distributor in the area, and one of the main drug distributors in all of Belo Horizonte.

Information regarding violence in the favela garnered from the officers' accounts helped me anticipate the challenges of the fieldwork, which would require attentiveness, intense involvement, and exposure to unpredictable and risky situations. Additionally, as an insider to Brazil but an outsider to the favela, I found it necessary to reflect on how my liminal status would affect certain fieldwork aspects such as accessing information, creating rapport, interacting with both parties in the study, and developing strategies to deal with safety issues.

Conducting fieldwork with law enforcement

My fieldwork with police officers shed light on their main concerns with violence in the favela, as well as their perceptions of how environmental features pose challenges to ensuring safety. My initial acquaintance with police officials, as described earlier, was integral in creating rapport and interviewing low ranking officers as well as to further accompanying police officers on ride-a-longs and foot patrols; gaining their trust was also vital in facilitating my access to homicide data.

One of the most crucial elements in conducting research with law enforcement as participants is establishing the trust that is required between academics and officials (Hunt, 1984). Conventionally, as part of a hierarchical organization, law enforcement officers are not only reluctant in providing information about their daily activities, but are also cynical and suspicious of researchers and how they will use their findings. However, my teaching stint at local police academies and my credentials as a police researcher at the local university helped me strengthen my reputation and my personal network of police officials. This experience and my status as a quasi 'outsider-insider' to the police were pivotal to opening the doors of law enforcement to my research. Even with these advantages, I also had to adhere to the police's bureaucratic system when acquiring official approval; nevertheless, my acquaintance with police officials hastened the approval process and made it easier to carry out the required scientific procedures of conducting field observations.

After obtaining the necessary approval from the top official, I began the fieldwork at the local police precinct with a series of visits in order to cultivate rapport with the commander, who gave me a 'free pass' to communicate with his personnel at any time. The local commander's democratic management style afforded middle-ranking police officers their unsolicited input and allowed for the use of broad discretionary power in decision making, which generated a palpable atmosphere of 'team spirit' at the precinct. This was in sharp contrast to the typical hierarchical structuring of the military police operation. Lieutenants and sergeants here seemed to be less resistant and suspicious in allowing me to participate as an observer at police meetings and to accompany outings, even including coffee breaks.

At first glance, in my first weeks of establishing a working rapport with top commanders and middle-ranking officers it seemed that my status had been elevated to a higher level than that of a mere outsider. Being a quasi 'outsider-insider' and having made the acquaintance of senior top officials turned out to be more beneficial that I had expected, which, as I have mentioned, led to my initial approval and acceptance of my research work. Although this provided me with free reign to meet and talk with other officers, I had to be careful to maintain a formal relationship and not allow myself to become too personal. As a female in a male-dominated organization, I am aware of the fact that in general many women are subjected to harassment (Steinþórsdóttir & Pétursdóttir, 2017). To avoid any misinterpretation of my work as a researcher and to maintain a relationship with higher standards of respect, I always addressed all officers by their specific rank. I also assured the commander that

I would keep him updated as to my progress, including visits to the precinct, without jeopardizing the anonymity and confidentiality of information received from other officers. Nonetheless, it should be mentioned that no male-dominant organization can be totally free of sexual harassment. Although, I myself was treated with courtesy and cordiality during my fieldwork with top police executives, many police officers showed enthusiasm in sharing their knowledge regarding violence in the favela merely because they desired interaction with – and the chance to show off to – a woman.

During my field observations at the police precinct, I sat in as an observer during large police meetings involving the majority of staff members. I was also privy to smaller operational meetings conducted by the commander and a number of high-ranking officers in the Group Specialized in Policing Risk Areas (GEPAR) and the Tactical group. The Tactical Group, quite similar to the SWAT team, responds to emergency calls related to violent crimes. It is comprised of four officers and systematically conducts proactive foot patrols in the favela, particularly on gang turfs. On the other hand, GEPAR not only patrols the favela 24/7, but is also in charge of controlling and monitoring gang groups. In addition, GEPAR officers are responsible for community policing aimed at fostering relationships with local residents. Three groups of GEPAR are deployed in the favela in this study. Each one is made up of a team of four officers working split shifts of eight hours each. During my encounters with the high-ranking officers of both groups, I expressed an interest in their daily routine and was thereby able to gain knowledge of their experience of violence in the favela.

Interviews with ranking officers

Interviews with ranking officers was a valuable opportunity to immerse myself in the favela from the officers' standpoint, as they had at least 10 years of extensive experience patrolling that environment. In fact, some of the police officers were born and, at the time of the study, resided in the favela. Such knowledge provided a deeper understanding of local police officers' perspective of the violence, the challenges they face when patrolling the area, and their frustrations and expectations regarding crime control and prevention.

The interviews were conducted with a total of 12 police officers: four officers of the GEPAR team; four officers of the Tactical Group; two officers working at the Statistics and Crime Analysis Unit, and two other officers working in the Intelligence Unit. These interviews, which lasted approximately between 1 and 2 hours each, were conducted at the local police precinct. As part of my methodology plan, I also established a rapport with two sergeants in charge of the Statistics Unit and two officers of the Intelligence Unit. This played an important role in my having access to homicide reports. Contact with these officers kept me updated on the dynamics of local gangs, which further helped me to secure interviews with key gang members. Verbal consent from those being interviewed was required, and nothing was recorded. However, I did take many notes, which I later organized into a full report, and managed to preserve the confidentiality of all those involved by using fictitious names. Notes and observations were secured in a safe place.

Maintaining the researcher's safety during outings with officers into the favela

Ride-a-longs and foot patrols gave officers the opportunity to willingly discuss their own experiences with gang members as well as other challenges in their line of work. However, listening to officers 'live' was challenging: I needed to remain fully focused and in the moment, listening attentively in order to decipher all the new information they offered as well as to recognize its link to my previous research, while simultaneously also observing the favela's surroundings. Similarly, the police officers needed to be alert in order to ensure everyone's safety.

I participated with officers of the Tactical Group in two ride-a-longs from 2:00 p.m. to 10:00 p.m. and three foot patrols from 10:00 p.m. to 1:00 a.m., completing a total of 22 hours. After solving the initial issue of obtaining permission to be part of these outings, the second major concern was for my safety. The ride-a-longs had to be well-planned to avoid my being identified by gang members, including disguising my physical appearance. This became paramount. I wore my hair in a ponytail covered by a hat and dark glasses. I also decided to dress in slacks and a long sleeved shirt, similar in color to the light brown police uniforms. To be in sync with the police – as well as for my own physical protection – I dressed in a bulletproof vest and boots. I always sat on the back seat between two officers to further conceal my identity.

To reduce the likelihood of any confrontation with gang members, foot patrols were conducted late at night, from 10:00 p.m. to 1:00 a.m., on quiet days such as Mondays and Tuesdays, when no drug activities could be observed. The Group Tactical commander considered this 'safety time,' which had many advantages from a methodological perspective. For instance, I was able to maintain my connection with the police and learn about their perspective while minimizing the chances that someone would actually spot me in their company; typically, if dealers and lookouts saw me with the police, I would be deemed a snitch, thus jeopardizing my safety.

The geography of the favela and its impact on crime and policing

Environmental Criminology posits that all human behavior results from the interaction between an individual and an immediate situation (Wortley & Townsley, 2017). Therefore, a complete understanding of crime involves a precise knowledge of how specific elements of the immediate environment or situation influences individuals' perceptions and behavior as well as their subsequent decision to either commit crime or attempt to prevent it. The direct observation of crime scenes through the eyes of those who are responsible for safety in the favela was valuable in identifying and examining situational factors that explain crime patterns and their variations in time and space.

During the ride-a-longs, which were conducted during the daytime, I gained a general overview of the landscape of this and other neighboring favelas. Furthermore, I was also able to observe some known drug dealing locations in accessible areas, including specific spots in open streets (as opposed to the alleyways where drug deals were most prevalent). These open spots were on the borders, often connected to main highways and avenues, which provided easy access to outside buyers. Lookouts were strategically positioned on hilly parts of the favela, which provided an unobstructed view of any outside arrivals. I observed a total of 37 locations of street drug dealing.

In addition, I had the unique experience of being immersed in some of the most hidden parts of the favela, including alleys and local bars where drug activities are widespread, the houses where most well-known drug dealers reside, and spots where homicides have occurred. Observing alleys at night with police officers provided me a direct experience of the time and place in which the majority of homicides transpire. Although the favela is generally well-lit, its alleyways tend to be less illuminated. I was able to observe how the silence and emptiness that characterize these closed parts of the favela create an ideal site for homicides. It is in these areas that many of the drug dealers, murderers, and their victims live and die.

One crime scene I observed during a ride-along is worth recounting to illustrate how the experience helped me understand the role the environment plays in shaping locals' reactions to a murder scene. It was past midnight when the Tactical Group was called to attend to a homicide that had occurred in front of a bar. Upon our arrival, many local residents had surrounded the body, including young adults, children, and seniors. Observing the locals' apathy and silence, I had the impression that they saw this scenario as normal – that a young man shot to death was 'just one more death on the streets.' Because this is the daily reality of living in a violence-ridden favela, for them the victim was not a person, but a statistic.

The ride-a-longs and foot patrols provided the opportunity to gain deeper insight into the favela's environmental features. The irregular terrain and the built landscape of the favela not only challenge police surveillance, but also play a major role in an offender's decision to commit crime at specific locations. For example, police officers explained that the houses, which are built adjacent to each other, with no spaces in between, offer criminals the advantage of escaping via rooftops as well as easy access to others' houses to hide themselves, drugs, or weapons by means of breaking and entering. Because of this cluttered environment, drug dealers feel secure in their control of the area. Another challenge for the police is the existence of gated alleyways in areas where shootings and homicides frequently occur. These gated alleyways are symptomatic of the residents' attempt to control their own 'territory' and to protect themselves, yet they also inhibit police surveillance.

In short, I was able to observe and reflect on how geographical details and the physical environment shape criminal activity. The opportunity to do this without time constraints and with direct access to the perspective of the police alleviated any doubts I may have had related to the link between environmental factors and crime events. Take, for instance, the challenge of police surveillance of the entry points to the largest gang turf in the favela, a 9.77-hectare residential area in the northeast. According to the police, this is considered the most densely populated part of the favela, corresponding to about 10% of the total area. The police sergeant leading our group explained that the area's layout is loop-shaped, which has made the entire location a large 'boca de fumo.' Illegal drug commerce operates freely there while armed dealers' 'security guards' are vigilant around entrances and exits. The area's layout also complicates police surveillance as it has numerous entrances and exits leading to other interconnected alleys surrounding the area.

In another scenario, we were on foot patrol and standing on the center of an alley where, according to the police, significant drug activity had occurred. Because so much of the favela is oppressively narrow and cramped, the police are restricted to foot patrol, which has many drawbacks. The police admitted that, because of the large network of alleys, criminals can move across the entire favela without ever being seen by officers. Criminals therefore rarely need to find a new place to hide.

Furthermore, the hilly, curved terrain restricts visibility, and the labyrinth of alleys obstructs their view of criminal activity, making it difficult to identify perpetrators, their hangouts, and other hidden spots. The hills also make it more difficult to pursue a criminal and the criminals' familiarity with the area and knowledge of shortcuts allows for a quick escape from law enforcement. Not only is foot patrol strenuous for officers, but it also makes them vulnerable to being trapped by criminals. While confrontations between police officers and criminals are rare (as criminals tend to avoid them), the claustrophobic nature of these closed areas significantly increases the chances of confrontation between an offender and a police officer compared with more open areas. As a result, it is distinctly possible that the police may end up as victims themselves.

The complicated geography of the area requires alternative strategies for police conducting foot patrols. Officers employ military discipline and tactics to enter the favela and curtail their vulnerability, as well as to reduce danger. To catch criminals off guard, they rarely take the same route when arriving in high-risk areas. Usually, Tactical Group officers enter the favela in units of four. They walk through the alleys with guns in hand, one behind the other, several feet apart. The first officer in line operates almost as a scout. The second officer is responsible for looking out for the man in front of and behind him. The third officer is always the commander of the group. The officer behind the commander watches the rooftops for criminals and watches the rear to protect the group from assault. When accompanying the Tactical Group on foot patrol I was between the commander and the last officer in line. This is part of the Military code and was useful in protecting my identity. We often walked through dark alleyways and secluded areas, which were often deserted. The barking of dogs was audible in the background. Several officers of the GEPAR unit were strategically positioned at the entrances of these areas to help protect the group from the unexpected arrival of anyone who might create confrontation. The main idea of patrolling the favela is to send a critical message that criminals do not have control despite the physical barriers of the terrain, as explained below by the Tactical Group sergeant:

> There's no specific way for us to move in there. You face different obstacles in every situation and in every approach. If we move in one hundred times, it'll be one hundred unique strategies. What my team often does is to never move in through the same place. There are many entrance points. So I try to not always use the same entrance point because they could be on to us and if they try to set a trap for us tomorrow, it would be that much easier for them to do so. That's why I never use the same spot when moving in."

From a methodological perspective, the ride-a-longs and foot patrols provided the opportunity to gain a deeper insight into the favela's environmental features and how they played a role in an offender's decision to commit crimes at specific locations, as is assumed by Environmental Criminology.

Fieldwork with gang members in the favela

Armed with as much information as possible, I proceeded with my plan to interview active gang members in order to explore their stories and perceptions of the police, violence, and life in the favela. Despite the fact that my informant would initiate contact and facilitate my encounters with the gang members, I myself needed to deal with several other issues, including coming up with strategies of establishing rapport and trust, ensuring safety and, finally, deciding on an appropriate location to meet.

Gang members in this study, all of them in their early twenties, agree that the story of violence in the favela can be traced back to ages-old rivalry and retaliation among previous generations of outlaws. On the one hand, the favela's *de facto* law 'to kill and to be killed' can be considered a 'reward,' as it allows criminals to keep their 'status' and settle scores. On the other hand, it also embodies the 'costs' of living in the criminal underworld; gang members have admitted that the favela negatively affects their daily life, as they become confined to their turfs and cannot break free of the cycle of criminal activities. Police officers also perceive the environment of the favela as favoring criminal activity.

Gaining access to the favela and its inhabitants

I conducted my first solo trip to the favela in late 2005. The aim was to improve my grasp of the area and thereby anticipate safety issues and other potential problems as I prepared for my contact with gang members. I also wanted to immerse myself in the favela atmosphere to obtain my own impressions and firsthand information. I took 40-minute bus ride from downtown to the favela. I had planned to get there around 4:00 p.m., as I thought it would be a safe and appropriate time because of the high level of pedestrian activity. Despite already being in the favela during my ride-a-longs with the police, I found that visits alone and on foot enabled me to observe a significantly different scene than previously encountered.

The moment the bus entered the favela, my first impression was that it was similar to other neighborhoods in the city. Its urban development, with bustling traffic and busy commercial activity, made me feel I was in a typical low-income urban neighborhood. There were some signs of poverty in the distance, subtly signaled by a row of unfinished brick houses, but nothing was highly distinctive.

I decided to wear plain and inconspicuous clothes to avoid being seen as an outsider. Unfortunately, my so-called disguise had not been successful. Immediately upon my arrival, I was approached by a man standing in front of a store who asked me what I was doing there. He advised me to exercise caution, as the area was full of drug dealer lookouts, and then identified an individual in the vicinity as one. Feeling quite shocked, I simply replied that I was meeting some friends and went on my way. After a few blocks, the individual he had identified as a lookout drew near to me. I then decided that it was time to leave, as I was really frightened at this point.

This first solo trip was brief, but productive nonetheless. Planning my interviews with gang members would clearly be impossible without serious consideration for my safety. I learned how important it was to accurately plan dates and times to avoid confrontations. Upon reflection of the risk to which I had exposed myself out of an impetuous desire to acquire my own impression of the favela, I realized that there were some key ethical issues regarding the extent to which a researcher should endanger him- or herself to obtain information. Despite my reservations, my brief solo experience of the favela convinced me that I would need an informant to assist me, not only to have access to the favela and recruit gang members, but also to accompany me in my interviews with them.

Acquiring an informant

From February to April 2006, I invested more time conducting my own personal observation of the favela in the company of my informant as well as interviewing the gang members who lived there. Since I intended to establish contact with gang members, obviously the ideal informant would be one most knowledgeable about gangs and familiar with the area. Following the advice of the local commander, I was able to contact the coordinator of a local government crime prevention program called *Fica Vivo* (Staying Alive) who helped me to recruit one of the program's participants who had demonstrated interest in assisting me. My informant, whom I will refer to only as 'Mark,' was 26 years old, born and raised in the favela, and had been a gang member as a teenager. He was the perfect informant for a researcher like me: knowledgeable, self-motivated, and fully engaged in assisting me. For two weekends, he took me on a tour of the area, guiding me through mazes of alleyways and revealing places I could not have possibly discovered alone.

My visits to the favela with my informant allowed me to observe the favela in the daytime when the streets and business areas were relatively busy. I witnessed the favela's social backdrop in motion while ensuring my safety. Mark was helpful in showing me hangouts such as specific corners, bars, and alleyways that were popular among gang members. Most importantly, these visits created opportunities for locals to see me in Mark's company, making me seem like I belonged, which might help me to create rapport with gang members in the future.

Contact with gang members and drug lords

For my interviews with gang members, I selected six of the most well-known drug dealers based on the police data, each of whom was recruited with the assistance of my local informant Mark. However, I was only concerned with those who were currently active and not incarcerated. Initially, only two drug lords were contacted. Four others were introduced to me by Mark. Ultimately, I met six active gang members, all of them males in their 20s, who verbally agreed to talk with me provided that their confidentiality would be assured. My informant not only helped me to decide on meeting places and times, but also accompanied me during the interviews, which I will describe further on.

These interviews were conducted at different locales depending upon the requirements of each participant. I requested their permission to use a tape recorder, and afterwards, the interviews were typewritten and kept in a safe place together with other information that I had collected. All the participants' names were kept confidential, as well as their gang affiliations.

Establishing a good rapport and acquiring trust with gang members

During my contact with gang members, I was keenly aware that my various social identities could drastically affect my reception by and interactions with them. Despite the minimal risk of being target by the participants, it was a concern that required my utmost attention, in part because I am a woman and women are typically less respected by men in gang culture (Jody, 1998a; Miller & Brunson, 2000) Furthermore, it was necessary for my own protection that I not reveal my connections to the police. It was of the utmost importance that I gain gang members' trust and convince them that I was purely doing research and had no ulterior motives. As each meeting with gang members was unique in terms of what contingencies might and did occur, I had to constantly temper my own anxiety before these encounters.

Being constantly accompanied by my informant, a former drug dealer and well-known among the participants, helped not only to create an easy rapport with my subjects, but also helped to mitigate any issues that might have arisen due to my gender. However, establishing rapport was far less challenging than acquiring actual trust. As my interactions with the gang members progressed, I found myself continuously having to deal with issues of mistrust that opened onto concerns for my own safety. The participants in the study were always concerned that they might be dealing with a snitch, and as a result, I was threatened with a number of serious repercussions should I fail to convince them that I was worthy of their trust. I was inundated with threats ('If I find out that you are a police officer or working with the police, I will find you and your family'), leery questions ('Why are you studying us? We are amateurs. You should study violence in Rio') – referring to another large Brazilian city, and dismissals ('We are more interested in doing our 'business' and making money than in having problems with the "men" [the police]').

I had to convince gang members that I had no police connections, which put me in a rather precarious position because this was untrue. Such circumstances forced me to learn how to manage the relentless fear that if I were caught in a lie and if my connection with the police was ever revealed my family and I would be at risk. This anxiety always lurked in the back of my mind during each encounter. However, I had taken some methodological precautions to make sure that my relationship with the police was remained hidden from the eyes of local residents and gang members. For instance, interviews with police officers were conducted at the local police jurisdiction near the favela, not at the favela itself, and the ride-a-longs and foot patrols were kept to a reduced number, conducted on specific times and days when there was little chance of me being seen. I finally was able to reach the point where open collaboration was achieved.

Aside from the reassuring presence of Mark and my concealment of my associations with law enforcement, two major factors contributed to reducing any distrust that might arise. First, I demonstrated no interest in investigating details of the gang members' current illicit activities, emphasizing that the main focus of my study was to understand whether or not the conditions of the favela environment can influence the rational decision-making process in committing crime at specific places. This allowed them to feel more comfortable and willing to participate. Secondly, I tried to make our encounters feel as informal as possible. Although the interviews were planned ahead of time and for a specific purpose, which gives them some elements of formality, I made sure that the give and take of the discussion was more conversational and felt less like an actual interview. This strategy induces a sense of confidence and motivates the subjects to divulge real experiences and beliefs. In order to pull off the illusion of the 'informal' interviews while still effectively obtaining the information I was seeking, I needed to be highly attentive and interpret the subjects' verbal and body language, adjusting my approach as necessary to make them feel comfortable. During my encounters, the turning point was to convince gang members, who traditionally live in an underground and marginalized world and are constantly targeted by the police, that I was interested in listening and writing about their lives and their perceptions of the favela and the police.

Although cultural anthropologists and ethnographers generally believe that, in order to obtain trust, it is necessary to immerse themselves completely within the world of the participants in the study (Bourgois, 1995), I was able to acquire a significant degree of trust without taking such measures; even if it was constrained to the specific context of the interview, I was able to give the subjects a feeling of self-worth and thereby earn their trust for a short period of time. Yet obviously, my short interaction with them could not create bonds as deep as those generated by the ethnographer's total immersion in the subjects' lives, and this often led me to wonder if some of the participants' statements were entirely truthful or simply fabricated with the intent of self-promotion.

Another important issue was meeting with active gang members in locations they saw as havens. Gang members usually remained on their own turfs located in the hidden parts of the favela, where they could walk about freely without any threats from rival gangs, and they tended to avoid awkward situations, for instance, confrontation with the police.

Therefore, the location of each encounter had to suit the specific requirements of each participant. A well-know and established drug lord prefers to meet on his own turf, typically in an alley close to his residence. Offenders, similar to law enforcement personnel, recognize the presence of alleyways as a favorable factor for crime, since these facilitate the escape of offenders and their subsequent disappearance into less accessible areas of the favela, which are rarely reached by the police. As they explained, the maze of alleys provides natural protection for them and, in turn, a massive risk for police officers. A drug lord also prefers being in the company of his comrades. In such a circumstance, the main issue is dealing with unpredictability, particularly in a favela identified as a hotbed of violence. Our meeting could be disrupted by shootings, other gang conflicts, or even by the unexpected arrival of the police, which made me feel apprehensive of the risks involved in meeting gang members in such a setting. Overall, I was unable to completely anticipate how these encounters would unfold.

My experience proved that unpredictability is a reality that researchers must confront when conducting these types of studies. For example, my informant and I met with a drug lord in the dead-end alleyway of his residence. My informant had notified me that four other gang members would be present as well, which severely troubled me and cast doubt on whether I should attend such a meeting. I wondered, how would this meeting evolve? Would they be armed? While the gang members never threatened me, I was nonetheless intimidated by the presence of weapons. Notwithstanding, having taken the precaution of communicating the time, day, and location of this meeting to the commander of the jurisdiction, I took the chance and attended. And yet, however appropriate I felt this precaution might be, it also raised ethical concerns: while I was cautious never to jeopardize the confidentiality of the information I acquired in my meetings with gang members, I questioned whether I was just in informing the police of my whereabouts without the gang's knowledge or permission. Furthermore, I thought about how much information about my own identity I should conceal from gang members and whether it was unethical to deceive in this circumstance. My final decision was to trust the commander's affirmation that safety would be assured to all of us.

Conclusion

Employing different strategies in my fieldwork allowed me not only to reflect on some ethical and methodological issues, as previously described, but also yielded some insights that can guide researchers, particularly those following the tradition of Environmental Criminology, who are interested in advancing comparative and international research in order to understand the ecology of crime in dangerous environments.

First, fieldwork provided more advantages than if I had simply examined statistics or crime mapping technology. Official data related to homicide locations in the complex environment of favelas is often compromised by incomplete addresses and problems with recording addresses. This might be explained by the fact that the locations of homicides can become confused due the unclear borders separating favelas and the disorderly numbering of addresses. The deficiencies and inaccuracies of the information related to homicide locations reflect a complex problem related to the disorganized process of urban occupation of favelas in addition to signaling the difficulties municipal authorities face when they try to update addresses and other information in these areas. The absence of logical numerical sequences for street addresses is very common in favelas, especially where there is a concentration of streets connected to alleys. This lack of proper numbering leads to the same problem in adjacent alleys, thus perpetuating faulty address sequencing throughout entire favelas.

Another obstacle to maintaining any semblance of order in record keeping is that residents commonly create their own address numbers or create unofficial names for alleys; this frequently confuses police who are unfamiliar with the favela, and makes it necessary to constantly update the official address database. The process of updating addresses is a slow one, because verification is undertaken on foot by professionals who are unfamiliar with the area. Furthermore, the presence of armed drug dealers in certain parts of the favela makes access difficult for the municipal employees responsible for updating address registers. This also complicates mapping the favela using technology such as Google Street View. As a result, law enforcement personnel unfamiliar with the urban layout of the favelas to which they are assigned can commit costly errors in registering addresses where crimes have occurred. Additionally, law enforcement's unfamiliarity with the area makes it very challenging for them to identify the addresses where homicides occurred, and limits their ability to anticipate risks that might jeopardize their arrival and investigative work in these areas.

Due to the cluttered environment of the favela, favelas have rarely been mapped completely. Not surprisingly, in the case of the favela in this study, mapping technology was not able to capture detailed images of alleyways and pedestrian paths. In addition, many other features of the favela cannot be conceptualized and measured by using only quantitative methods; the quantitative must be supplemented with the crafted methodology of qualitative fieldwork in order to realize the larger picture. Such features include the existence of gated alleys, the presence of drug dealers' lookouts and open drug dealing spots, and the variation of the social dynamics and crime activities during different hours.

Second, conducting interviews with subjects traditionally on opposing sides, such as law enforcement and gang members, poses challenges for the researcher, who must establish trust with all participants. My bond with the police was built on constant collaboration and cooperation. I frequently visited the local police station, not only to update my research with the most current information available, but also to foster good rapport. I did my utmost to promote trust between the police and myself, while exercising diligence in making sure that it would not interfere in my relationship with gang members. In creating rapport and trust with gang members, concealing my identity was necessary not only so as to make it easier to gain the subjects' confidence, but also to ensure my own safety. Ultimately, this issue was irresolvable, as my connections to the police meant that any relationship with gang members was temporary at best. Additionally, managing the proper dates and times to conduct fieldwork, as well as selecting appropriate locations to meet participants, was fundamental in being able to maintain both parties' safety.

Furthermore, it is important to note that there is no methodological guide able to predict how the intersectionality of social identities of the researcher might impact the relationship with the research subjects. The interactions between the researcher and those being interviewed are always uniquely impacted by the social identities of both parties (Belur, 2014).

Safety was perpetually an issue to be dealt with in conducting my research. I was constantly at risk during my outings in the favela, and when I was compelled to conceal my connections with the police during my interviews with gang members, I was placed into an even more precarious position – that of lying to subjects who would not hesitate to harm me if they found out. Yet it must be stressed that the qualitative information that fieldwork yields makes it well worth the risk. Subsequent research should continue to explore the practical and ethical issues of safety that arise from this kind of fieldwork.

As is common in qualitative research, an issue that arose during my study was the threat to the validity of field observations, since information obtained from gang members and the police are vulnerable to self-report bias (Hammersley & Atkinson, 2007). Furthermore, I needed to consider to what degree my contact with offenders and with the police may have influenced the responses from both groups; also, a common problem in qualitative research, this phenomenon is known as reactivity (Hammersley & Atkinson, 2007). In dealing with both validity problems, I was able to validate the information that I obtained from my own work and collected material by testing police narratives against the narratives of offenders as well as against police data.

To sum up, collecting information from different sources – a process well-known as triangulation – reduces the risks inherent to relying on a single source of information (Maxwell, 1996). The triangulation process was integral in understanding the perspectives of different groups and illuminating how their perceptions of the environmental mechanisms shape crime patterns as well as policing in the context of a dangerous favela in Brazil; this in turn aided in answering the main research questions. Although the favela presented a unique situation, the results of fieldwork provide new and far-reaching insights that are beneficial for researchers studying opposing groups in dangerous areas.

Acknowledgments

This study would not have been possible without the support of the commander of the Military Police in Belo Horizonte, Brazil and all the participants. Special thanks to Col. Marco Antonio Bicalho for facilitating this research.

Disclosure statement

No potential conflict of interest was reported by the author.

References

Arrigo, B.A. (1998). Shattered lives and shelter lies? Anatomy of research deviance in homeless programming and policy. In J. Farrell & M.S. Hamm (Eds.), *Ethnography at the edge: Crime, deviance, and field research* (pp. 44–64). Northeastern University Press.

Belur, J. (2014). Status, gender and geography: Power negotiations in police research. *Qualitative Research Journal. Sage Publications, 14*(2), 184–200.

Bourgois, P. (1995). *In search of respect selling crack in El Barrio*. Cambridge University Press: San Francisco University.

Brown, J. (1996). Police research: Some critical issues. In F. Leishman, B. Loveday, & S. Savage (Eds.), *Core issues in policing* (pp. 178–190). Harlow: Longman.

Clarke, R.V. (2004). Technology, criminology and crime science. *European Journal on Criminal Policy and Research, 10*, 55–63.

De Souza, E. (2010). *Situational Factors in Homicides in a Violence-Ridden Brazilian Favela*. doi:10.7282/T31V5F26

De Souza, E., & Miller, J. (2012). Homicide in the Brazilian Favela: Does opportunity make the killer? *British Journal of Criminology, 52*(4), 786–807. Retrieved from http://www.jost.org/stable/4417357

Ferrari, J.M. (2013). *Segragacao socioespacial em Belo Horizonte: Desafio historico para a habitacao de interesse social* [Socio-spatial segragacao in Belo Horizonte: Historical challenge for housing of social interest]. Belo Horizonte: Revista Conexao Gerais.

Ferrell, J., & Hamm, M.S. (1998). True confessions. In J. Farrell & M.S. Hamm (Eds.), *Ethnography at the edge: Crime, deviance, and field research* (pp. 2–19). Boston: Northeastern University Press.

Hammersley, M., & Atkinson, P. (2007). *Ethnography: Principles in practice* (2nd ed.). New York: Routledge.

Huggins, M., & Glebbeek, L. (2003). Women studying violent male institutions: Cross-gendered dynamics in police research on secrecy and danger. *Theoretical Criminology, 7*(3), 363–387.

Instituto Brasileiro de Geographia e Estatistica—IBGE Census. (2010).

Jacobs, B.A. (1998). Researching crack dealers: Dilemmas and contradictions. In J. Farrell & M. S. Hamm (Eds.), *Ethnography at the Edge: Crime, Deviance, and Field Research* (pp. 160–177). Boston: Northeastern University Press.

Maanen, J.V. (1995). An end to innocence: The ethnography of ethnography. In J. Van Maanen (Ed.), *Representation in ethnography* (pp. 1–35). Thousand Oaks, CA: Sage.

Maanen, J.V. (2011). *Tales of the field – On writing ethnography*. Chicago and London: The University of Chicago Press.

Manderson, L., Bennett, E., & Andajani-Sutjahjo, S. (2006). The social dynamics of the interview: Age, class and gender. *Qualitative Health Research, 16*(10), 1317–1334.

Meuser, M., & Löschper, G. (2002). Introduction: Qualitative research in criminology [26 paragraphs]. *Forum Qualitative Sozialforschung/Forum: Qualitative Social Research, 3*(1). Art. 12.

Miller, J. (1998a). Gender and victimization risk among young women in gangs. *Journal of Research in Crime and Delinquency, 35*, 429–453.

Miller, J., & Brunson, R.K. (2000). Gender dynamics in youth gangs: A comparison of males' and genders' accounts. *Journal of Justice Quarterly*, *17*(3), 49–448.

Misse, M. (1997). As Ligacoes Perigosas: Mercados Ilegais, Narcotrafico e Violencia no Rio [Dangerous ligands: Illegal markets, narcotics and violence in Rio]. *Comtemporaneidade e Educacao*, *1*, 93–116.

Misse, M. (2007). Illegal markets, protection rackets and organized crime in Rio de Janeiro. *Estudos Avancados*, *21*(61), 139–157. Sao Paulo Sept/Dec. Print version ISSN 0103-4014.

Oliveira, E.D., & Hsu, K. (2018). Exploring places of street drug dealing in a downton area in Brazil: An analysis of the reliability of Google street view in international criminology. *International Journal of Criminology and Sociology*, *7*, 32–47. Lifescience Global.

Ratcliffe, J. (2010). Crime mapping: Spatial and temporal challenges. In A.R. Piquero & D. Weisburd (Eds.), *Handbook of quantitative criminology*. springer science+Business media, LLC. doi:10.1007/978-0-387.77650-7-2@

Reiner, R. (2000). Police research. In R. King & E. Wincup (Eds.), *Doing Research on Crime and Justice* (pp. 205–227). New York: Oxford University Press.

Spradley, J.P. (2016). *The ethnographic interview*. Long Grove, IL: Waveland Press Inc.

Steinþórsdóttir, F.S., & Pétursdóttir, G.M. (2017). Preserving masculine dominance in the police force with gendered bullying and sexual harassment. *Policing: A Journal of Policy and Practice*, *12* (2), 165–176.

Tewksbury, R., Dabney, D.A., & Copes, H. (2010). The prominence of qualitative research in criminology and criminal justice scholarship. *Journal of Criminal Justice Education*, *21*(4), 391–411.

Vandeviver, C. (2014). Applying Google maps and Google street view in criminological research. *Crime Science - An Interdisciplinary Journal*. *3*(1), 13. Springer.

Weisburd, D., Bushway, S., Lum, C., & Yang, S.M. (2004). Trajectories of crime at places: A longitudinal study of street segments in the city of Seattle. *Criminology*, *42*(2), 283–322.

Weisheit, R.A. (1998). Marijuana subcultures: Studying crime in rural America. In J. Farrell & M. S. Hamm (Eds.), *Ethnography at the edge: Crime, deviance, and field research* (pp. 178–203). Northeastern University Press.

Wortley, R., & Townsley, M. (2017). *Environmental criminology and crime analysis* (2nd ed.). Crime Science Series, Routledge.

Zaluar, A., & Alvito, M. (Eds.). (1998). *Cem anos de favela* [One hundred years of favela]. Rio de Janeiro: FGV.

Exploring the influence of daily microroutines on residential guardianship and monitoring patterns

Emily Moir, Danielle M. Reynald, Timothy C. Hart and Anna Stewart

ABSTRACT

Everyday routine activities affect the convergence in space and time of motivated offenders, suitable targets, and capable guardians. When locations of convergence are studied in this context, they tend to be viewed as part of a much larger pattern of movements through one's normal activity space. Although our understanding of crime and victimisation risk has been advanced considerably by studying places where incidents occur and our movements to-and-from them, far less is known about our everyday routine activities *within* locations that are part of our daily activity patterns and how our behaviour while at these places influence criminal opportunities – including opportunities for preventing crime. In response, the current study explores the impact of individuals' daily microroutines undertaken while at home on opportunities to supervise and act as guardians over their suburban surroundings. Using a sample of Brisbane suburban residents who completed semi-structured interviews (*N* = 20), we show how daily macroroutines affected when residents are home; but more importantly, how their daily microroutines influenced when – and for how long – they are able to engage in supervision over their residential areas. Implications for opportunity theories in general and measurement of guardianship behaviour, in particular, are discussed.

Our lives are defined by a handful of daily routine activities that often include coming and going to work or school, engaging in housework, shopping, and undertaking social and leisure activities at malls, entertainment venues, or our friends' homes (Cohen & Felson, 1979). Routine activities determine when we are in certain places, how much time we spend there, and how we travel to and from them (P.L. Brantingham & Brantingham, 1993). When and where our daily routine activities take place can create opportunities to offend (e.g. Miller, 2012; Osgood, Wilson, O'Malley, Bachman, & Johnston, 1996), increase risks of victimisation (e.g. Massey, Krohn, & Bonati, 1989; Miethe, Stafford, & Long, 1987; Miethe, Stafford, & Sloane, 1990; Sampson & Wooldredge, 1987), or provide opportunities for people to guard against crime (see Hollis-Peel, Reynald, van Bavel, Elffers, & Welsh, 2011). However, most research that examines our everyday routine activities view our movements and corresponding behaviours as part of a broader macro-level daily pattern. Such research is useful in understanding *when* people are present in certain locations, but does not explore the micro-level routines of *what* people do in such locations.

For many of us, the majority of our daily routine activities are spent at home (Hart, Birks, Townsley, Ruiter, & Bernasco, 2018; Wikström, Ceccato, Hardie, & Treiber, 2010) and existing criminological research shows that residents have the opportunity to act as capable guardians by supervising their surroundings while there (Hollis-Peel & Welsh, 2014; Moir, Stewart, Reynald, & Hart, 2017; Reynald, 2009). Most research on this topic takes a macroscopic view of routine activities and measure guardianship through indicators of how much time residents spend at home (e.g. Cohen & Felson, 1979; Lynch & Cantor, 1992; Massey et al., 1989; Robinson, 1999). While this research provides important insights into the relationship between guardianship and crime (see Hollis-Peel et al., 2011), this type of measurement views activity at home as static (i.e. if someone is home, guardianship is automatically provided). While availability at home can prevent some crime types (e.g. Nee & Meenaghan, 2006) availability at home is not a good indicator of actual guardianship behaviour (Reynald & Elffers, 2015). Supervision is therefore considered to play a critical role in local crime prevention by enhancing the level of guardianship intensity over places (Felson & Eckert, 2016). As such, this paper focuses on how supervision patterns could be impacted by residents' microroutines. We argue that people will have regular residential routines *at* home which determine when and where they are in particular locations of their homes or properties. We surmise that different activities will provide different opportunities for residents to watch over their surroundings.

The present study begins to fill this gap in the literature by answering the research question, *'How do residents' microroutines at home affect guardianship patterns?'* In particular, we investigate how daily residential microroutines enable and facilitate supervision by suburban residents. In doing so, this exploratory study makes contributions to the routine activity literature by treating guardianship as a layered activity influenced by both residents' macroroutines (i.e. when and for how long they are home) and microroutines (i.e. what they do when they are home). Before the impact of microroutines on guardianship patterns is explored, relevant literature related to routine activities and guardianship is reviewed, followed by a summary of the sample, data collection process, and analytical method.

Guardianship and routine activities of everyday life

Theories of human ecology and environmental criminology provide explanations of the regular patterns and activities people are involved in, the paths they travel to get to those activities, and the impact this movement has on victimisation, offending, and crime prevention (P. L. Brantingham & Brantingham, 1993; Cohen & Felson, 1979). People have regular daily routines, such as work, leisure activities, and household chores that follow fairly consistent temporal and spatial patterns (Cohen & Felson, 1979). These routines influence the convergence of those likely to commit crime, targets or people who may become victims of crime, and those who prevent victimisation. Early scholars identified three elements of time organization that influence the spatial-temporal patterns of regular activities: (a) tempo – the number of events per unit of time, (b) rhythm – the regular period in which events occur (such as work), and (c) timing – the intersection of people's rhythms (Hawley, 1950). While Hawley's ideas have generally been used to explain offenders' behaviours in relation to crime (Felson & Poulsen, 2003), this paper applies such ideas to preventative behaviour (i.e. capable guardianship).

Daily macroroutines

The majority of past research examining daily routines, guardianship, and its impact on crime have generally used broad indicators of macro-level activities. These macroroutines are used to estimate the amount of time spent at home to approximate the level of guardianship at certain places. Many studies have used measures of employment as a proxy for routine activities to indicate how much time people spend at home; and therefore, could theoretically provide guardianship (Cohen & Cantor, 1980; Massey et al., 1989; Moriarty & Williams, 1996; Wickes, Zahnow, Schaefer, & Sparkes-Carroll, 2017). Other common measures of people's routine activities (and therefore potential guardianship over places) include the number of household members (Sampson & Wooldredge, 1987; Tseloni, Wittebrood, Farrell, & Pease, 2004; Wilcox, Madensen, & Tillyer, 2007), and measures of day and night-time activity (Garofalo & Clark, 1992; Lynch & Cantor, 1992; Miethe & Meier, 1990; Miethe et al., 1990). Importantly, a majority of these studies found that higher levels of guardianship were associated with lower levels of property crime (see Hollis-Peel et al., 2011). These studies provide a starting point for understanding the impact of broader macroroutines on crime; however, they do not measure what residents do when they are at home, including how and when people actually engage in guardianship over their surroundings. As a result, guardianship is treated as a static behaviour that is automatically provided when someone is home (Reynald, 2009). This perspective contradicts recent studies showing that availability at home does not always translate into capable guardianship.

Studies of guardianship in action

Using observational methods, Guardianship in Action (GIA) studies have found that being at home does not make a resident a capable guardian, *per se* (Hollis-Peel & Welsh, 2014; Moir et al., 2017; Reynald, 2009). Existing GIA studies utilise direct observation methods to observe (a) whether residents were present at home, (b) whether those residents were monitoring their surroundings and the researcher on the street, and (c) whether they intervened with an unfamiliar person (i.e. the researcher) on their street. Results suggest that 9% of The Hague residents who were available at home did not monitor their street (Reynald, 2009). In Brisbane and Boston, these figures were 23% and 89%, respectively (Hollis-Peel, Reynald, & Welsh, 2012; Moir et al., 2017). These GIA studies show that being at home does not automatically equate to capable guardianship and that when residents monitored and intervened with observers, lower levels of property crime were reported in The Hague (Reynald, 2009) and Boston (Hollis-Peel & Welsh, 2014).

GIA research also demonstrates that guardianship intensity fluctuates over time of day and day of week. For example, Reynald (2011b) found that observable availability at home was significantly higher during evening periods than during the day. Additionally, Moir et al. (2017) found occupancy was significantly higher on weekends in suburban Brisbane, which they argued was a result of fewer residents having work commitments during this time. Further, multiple studies have shown meaningful differences in self-reported supervision intensity by Dutch residents over the course of the day (Reynald & Elffers, 2015; Reynald & Moir, 2018). Self-reported levels of monitoring were highest during afternoon periods and lowest during late-night and early evening hours. Such studies indicate that daily routines affect availability at home and provide a starting point to understand crime control behaviour of residential guardians. We are interested in exploring how microroutines at home affect supervision patterns in residential areas.

Theoretical development of microroutines

Recent empirical and theoretical work has begun to reveal that people's activities and movements in time and space are dynamic and influenced by both macro and micro-level routines (Olaghere & Lum, 2018). Macroroutines affect the convergence of offenders, victims, and guardians in a location, whereas microroutines affect what those people do in that space. In this paper, we define microroutines as the activities undertaken within a specific location. Understanding the routine activities of individuals within micro-environments can develop our understanding of how opportunities for crime and guardianship arise.

The notion of microroutines builds on theoretical tenets from crime pattern theory, crime script development, and person–situation interaction frameworks. As asserted in crime pattern theory, people have general daily macroroutines which shape when and how people travel to and from places (P. L. Brantingham & Brantingham, 1993). However, people will develop sub-patterns of behaviour in specific places (i.e. microroutines). For example, a person might follow a daily residential microroutine of coming home from work, having a drink while sitting on their balcony, cooking dinner in their kitchen, watching television in their living room, and then going to sleep in their bedroom. Based on these microroutines, residents will spend different amounts of time in various parts of their homes and regular paths are used to travel in between rooms (P. J. Brantingham, Brantingham, & Andresen, 2017). While awake, residents will spend more time in some rooms than others – called 'active rooms' (Armitage, 2013). For example, kitchens and living rooms are active rooms, whereas bedrooms and bathrooms are not. When active rooms provide high levels of visibility to the street and surroundings, residents can more easily act as guardians as opportunities for passive surveillance are higher. Overall, the ideas about the movement from crime pattern theory can be applied at a finer level to understand the specific and micro-level movements of residents at home and how these activities may provide opportunities for guardianship.

Insights into the importance of microroutines can also be found in the crime script literature (Olaghere & Lum, 2018). Crime scripts view crime as a sequence of events and decisions that offenders (and guardians) may go through to successfully complete or thwart a crime event (Cornish, 1994; Leclerc & Reynald 2017). Scripts break down events into a series of micro-behaviours before, during, and after a crime, and have generally been applied from an offender's standpoint (see Leclerc, 2017). Recent work has applied ideas about scripts to guardianship action in public settings, which shows that capable guardianship is not an automatic, static behaviour, but one that goes through a sequence of decisions and micro-events (Leclerc & Reynald, 2017). In all, scripts have moved our understanding of crime opportunities forward by analysing events in small, micro-steps.

Microroutines can be also be influenced by a variety of person–situation interactions (Wikstrom, Oberwittler, Treiber, & Hardie, 2012; Wortley, 2012). People will have different propensities to offend and situations will provide a different number of criminal opportunities. Behaviour is then the consequence between an individual's characteristics and the locations in which they find themselves. While person–situation interactions have been applied to anti-social behaviour, they have yet to be applied to guardianship (a prosocial behaviour). In applying these ideas to guardianship, people (a) will have different propensities to act as residential guardians (i.e. differing levels of responsibility/capability; see Moir, Hart, Reynald, & Stewart, 2018; Reynald, 2010; Reynald & Moir, 2018), (b) live in homes that offer different opportunities to monitor their surroundings (Armitage, Rogerson, & Pease, 2013; Hollis-Peel et al., 2012; Reynald, 2009, 2011a), and (c) live on streets which encourage or discourage civilian action against crime and incivilities (Jacobs, 1961). Therefore, people are more likely to guard against crime when they have a propensity to do so, the environment is conducive to surveillance, and the context in which they live supports crime control by residents.

Microroutines and crime events

So far, limited empirical work has tested the effect of microroutines on crime opportunities. To our knowledge, only one criminological study has included measurements of specific household activities to examine how microroutines affect crime and victimisation. Messner and Blau (1987) used indicators of television watching as a way to approximate leisure activities at home.[1] Their results suggested that activities outside the home were associated with higher victimisation risks, while activities at home decreased this risk. From this study, it could be surmised that microroutines at home could affect a person's ability to act as a guardian. Further, recent work revealed specific microroutines drug offenders took before, during, and after illicit drug activities (Olaghere & Lum, 2018). While Olaghere and Lum (2018) work was the first known study to explicitly refer to the idea and measure microroutines, it focused on offender behaviour. So far, no known study has examined residents' routine activities at home and how this could influence guardianship and levels of supervision over residential areas.

In summary, prior research has provided an important basis to understand the link between routine activities, guardianship levels, and crime. However, these studies do not investigate individuals' routine activities and *how* and *why* such routines offer opportunities to act as crime controllers. This research is driven by the question, *'How do residents' microroutines at home affect guardianship patterns?'* We hypothesise that residents' daily microroutines at home will affect when and for how long they are able to monitor their surroundings; and therefore, affect their ability to act as a guardians over their residential micro-spaces. The following sections outline the data and methodology used to answer this question.

Data and methodology

Data used in the current study were collected from semi-structured interviews conducted with 20 suburban Brisbane residents. Study participants lived in one of two suburbs in north Brisbane, Australia: Wavell Heights and Northgate-Virginia. To investigate residents' microroutines participants were asked about their daily routines and what they did while at home on an average weekday and weekend. They were also asked to describe the line-of-sight views from various places within their residence (i.e. their kitchen, bedroom, balcony, etc.) to the street and neighbouring properties. This information enabled us to understand what surveillance opportunities were available to participants while inside their properties. Study participants also discussed their monitoring habits during the interviews. For example, if they answered in the affirmative to a question about whether they monitored their surroundings while at home, they were asked where in their house or their property they monitored from, what times of day they monitored, and whether they had a specific reason for monitoring. For the purposes of this study, a resident's surroundings refer to their home and property, their neighbours' homes and properties, and the street/s in which they live on. Interviews were recorded and later transcribed.

Study site selection

The two Brisbane suburbs chosen for the current study were purposively selected, based on their respective property crime rates, using Conjunctive Analysis of Case Configurations[2] (CACC; Miethe, Hart, & Regoeczi, 2008). To do this, CACC was used first to match Brisbane suburbs based on similar demographic characteristics: (a) population growth, (b) disadvantage,[3] (c) ethnic presence, (d) proportion of family households, (e) residential mobility, and (f) proportion of male youth (i.e. potential offenders).[4] Next, matched suburbs were grouped into one of two groups: (a) having a *lower*-than-average property crime rate, and (b) having a *higher*-than-average property crime rate for Brisbane between December 2010 and December 2013. The property crimes included unlawful entry, motor vehicle theft, property damage, and other theft. These procedures generated two demographically similar suburbs, with disparate property crime rates: Wavell Heights (low crime) and Northgate-Virginia (high crime). Wavell Heights is a predominately residential suburb with low levels of mixed land-use. Northgate-Virginia includes a large industrial estate, and a trainline and an arterial road also run through this suburb. Lot sizes typically range from $400m^2$–$600m^2$. As presented in Figure 1, houses are built close together and have small front yards. From these two suburbs, 12 street segments were randomly selected. A total of 379 unique addresses, associated with 278 unique properties, belonged on the randomly selected street segments.

Participant sample

Doorknocking took place in the two suburbs from June to August 2015 to identify interviewees willing to participate in the current study. Two researchers went from property to property, along sampled street segments, doorknocking from 9:00 am – 4:00 pm. If no one

Figure 1. A typical suburban street in Brisbane.

was home, a letter with details of the study was left in their mailbox. Approximately a quarter of properties were not contactable because either (a) no one was home, (b) there was a 'No Doorknocking' sign on their property or (c) there were 'No Junk Mail'/ 'Australia Post Only' stickers on their letterbox.

Twenty residents agreed to participate as a result of doorknocking. Eleven residents lived in the low-crime suburb (i.e. Wavell Heights), while nine lived in the high-crime suburb (i.e. Northgate-Virginia). Interviews took 30 minutes to complete on average. The average interviewee was in their mid-40's (M =46.8 years, SD = 14.5), and lived at their current address for nearly a decade (M= 9.4 years, SD = 7.9). Table 1 presents other socio-demographic characteristics of the interviewees and show the majority were female, had completed an undergraduate degree, were married and lived with their family, were Australian born and were employed full time at the time of this study. The sample used in the current study had higher education levels than the Brisbane population more generally (Australian Bureau of Statistics, 2011a).

Analytic approach

Interview data from the 20 participants was analysed through creating an informant-by-variable matrix (Miles, Huberman, & Saldana, 2014). There are three stages of qualitative data analysis using this approach: data reduction, data display, and conclusion drawing/ verification. First, data were reduced through coding. As the sample size was small, manual coding of the transcripts was deemed suitable (Saldana, 2013). Each transcript was read line-by-line to understand what participants were trying to communicate and codes were attached. As suggested by Miles et al. (2014) pre-determined codes were used based on research questions and theoretical frameworks but remained an iterative process, resulting in additional codes being added through analyses. Eight codes were used reduce data: (a) perceptions of area, (b) relationship with neighbours, (c) surveillance opportunities, (d) contextual awareness, (e) routine activities, (f) witnessing of incidents, (g) monitoring behaviours, and (h) intervention.

Table 1. Characteristics of interview participants (*N* = 20).

	n	%	Min	Max	$\bar{x}$	*SD*
Gender						
Male	8	40.0				
Female	12	60.0				
Education						
10th grade or below	0	0.0				
12th grade	2	10.0				
Diploma	2	10.0				
Undergraduate degree	10	50.0				
Postgraduate degree	6	30.0				
Relationship status						
Single/Never married	1	5.0				
Married/De-facto	17	85.0				
Divorced	2	10.0				
Widowed	0	0.0				
Australian born						
Yes	19	95.0				
No	1	5.0				
Employment						
Unemployed	1	5.0				
Full time	10	50.0				
Part time/casual	6	30.0				
Not in labour force	3	15.0				
Living status						
Live with partner	7	35.0				
Live with partner and children	10	50.0				
Live with children	1	5.0				
Live with other family	0	0.0				
Live with parents	0	0.0				
Live with friends	0	0.0				
Live alone	2	10.0				
Age (years)			24	83	46.8	14.5
Length of residence (years)			0.5	32	9.4	7.9

The second stage involved displaying this coded data in an informant-by-variable matrix in which rows represented the 20 interviewees (i.e. informants) and columns represented the codes (i.e. variables) described previously. This type of matrix was selected as (a) each participant can be individually examined, (b) similarities and differences between participants can be inspected, and (c) interactions and relationships between key variables can be explored. Miles et al.'s (2014) '10 rules of thumb' were followed to ensure data was entered into the matrix appropriately including the use of decision rules, supplying page numbers with text, identifying where data is missing, and having the matrix reviewed early in the process. Evidence to support or contradict participant statements were sought to understand their representativeness and validity. Text in each cell consisted of short blocks of texts, direct quotes, and researcher explanations (Miles et al., 2014).

Conclusions were drawn and verified by first reading across each row to examine the experiences of each participant followed by reading down the columns to make comparisons between participants. This cross-case analysis enhanced generalizability and helped to understand whether people's behaviours and experiences were idiosyncratic, or if broader trends and processes could be identified. Miles et al.'s (2014) 11 guidelines were then used to draw conclusions including noting patterns and themes, exploring similarities and differences between participants, including specific examples of themes, looking for contradictory evidence, and re-checking preliminary conclusions with raw data and transcripts. The final matrix was approximately 42 pages and 23,000 words long. The results that emerged from this analytical procedure are outlined in the next section.

Results

The current exploratory study addresses one main research question: *'How do residents' microroutines at home affect guardianship patterns?'* A number of themes emerged between microroutines and opportunities for residential guardianship, as presented in Table 2. The table first identifies each participant and whether they lived in the low crime or high crime suburb. Outlined second is whether participants general day-to-day microroutines at home and affected opportunities for monitoring in positive or negative ways (i.e. they were coded as 'positive' if their general microroutines provided opportunities for supervision). Presented third is whether participants had active rooms in their homes that enabled supervision over their surroundings. Whether participants reported familiarity with their surroundings is presented fourth, followed by whether they reported motivations for acting as guardians. Last, categories of passive and active monitoring were created to show whether participants reported monitoring for a deliberate purpose (i.e. active monitoring) or whether the majority of time they spent watching over their surroundings was unintentional or accidental (i.e. passive monitoring). Each category presented in Table 2 is expanded upon in the following sections.

Table 2. Participants' microroutines and presence of factors found to affect monitoring (N= 20).

Participant	High or low crime suburb	Microroutines	Active rooms	Contextual familiarity	Motivation	Active or passive monitor
Wayne[a]	Low	Positive	Yes	No	No	Passive
Greg	Low	Positive	No	Yes	No	Passive
Jacqui	Low	Positive	Yes	Yes	Yes	Both
Jane[b]	Low	Positive	Yes	Mixed	No	Passive
Brian	Low	Positive	Yes	Yes	No	Passive
Theresa	High	Positive	Yes	Yes	Yes	Active
Louise	High	Positive	Yes	Yes	Yes	Active
Gloria	High	Positive	Yes	Yes	No	Passive
Matthew	Low	Positive	Yes	Yes	No	Reactive
Helen	High	Positive	Yes	Yes	Yes	Both
Sam	High	Positive	Yes	Yes	Yes	Both
Heather	Low	Positive	No	Yes	No	Reactive
Diana[c]	Low	Mixed	Mixed	Yes	No	Passive
John	Low	Mixed	No	Yes	Yes	Active
Eric	Low	Negative	Yes	Yes	No	Passive
Ruth	Low	Negative	Yes	No	No	Neither
Mary	High	Negative	No	No	No	Neither
Melissa	High	Negative	No	No	No	Neither
Hannah	High	Negative	No	No	No	Neither
Ryan	High	Negative	No	No	No	Neither

[a] All names are pseudonyms.

[b] Jane's contextual familiarity was coded as 'Mixed' due to the social context of her street. On her side of the street, there were singular detached houses, however, the opposite side of the street was exclusively large apartment blocks in which in-movers and out-movers were frequent. She knew her neighbours on her side of the street, however, knew very little about who lived on the opposite side.

[c] Active rooms for Diana was coded as 'Mixed' as opportunities for surveillance were vastly different depending on what location at the front of the house you were in. The right side had a verandah which provided clear views to the street, however, the left side was obstructed by landscaping and the slope of the street.

Microroutines and guardianship

First, residents spoke of how they spent their time at home and the regular daily microroutines they engaged in. Examples of microroutines included: relaxing outside, cooking, watching television, studying/working, and caring for children. As presented in Table 2, microroutines at home positively affected 60% of respondent's opportunities for surveillance to act as guardians. For instance, Jacqui spent about 90 minutes per day on her front balcony before and after work on weekdays, and additional time on weekends. Jacqui primarily sat outside for enjoyment and to spend time in the sun. As the balcony provided unobstructed views to the street and surrounding properties, this enabled passive surveillance of the street and neighbour's homes. Likewise, when Wayne worked on his computer at home, he stated, *'I can have a peep through where I'm working at the computer table.'*

Second, microroutines hindered the ability to act as a guardian for six respondents. For example, while Eric spent a lot of time at home, he stated he monitored, *'Very rarely. I'm normally concentrating on what I'm doing inside the house.'*

Third, for a minority of residents, their microroutines reportedly had mixed effects on whether they facilitated or hindered opportunities to monitor: it depended on the time of day and what activity they were engaged in. For instance, Diana, used to study on her front balcony, which facilitated her ability to watch over her street, *'I'll often sit out there [balcony] and read, so that kind of, you're more aware of what's going on out the front.'* However, during the day she explained, *'I don't spend much time looking out the window'* as she was a stay-at-home parent who was occupied caring for her two young children.

As illustrated in this section, activities and behaviours at home are not static, and the activities residents engaged in while at home influenced their ability to watch over their surroundings and act as guardians. As the next sections will show, additional features helped to extend the relationship between microroutines and guardianship opportunities.

Active rooms, microroutines and guardianship

A number of findings emerged from the relationship between active rooms, microroutines, and guardianship. First, a majority of residents had microroutines which took place active rooms which facilitated monitoring. Second, a sub-set of residents did not have active rooms with good visibility to the street, blocking opportunities for monitoring. Third, even when residents were not motivated to monitor, they were able to passively monitor their surroundings while completing daily tasks in active rooms.

Forty-five percent of respondents reported being able to engage in guardianship over their surroundings due to the interaction between their microroutines and the design of their house (i.e. in Table 2, they have been recorded as having active rooms present and having microroutines that positively facilitated monitoring). Specifically, if residents had microroutines in 'active rooms' which faced the street, opportunities to monitor the street were enhanced. For instance, Helen spent a lot of time cooking during the day and watching television in the evening. She lived in a home where the living room and kitchen were positioned at the front of the property and there were no obstructions of visibility of the street. As a result, when asked if she monitored the street, she replied, *'Oh all the time...Because I spend a bit of time in the kitchen cooking, I'll just naturally be looking out.'*

On the other hand, when active rooms were located at the back of the property, residents' ability to monitor was hindered. Thirty-five percent of residents did not have active rooms that provided views over their surroundings. For example, Hannah was a student and most of her time at home was spent in her living room studying and caring for her young daughter. The living room was at the very back of the property and only had views of the backyard. As she stated, *'I don't see what's happening on the street.'*

The placement of active rooms and visibility were important design features as they enabled passive surveillance for residents who were generally not motivated to monitor. Eric, for example, generally did not monitor his surroundings as believed he did not need to and was generally preoccupied with other household tasks. However, his kitchen provided direct views of the street and while he was engaged in microroutines such as cooking or washing dishes, he stated, *'Yeah, I do [look outside]. It's just a natural habit to look out.'* From this time spent looking out from the kitchen, he was able to build an awareness of who did and did not belong on his street. Overall, it is not just about *what* and *when* residents do at home, but more importantly, *where* that microroutine takes place and the opportunities provided for supervision from that area. When residents could monitor, this increased their understanding of the normal patterns and people of their street.

Contextual familiarity, microroutines and guardianship

Over time, continual monitoring helped enhance contextual awareness of what normally occurred on residents' streets and to recognise other residents and regular visitors (hence, they could easily identify strangers or 'outsiders'). From the data, key patterns emerged from residents who had high contextual familiarity compared to those who did not. Out of the 65% of residents who were categorised as having high contextual awareness, eight had both active rooms and microroutines that provided opportunities for surveillance. For instance, Samuel often played with his young children (microroutine) in his front yard (area of his property with clear views to the street). While the primary objective of this microroutine was family time, it also enabled Samuel to observe who lives near him. As he explained:

> *"For me, I like to know a bit about the people here, who are the sort of people in the city and neighbourhood, and sometimes, if I can see people out the front, some of their faces and what sort of jobs they're in and that sort of gear. Just for myself, if I see them in the area, then I know what they are here for, or if somebody looks a bit out of place."*

As a result, he could recognise unfamiliar people and cars, which increased his ability to be an effective guardian. Similarly, Jane generally spent a few hours on her balcony relaxing and reading. As Jane explains, *'I've got a fairly good idea of who's around. If there's different sounding cars or trucks, you'll have a look, see what's going on.'* Although surveillance was not the primary purpose of spending time outside, these residents would naturally and passively observe what was going on around them. The ability to monitor was further enhanced by the location of their microroutine.

Six residents reported low contextual familiarity. Out of these, two-thirds were categorised as having poor visibility from active rooms and microroutines that impeded opportunities to monitor. Mary spent much of her time on days off in her painting studio, which had poor visibility to any surroundings. *'You can't see anything,'* Mary stated when asked what views of her surroundings she had. As a result of the interaction between this microroutine and poor surveillance opportunities, she was not able to watch over her street and commented that, *'I wouldn't have a clue who lives next door to us now.'*

Overall, there is an unintended consequence of microroutines taking place in areas of a resident's home or property that provide good opportunities for surveillance: it builds contextual familiarity. While residents were undertaking their microroutines in these locations of their property, they were able to see what was going on around them (either deliberately or passively). By repeating this activity regularly, contextual familiarity was built around what normally happened on their street, what cars belonged to residents, and regular visitors to their street enhancing residents' capacity to act as capable guardians.

Motivation, microroutines and guardianship

For a small subset of residents' (30%), guardianship was a deliberate part of their microroutines at home. They purposefully and routinely conducted surveillance at specific times of the day as a form of personal security. Residents did this for two main reasons: (a) as a result of prior victimization, and (b) to ensure safety of their neighbours. As John explained:

> *"I monitor every night. I check the front out here before I go to bed...and if I drive down the street, I'm conscious of whose wandering around the streets and pay special attention to who they are."*

Louise frequently monitored her street during the week, *'Just to make sure that nothing happens to myself of the neighbours.'* For these residents, personal motivation and perceptions of responsibility were important catalysts for supervision that became part of their regular routine while at home.

The remaining 70% did not report a deliberate motivation for monitoring, however, two key groups emerged. First, there were those residents' (57%) who were able to passively engage in this behaviour due to microroutines and active rooms. The remaining 43% did not report motivations to monitor and had active rooms and microroutines which inhibited supervision. For example, when asked if Melissa regularly monitored her street, she replied, *'if I hear something out of the ordinary.'* When she was at home, she was either working or completing household tasks and it was very hard to see neighbouring houses and the street. Coupled with a lack of motivation, this meant Melissa had poor contextual familiarity and didn't even know, *'if anyone is living there [next door] at the moment.'*

Therefore, while some residents were often home, they did not have either the motivation or capacity to conduct regular surveillance. This suggests the existence of an interconnected relationship between motivation, microroutines, and visibility in providing opportunities for residents to act as guardians.

Active and passive monitoring, microroutines and guardianship

As depicted in Table 2, 15% of respondents were categorised as predominately 'active' monitors – that is, they had a reason or motive for monitoring their surroundings. An additional 15% were classified within both categories: sometimes they monitored with a specific goal in mind (e.g. to look after their neighbours), while at other times they were able to passively monitor due to their microroutines and levels of visibility to the street. For example, Theresa had high contextual familiarity over her street, so she would monitor to look for unfamiliar people or cars, *'If any [cars] stop or park or anything, I would watch out there, and I would look at anyone who came to either of those neighbours' yards.'*

Thirty-five percent were classified as 'passive' monitors. While these residents did not purposefully supervise their surroundings, they were able to due to the combination of two key factors: (a) their daily microroutines, and (b) the presence of active rooms with good levels of visibility over their surroundings. For instance, Gloria worked from home during the day and was able to passively watch over her street even though she did not actively decide to engage in this behaviour, *'I don't really think about it, but, I guess it's a subconscious thing...checking what the neighbours are doing, making sure that there's no strangers walking around.'* Further, Greg explains how his daily routines created opportunities for passive surveillance, *'I don't necessarily look out, but as I go and come and go all day, I – not intentionally – but I see their houses regularly and what's going on.'*

The remaining 35% were classified as either 'neither' or 'reactive' in Table 2 as they generally did not monitor or only monitored in response to an unfamiliar noise. For those respondents who were classified as 'neither', all had microroutines that were not compatible with opportunities for surveillance. Likewise, all reportedly did not have a specific purpose or motivation for acting as a guardian. As Ryan explains, he was not motivated to watch over his street, *'There's just no motivation too. Unless there's a reason for it then I don't see the point being nosy around the street. I don't really need to actually look out.'*

Crime, microroutines and guardianship

As presented in Table 2, there were some slight differences between participant behaviour in the low and high crime suburbs. For example, out of the five residents who generally did not monitor (i.e. classified as 'neither'), 80% of them lived in the suburb with higher crime. These residents all had microroutines that were not conducive to surveillance and had limited opportunities for surveillance. A lack of monitoring had negative consequences for their level of contextual familiarity. Further, 90% of those living in the low crime suburb were familiar with the people and regular routines that occur on their street, compared to 55% of residents living in an area with higher levels of crime. Interestingly, a higher proportion of residents living in high crime areas reported specific motivations for monitoring. Such a finding illustrates that guardianship may be both protective and reactive behaviour.

Depicted in Figure 2 are the overarching relationships between these results. First, people's motivations influenced their guardianship and monitoring patterns. When residents were motivated and felt a responsibility to prevent crime in their area, they were more likely to monitor their surroundings. Second, data from the current study support that microroutines affect opportunities for monitoring. Further, monitoring was

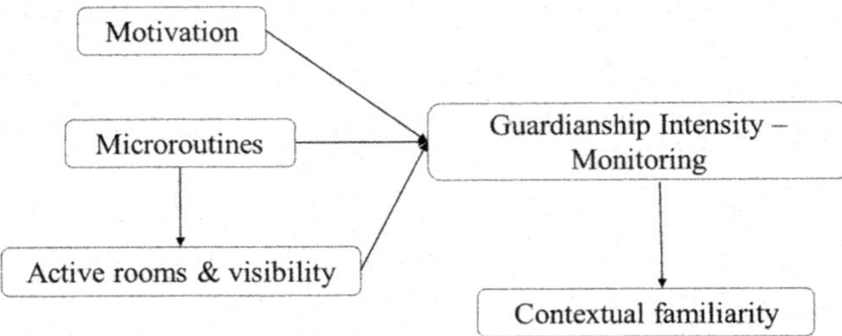

Figure 2. Summary of results theorising interactions between microroutines, physical and social factors, and monitoring.

enhanced when residents had microroutines that took place in active rooms which provided visibility to the street. Contextual familiarity was strengthened through consistent monitoring, which then made the role of active guardian easier for residents. Overall, residents who had (a) microroutines that facilitated opportunities for surveillance, (b) had good sight lines over their surroundings, and (c) were motivated to act as guardians, were most likely to act as guardians and most likely to be able to act as capable guardians due to high contextual awareness.

Discussion

Semi-structured interviews were conducted with 20 residents living in suburban Brisbane, Australia to understand the influence of daily microroutines on guardianship patterns. Overall, this exploratory study sought to address one main research question: *'How do residents' microroutines at home affect guardianship patterns?'* From this research, conclusions about the importance of daily microroutines that take place while residents are at home, and the interactions between the social and physical environment and guardianship can be drawn.

First, this paper makes a distinction between types of routine activities that affect residential guardianship behaviours. These are macroroutine activities that take place *outside* of the home, such as employment and recreational activities. Such macroroutines affect residents' availability at home and will determine the convergence of offenders, victims, and guardians in specific places at specific times (Cohen & Felson, 1979). However, a person's macroroutines do not inform us of what they do in such places. When residents are home, there are daily microroutines such as cooking, child-rearing, and other household chores. While macroroutines will affect when a person is home, it is the timing and location of residential microroutines that affect when and for how long residents monitor. As Reynald and Elffers (2015) assert, availability does not equate to supervision, so it is important to understand *where, when*, and *what* a person does when they are at home and how this can affect residential guardianship opportunities. Consequently, we suggest that it is what residents do while they are at home that may have the more proximal effect over guardianship and supervision patterns. Our conclusion aligns with Olaghere and Lum's (2018) research which shows that microroutines are just as important to consider as macroroutines in understanding crime opportunities..

Second, there are important interactions between daily microroutines, property design, and feelings of responsibility. Specifically, residents who spent a lot of time in 'active rooms' at the front of their property or in rooms that offered clear lines of sight to the street and other properties were able to engage in non-purposeful (i.e. passive) surveillance, providing support for Armitage's (2013) arguments about good housing design and crime prevention. Further, results suggest that even if a resident spends a lot of time at home, if the design of their property has poor views, they cannot act as guardians. In this way, people who are present at home but cannot see what's going on around them can create opportunities for crime (Felson & Eckert, 2016). Therefore, it is not simply how much time residents spend at home or in 'active rooms' that is important, but rather where these rooms are located and the views they offer of outside surroundings. Further, when residents could see their neighbour's properties and the street, they were able to build an awareness of the people that lived near them and regular patterns of people and activities on their street. The more engaged residents were in monitoring their surroundings, the more responsible they felt for caring for others on their street. As a result, residents' microroutines and housing design determined monitoring habits, which increased contextual familiarity and feelings of responsibility. This, in turn, further facilitated effective residential guardianship.

Third, for a number of residents, monitoring was not the objective of their residential microroutines but was a by-product. So while a minority of residents monitored as part of their security routine (Ekblom, 2011), for most residents this behaviour occurred passively while going about their micro daily routines at home. Monitoring was facilitated by housing design and active rooms. Residents could spend time in their active rooms and passively watch over the street. Regardless of the intention, passive surveillance still contributed to residents' contextual familiarity of their residential areas (Reynald, 2010). Contextual awareness enabled residents to identify legitimate users of their space, and detect unfamiliar or suspicious people or events, making them more efficient and effective guardians.

Fourth, while daily routines were an important prerequisite for residential supervision, other individual factors emerged that should be considered. The current study found that motivation influenced supervision habits. Further, as Moir et al. (2018) found, both the built environment and individual factors facilitated residential guardianship. As such, it is not simply housing design that facilitates surveillance, but the person within that house also needs consideration: their characteristics, their motivations, and feelings of responsibility for guarding (Reynald, 2010; Reynald & Moir, 2018). Additional perspectives such as Wortley's (2012) person–situation interaction or situational action theory (Wikstrom et al., 2012) could also be useful in understanding guardianship by including both physical and individual factors into explaining this behaviour. This has important methodological and conceptual implications for future research, as we cannot rely solely on one factor to study and explain guardianship.

Limitations and future research

One of the inherent limitations of this study is the small and fairly homogenous sample. The majority of interviewees were Caucasian, middle-aged Australians who were highly educated and lived with their children. Residents from ethnically or linguistically diverse backgrounds are under-represented in the current work. Further, interviews took place in two suburbs that were both relatively advantaged, and comparative to other European and

U.S. cities had low property crime rates. Consequently, results may not be generalizable to areas with higher levels of crime and disadvantage. It would be interesting to examine how microroutines interact with physical and individual factors to facilitate crime control in such suburbs. Further, the current work relied upon self-report data from people who were available at home during weekday, who may have different microroutines to those who are away during the day. As supervision is dependent on the time of day (Felson & Eckert, 2016; Reynald & Elffers, 2015), opportunities for further research arise in sampling a broader section of residents with different weekly routines. Finally, this study did not examine the impact of residents' surveillance on crime events – we did not measure whether a resident's supervision stopped or prevented a crime event from occurring. Future research could delve into this process in more detail to explore the impact a guardians behaviour has on an offender's behaviour.

Policy implications

Whilst the study sample is small and exploratory, the current work has important implications for housing design to facilitate crime control behaviour in residents. Several authors consistently stress the importance of good housing design with clear views to enable residents to see their street and their neighbour's properties (Armitage, 2013; Reynald, 2011a). The ability for a resident to watch over their surroundings is the first step in facilitating residential guardianship (Felson & Eckert, 2016). Therefore, promoting guardianship in residential places requires good housing design and residents who feel personally responsible for controlling crime in their surroundings. By implementing housing design that facilitates supervision, secure residential environments can be built to naturally prevent crime (Armitage, 2013). Further, strategies that aim to bolster guardianship should focus on defining responsibility for residents to guard over their immediate areas. Ekblom's (2011) CLAIMED approach outlines strategies to empower and mobilise citizens to act as crime preventers and could be applied to residential areas. CLAIMED is a set of tasks that practitioners can use to encourage others to be engaged in local crime prevention. The process seeks to *clarify* what action/s needs to be taken against a crime problem, *locate* key individuals who are best placed to undertake such action/s, *alert* key individuals in their ability to prevent crimes, *inform* them of the crime problem and the role they can play in prevention, *motivate* change, *empower* them to undertake crime control strategies, and *direct* them on how to use those strategies. Examples of strategies include informing residents of their ability to stop/disrupt crime by acting as a guardian and supervising their streets, motivating residents to engage in more active surveillance, and providing them with the skills and knowledge of how to do so.

Conclusion

Routine activity theory argues that guardianship is affected by a person's macroroutines (e.g. work, shopping, and leisure activities). Routine activities are layered: macroroutines affect where and when a person is during the course of the day, but microroutines affect what a person does while in a specific location. The unique contribution of the current study finds that microroutines and what someone does while they are at home influences monitoring patterns. To gain a complete understanding of how crime opportunities arise and how they can be prevented, microroutines of offenders, guardians, and victims need to be examined. As such, we argue that routine activity theory can be advanced through continued focus and incorporation of microroutines.

Notes

1. Messner and Blau (1987) did not directly measure the amount of time people spent watching television at home. Rather, an aggregate measure that estimated television audience size was used.
2. CACC considers all possible combinations of variable categories simultaneously (Miethe et al., 2008). The number of possible case configurations depends on the number of independent variables, and the number of categories within each variable. As CACC requires categorical variables, variables were split into quartiles measuring the lowest and highest 25% and the average 50%. Seven independent variables, each with three categories were used in sample selection. A total of 2,187 combinations of unique socio-demographic profiles were possible (3^7 = 2,187). However, only 99 unique profiles were identified using CACC in Brisbane. The most common configuration which had both low and high property crime was average on all factors (except for potential offenders, which was low). Two suburbs were selected from this combination. These are neighbouring suburbs; however, they had very different property crime rates. Further, their environmental landscape differed with the high crime suburb having a higher level of mixed land use and accessibility through a main arterial road and two train stations. From these two suburbs, 24 street segments were selected – 12 from each suburb, resulting in a sample of 279 properties.
3. Levels of disadvantage were measured using the Index of Relative Socio-Economic Advantage and Disadvantage from 2011 (Australian Bureau of Statistics, 2011b). This is a 25 item scale with measures of advantage weighted positively and measures of disadvantage weighted negatively. A higher score reflects higher levels of advantage and lower levels of disadvantage.
4. Refer to Moir et al. (2017) for a detailed description of the sampling process for the suburb and street segments.

Disclosure statement

No potential conflict of interest was reported by the authors.

ORCID

Emily Moir http://orcid.org/0000-0001-6943-4788
Danielle M. Reynald http://orcid.org/0000-0002-4833-147X
Timothy C. Hart http://orcid.org/0000-0003-3274-3661
Anna Stewart http://orcid.org/0000-0002-5256-0400

References

Armitage, R. (2013). *Crime prevention through housing design: Policy and practice*. Hampshire, UK: Palgrave Macmillan.

Armitage, R., Rogerson, M., & Pease, K. (2013). What is good about good design? Exploring the link between housing quality and crime. *Built Environment*, *39*(1), 140–161.

Australian Bureau of Statistics. (2011a). 2011 Census Community Profiles. Retrieved Date from http://www.censusdata.abs.gov.au/census_services/getproduct/census/2011/communityprofile/3GBRI?opendocument&navpos=230

Australian Bureau of Statistics. (2011b). Census of population and housing: socio-economic indexes for areas (SEIFA), Australia, 2011. Retrieved from http://www.abs.gov.au

Brantingham, P.J., Brantingham, P.L., & Andresen, M.A. (2017). Geometry of crime and crime pattern theory. In R. Wortley & M. Townsley (Eds.), *Environmental criminology and crime analysis* (Vol 2, pp. 98–116). Oxon, UK: Routledge.

Brantingham, P.L., & Brantingham, P.J. (1993). Environment, routine and situation: Toward a pattern theory of crime. In R.V. Clarke (Ed.), *Routine activity and rational choice* (Vol. 5, pp. 259–294). New Brunswick, NJ: Transaction Publishers.

Cohen, L.E., & Cantor, D. (1980). The determinants of larceny: An empirical and theoretical study. *Journal of Research in Crime and Delinquency*, *17*(2), 140–159.

Cohen, L.E., & Felson, M. (1979). Social change and crime rate trends: A routine activity approach. *American Sociological Review*, *44*(4), 588–608. Retrieved from http://www.jstor.org/stable/2094589

Cornish, D.B. (1994). *The procedural analysis of offending and its relevance for situational prevention*. Monsey, NY: Criminal Justice Press.

Ekblom, P. (2011). *Crime prevention, security and community safety using The 51s framework*. Hampshire, U.K.: Palgrave McMillan.

Felson, M., & Eckert, M. (2016). *Crime and everyday life*. (5th ed.). Thousand Oaks: CA: Sage Publications.

Felson, M., & Poulsen, E. (2003). Simple indicators of crime by time of day. *International Journal of Forecasting*, *19*(4), 595–601.

Garofalo, J., & Clark, D. (1992). Guardianship and residential burglary. *Justice Quarterly*, *9*(3), 443–463.

Hart, T.C., Birks, D., Townsley, M., Ruiter, S., & Bernasco, W. (2018) *Activity nodes, activity spaces, and awareness spaces: Measuring geometry of crime's constructs with smartphone data*. Paper presented at the Environmental Criminology and Crime Analysis Symposium, Elche, Spain.

Hawley, A.H. (1950). *Human ecology: A theory of community structure*. New York: Ronald Press.

Hollis-Peel, M.E., Reynald, D.M., van Bavel, M., Elffers, H., & Welsh, B. (2011). Guardianship for crime prevention: A critical review of the literature. *Crime, Law and Social Change*, *56*(1), 53–70.

Hollis-Peel, M.E., Reynald, D.M., & Welsh, B. (2012). Guardianship and crime: An international comparative study of guardianship in action. *Crime, Law and Social Change, 58*(1), 1–14.

Hollis-Peel, M.E., & Welsh, B. (2014). What makes a guardian capable? A test of guardianship in action. *Security Journal, 27*(3), 320–337.

Jacobs, J. (1961). *The death and life of great American cities*. New York: Random House.

Leclerc, B. (2017). Crime scripts. In R. Wortley & M. Townsley (Eds.), *Environmental criminology and crime analysis*. (Vol. 2, pp. 119–141). Oxon, U.K.: Routledge.

Leclerc, B., & Reynald, D. (2017). When scripts and guardianship unite: A script model to facilitate intervention of capable guardians in public settings. Security Journal, *30*(3), 793–806.

Lynch, J.P., & Cantor, D. (1992). Ecological and behavioral influences on property victimization at home: Implications for opportunity theory. *Journal of Research in Crime and Delinquency, 29*(3), 335–362.

Massey, J.L., Krohn, M.D., & Bonati, L.M. (1989). Property crime and the routine activities of individuals. *Journal of Research in Crime and Delinquency, 26*(4), 378–400.

Messner, S.F., & Blau, J.R. (1987). Routine leisure activities and rates of crime: A macro-level analysis. *Social Forces, 65*(4), 1035–1052.http://www.jstor.org/stable/2579022

Miethe, T.D., Hart, T.C., & Regoeczi, W.C. (2008). The conjunctive analysis of case configurations: An exploratory method for discrete multivariate analyses of crime data. *Journal of Quantitative Criminology, 24*(2), 227–241.

Miethe, T.D., & Meier, R.F. (1990). Opportunity, choice, and criminal victimization: A test of a theoretical model. *Journal of Research in Crime and Delinquency, 27*(3), 243–266.

Miethe, T.D., Stafford, M.C., & Long, S.J. (1987). Social differentiation in criminal victimization: A test of routine activities/lifestyle theories. *American Sociological Review, 52*(2), 184–194. http://www.jstor.org/stable/2095447

Miethe, T.D., Stafford, M.C., & Sloane, D. (1990). Lifestyle changes and risks of criminal victimization. *Journal of Quantitative Criminology, 6*(4), 357–376.

Miles, M.B., Huberman, A.M., & Saldana, J. (2014). *Qualitative data analysis: A methods sourcebook*. Thousand Oaks, CA: Sage Publications.

Miller, J. (2012). Individual offending, routine activities, and activity settings: Revisiting the routine activity theory of general deviance. *Journal of Research in Crime and Delinquency, 50*(3), 390–416.

Moir, E., Hart, T.C., Reynald, D.M., & Stewart, A. (2018). Typologies of suburban guardians: Understanding the importance of responsibility, opportunities, and routine activities in facilitating surveillance. *Crime Prevention & Community Safety, 21*(1), 1–21.

Moir, E., Stewart, A., Reynald, D.M., & Hart, T.C. (2017). Guardianship in Action (GIA) within Brisbane suburbs: Examining the relationship between guardianship intensity and crime, and changes across time. *Criminal Justice Review, 42*(3), 254–269.

Moriarty, L., & Williams, J. (1996). Examining the relationship between routine activities theory and social disorganization: An analysis of property crime victimization. *American Journal of Criminal Justice, 21*(1), 43–59.

Nee, C., & Meenaghan, A. (2006). Expert decision making in burglars. *British Journal of Criminology, 46*(5), 935–949.

Olaghere, A., & Lum, C. (2018). Classifying "micro" routine activities of street-level drug transactions. *Journal of Research in Crime and Delinquency, 55*(4), 466–492.

Osgood, W.D., Wilson, J.K., O'Malley, P.M., Bachman, J.G., & Johnston, L.D. (1996). Routine activities and individual deviant behavior. *American Sociological Review, 61*(4), 635–655. Retrieved from http://www.jstor.org/stable/2096397

Reynald, D.M. (2009). Guardianship in action: Developing a new tool for measurement. *Crime Prevention and Community Safety, 11*(1), 1–20.

Reynald, D.M. (2010). Guardians on guardianship: Factors affecting the willingness to supervise, the ability to detect potential offenders, and the willingness to intervene. *Journal of Research in Crime and Delinquency, 47*(3), 358–390.

Reynald, D.M. (2011a). Factors associated with the guardianship of places: Assessing the relative importance of the spatio-physical and sociodemographic contexts in generating opportunities for capable guardianship. *Journal of Research in Crime and Delinquency, 48*(1), 110–142.

Reynald, D.M. (2011b). *Guarding against crime: Measuring guardianship within routine activity theory*. Surrey, UK: Ashgate Publishing.

Reynald, D.M., & Elffers, H. (2015). The routine activity of guardianship: Comparing self-reports of guardianship intensity patterns with proxy measures. *Crime Prevention and Community Safety, 17*, 211–232.

Reynald, D.M., & Moir, E. (2018). Who is watching: Exploring individual factors that explain supervision patterns among residential guardians. *European Journal on Criminal Policy and Research. Online first*. doi: 10.1007/s10610-018-9380-7.

Robinson, M.B. (1999). Lifestyles, routine activities, and residential burglary victimization. *Journal of Crime and Justice, 22*(1), 27–56.

Saldana, J. (2013). *The coding manual for qualitative researchers* (2nd ed.). Thousand Oaks: Sage Publications.

Sampson, R.J., & Wooldredge, J.D. (1987). Linking the micro- and macro-level dimensions of lifestyle-routine activity and opportunity models of predatory victimization. *Journal of Quantitative Criminology, 3*(4), 371–393.

Tseloni, A., Wittebrood, K., Farrell, G., & Pease, K. (2004). Burglary victimization in England and Wales, the United States and the Netherlands. *British Journal of Criminology, 44*(1), 66–91.

Wickes, R., Zahnow, R., Schaefer, L., & Sparkes-Carroll, M. (2017). Neighborhood guardianship and property crime victimization. *Crime & Delinquency, 63*(5), 519–544.

Wikstrom, P.O.H., Oberwittler, D., Treiber, K., & Hardie, B. (2012). Situational action theory. In P.O. H. Wikstrom, D. Oberwittler, K. Treiber, & B. Hardie (Eds.), *Breaking rules: The social and situational dynamics of young people's Urban crime*. (pp. 3–43). Oxford: Oxford University Press.

Wikström, P.O.H., Ceccato, V., Hardie, B., & Treiber, K. (2010). Activity fields and the dynamics of crime. *Journal of Quantitative Criminology, 26*(1), 55–87.

Wilcox, P., Madensen, T.D., & Tillyer, M.S. (2007). Guardianship in context: Implications for burglary victimization risk and prevention. *Criminology, 45*(4), 771–803.

Wortley, R. (2012). Exploring the person-situation interaction in situational crime prevention. In N. Tilley & G. Farrell (Eds.), *The reasoning criminologist: essays in honour of Ronald V. Clarke*. (pp. 184–193). London: Routledge.

Yelping about a good time: casino popularity and crime

Virginia Sosa, Gisela Bichler and Lianna Quintero

ABSTRACT

Electronic word-of-mouth (eWOM) is fast becoming a standard medium of communication when people are looking for information about where to go for a good time. Exploring the content of reviews posted online could expose criminogenic conditions associated with properties, thereby providing an opportunity to examine crime problems afflicting private facilities with public data. This study investigates whether Yelp comments, together with property characteristics, can account for crime and deviance occurring at or near casinos in Southern California. While a correlational analysis revealed that two Yelp-based variables – property magnetism and star ratings – were associated with fewer reported issues of crime and deviance, a multivariate analysis revealed the complex nature of risky facilities. Holding all other factors constant, perceived staff friendliness and casino magnetism are significantly related to higher crime rates. Notably, the presence of slot machines is associated with lower crime, irrespective of crime measure used. Study limitations restrict generalizability; however, these findings suggest that public data can be used to investigate the criminogenic capacity of risky-facilities.

Introduction

Modern casinos can be thought of as entertainment hubs, offering an assortment of adult recreation and leisure amenities (Maheshwari, 2016). While successful casinos draw large crowds and generate economic benefits that extend far beyond the facility, they are also linked to crime problems that affect patrons and neighboring communities (Williams, Rehm, & Stevens, 2011). A case occurring in San Diego in June 2017 illustrates this point. A Lucky Lady Casino patron was shot during the early morning while leaving the casino with his winnings. Two men followed him out of the casino, and as he drove out of the parking lot, the assailants intentionally rear-ended the car, causing him to stop at a gas station across the way. During the attempted robbery the victim was shot 4 times. While the victim survived, his assailants were not apprehended (KTLA5, 2017; see also CBS News, 2017). Given the pervasiveness of user generated electronic media, notorious incidents can have a significant impact on casino reputations and the communities that house them.

Two objectives drive this study. First, we adopt a risky facilities perspective, seeking to learn which property characteristics are associated with greater social media attention about reported onsite crime and deviance problems and observed crime in the vicinity of the property. Second, we aim to investigate the casino-crime nexus using information about a broad set of properties located in different communities. Aside from a few notable locations where many casinos co-locate (e.g., Las Vegas, Atlantic City, and Reno), communities tend to have one or a small number of facilities. To move beyond a case study approach, casino researchers must face the data challenges associated with multi-jurisdictional data collection. Moving the field forward, this study investigates violent and non-violent crime occurring at and within the vicinity of Southern California casinos using publicly available information, including: (1) incident data extracted from crimemapping.com; (2) property characteristics and reported onsite crime and deviance problems drawn from Yelp reviews; and, (3) a travel network, linking Yelp.com reviewers' home cities to the casino locations, to calibrate the magnetism or attractiveness of each property.

The paper proceeds as follows. First, we describe the different types of casinos in Southern California and review the ongoing debate about the economic benefits generated by casinos versus the potential criminogenic impact they have on their neighboring communities. Next, we provide a brief overview of two related theoretical frameworks – crime pattern theory and risky facilities. We also describe eWOM by explaining how the Yelp.com rating system functions. The sample, variables, and methodology used in the study are explained. Finally, we report our findings and discuss what these results suggest for investigating risky facilities and policing casino neighborhoods.

Project background

Casinos

Adult entertainment hubs

Gambling facilities located in California run the gamut from small, privately-owned card rooms, also known as card clubs, to Las Vegas style resort casinos located on large tracts of Indian lands. The legal distinctions between these types of properties are linked with facility features and gambling activities. Cardroom owners can conduct card games once they have registered with the Attorney General and have obtained facility approval and licensing from the local jurisdiction (Dunstan, 1997). The regulatory authority overseeing Indian casinos is delineated by a three-tiered system implemented by the National Indian Gaming Commission (NIGC). Class I consists of facilities hosting social games with minimal value prizes associated with traditional tribal ceremonies or celebrations and gaming oversight is completely under the tribe's jurisdiction; Class II gaming consists of limited card games, lotto, and bingo that are monitored by the tribe and the NIGC; and, Class III includes house-banked card games, all other games, and casino-style slot machines which are regulated by both the state and the tribe equally (Contreras, 2006).

Gambling facilities are important to study in Southern California as their functionality is complex. Many gambling facilities act as adult entertainment hubs (Maheshwari,

2016). As multipurpose facilities, casinos offer an array of amenities such as restaurants, bars, hotels, pools, spas, slot machines, gambling tables, and special event venues. By shifting the focus of activity from gambling to other pursuits, properties support social, physical, cultural, and entertainment activities for adults. A key factor driving casino development is the promise of economic benefits.

Economic benefits

Tribal and non-tribal gaming operations provide substantial economic benefits. Casinos generate considerable employment opportunities, associated with running the facility, operating non-gaming amenities, and new construction (De Anda, Levine, Schrader, & Thornberg, 2014; Dunstan, 1997). For example, studies show that in 2012, tribal casinos in California generated approximately $8 billion in economic output, which supported 56,000 jobs state-wide (De Anda et al., 2014); county-level estimates show that in the four years after an Indian casino opens there is a five percent increase in jobs (Evans & Topoleski, 2002); and, when a new casino opens, unemployment rates tend to decrease by 12 percent within the vicinity of that casino (Gerstein et al., 1999). Locally, communities with an Indian casino generate greater tax revenue (De Anda et al., 2014, Evans & Topoleski 2002) – even though tribal casinos do not pay into state and local taxes, their employees pay taxes (Dunstan, 1997). In addition, large, successful tribal casinos often donate earnings to non-profit organizations and civic infrastructure projects, thereby improving public services in the region.

Economic incentives may also drive the development of Las Vegas style resort properties. Examining the locus of revenue generation, gambling is not the most lucrative activity; rather, the amenities and other activities that a casino offers generate the most revenue (Dunstan, 1997). It follows that facilities that offer a full range of amenities, and attract overnight guests, will stand to generate greater economic impacts. Despite the noted benefits offered by gaming facilities, casinos can also contribute to crime problems in their host communities.

Crime/casino impact

Table 1 summarizes research investigating the association between casinos and crime. While the studies are diverse in scope and methodology, they are reasonably consistent in two ways. First, studies show that the presence or introduction of casinos is often associated with increased crime levels in the host community as recorded in official statistics. For instance, Stitt, Nichols, and Giacopassi (2003) discovered that larceny and liquor violations were significantly higher in casino communities. And, examining crime over a period of five years, Grinols and Mustard (2006) argue that although crime is low after a casino opens, it increases over time. These authors estimate that 8.6% of the observed property crime and 12.6% of the violent crime in casino counties are due to the presence of gambling facilities. To date, few studies refute the casino-crime connection. For example, using a mixed-method design that included focus groups with community residents, Belanger, Williams, and Arthur (2012) found no reported increase in crime following the introduction of casino facilities in two different First Nation's communities. Of note, the observed casinos were located in rural areas, operating within a 50-kilometer catchment area with less than 35,000 local residents. Although the

Table 1. Selected studies investigating crime at casinos.

Citation	Location	Focus	Crime	Time	Method	Purpose/Issue	Finding
Albanese (1985)	New Jersey	Atlantic City	Part I crimes	1978–1982	Correlational study	Casinos in relation to crime	Casinos have no effect on the serious crime; crime rose due to other factors
Hakim and Buck (1989)[1]	New Jersey: Atlantic, Cape May & Ocean Counties	64 Communities	Part I crimes	1972–1984	Pre/post	comparison	Casinos in relation to crime and population at risk
Crime was higher in post casino years and a spillover effect occurred in surrounding areas							
Chang (1996)	Mississippi	Biloxi	Part I crimes, other crimes & mischief	1986–1994	Pre/post	comparison	Measure the impact of casinos on local crime
Decrease in overall crime rates during the first full year of casinos opening; crime rates returned to the pre-casino level during the second year							
Grinols, Mustard, and Dilley (2000)	United States	3,165 counties	Part I crimes (excluding arson)	1977–1996	Correlational study; post-test only	Determine the relationship between casinos and crime	Casinos linked to higher crime except murder; crime increased beginning about 3 years after the casino opened
Gazel, Rickman, and Thompson (2001)	Wisconsin	all counties	Part I & other crimes	1981–1994	Pre/post	comparison	Examine the relationship between Native American casinos and crime levels
Counties with casinos showed an increase in crime rates; there was also a spillover effect with counties adjacent to casino-counties (higher crime rates)							

(Continued)

Table 1. (Continued).

Citation	Location	Focus	Crime	Time	Method	Purpose/Issue	Finding
Stitt et al. (2003)	Iowa, Missouri, Illinois, & Mississippi	8 cities	Part I & II crimes	1987–1998 Min. 4 yrs. pre & post casino opening	Pre/post	comparison	Effects of new casinos on crime and the quality of life in the area
Some communities experienced an increase in crime, others a reduction, and some remained the same: overall, crime rates do not increase							
Moufakkir (2005)	Michigan	City of Detroit & 3 counties	Part I, other crimes, & disorderly conduct	1996–2002	Pre/during/post	comparison	Examine crime volume in Detroit and its neighboring communities
Volume of crime did not materially increase when the 3 casinos opened							
Grinols and Mustard (2006)	United States	3,165 U.S. Counties	Part I crimes	1977–1996	Pre/post	comparison	Examines how the opening of new casinos affect crime
The effect on crime is low shortly after a casino opens, then increased over time							
Barthe and Stitt (2007)[1]	Nevada	15 casinos in downtown Reno	Part I crimes & other crimes	2003	Correlational study	Determine if casinos and their surrounding blocks are hot spots that generate crime	Almost 25% of Reno's crime, occurred within 1000 feet of the major casinos but factoring for population at risk, casinos do not appear to be 'hot spots' that generate crime
Wheeler, Round, Sarre, O'Neil (2007)	South Australia	111 local areas	Income & non-income-			generating crimes[b]	2002–2003

(*Continued*)

Table 1. (Continued).

Citation	Location	Focus	Crime	Time	Method	Purpose/Issue	Finding
Correlational study	Compare electronic gaming machine (EGM) expenditures to crime rates	Higher EGMs expenditures were significantly related to income-generating crime rates but not non-income-generating crime rates					
Barthe and Stitt (2009)[1]	Nevada	Reno	Violent crimes, property crimes, and disorder crimes	Not reported.	Correlational study	Compare casino and non-casino zones	Temporal trends in casino zones are not very different than those found in non-casino areas
Walker (2010)	21 casino-crime papers	locations throughout the United States	Overall crime rates of some or all Index I crimes	1985–2010	Systematic review	Examines the relationship between casinos and crime	Some studies suggested that casinos cause crime, while others argued that an increase in crime was more likely due to tourism
Belanger et al. (2012)[1]	Canada	Alberta: Dene & Eagle River (First Nations communities)	Casino-related crime	2006–2010	Pre/post	comparison	Assess crime & socioeconomic effects on rural communities
No reported increase in criminal activity; residents are aware of the financial and social realities of casino operations							
Pontell et al. (2014)	Macau & China	Macau & Hong Kong	White-collar & economic crimes	2009–2011	Case study	Examine economic and white-collar criminal activities	The growing casino industry has created a receptive environment for various forms of corruption to thrive
Falls and Thompson (2014)[1]	Michigan	83 counties	Robbery, burglary, larceny & motor vehicle theft	1994–2010	Correlational study	Impact of casinos on crime rates in the host and neighboring counties	The presence or size of a casino does not increase property crime rates in the host county or in the nearby counties

[1] Spatial aspect to the analysis of casino locations and crime.
[2] Income-generating crimes: robbery and extortion, burglary, break and enter, fraud, forgery, false pretenses and larceny. Non-income-generating crimes: offences against the person,

qualitative data did not suggest that crime increased, the focus group participants did identify an increase in drug activity in both communities.

The second take-away from the literature is that even though many of the studies purport to examine the impact of casinos on the community, geographic precision is missing from most analysis. Rather than investigating the immediate surrounds, the general impact of casinos is assessed in relation to crime in large administrative units, such as counties or cities. For instance, Falls and Thompson (2014) measured changes in four types of crime in 83 Michigan counties and Moufakkir (2005) examined crime volume before, during, and after a casino opened in Detroit, Michigan and 3 neighbouring counties. Again, the Belanger et al. (2012) study is the only noted exception. Rather than using administrative units, these authors examined the impact of casinos within 45 minutes, or a 100 kilometer drive from the facility. When compared to the facility-based research presented in studies focusing on liquor-serving establishments, a 100 km radius is still exceptionally large and would not accurately capture facility-based crime – a more reasonable radius is needed that accounts for the average facility size.

Casinos often house liquor serving venues. For this reason, we may be able to draw upon the large body of research examining the effect of liquor serving establishments on crime to determine an appropriate zone of impact. For instance, examining a range of drinking places that prepare and serve alcoholic beverages for immediate consumption such as bars, nightclubs, and taverns, Groff (2011) found that drinking places were associated with increased crime in the surrounding area that extended at least two blocks (244 meters) but no more than three blocks (366 meters); and, using a 1,500 foot radius in an urban area, Ratcliffe (2012) discovered that violence appeared to be highly clustered within 85 feet (25.9 meters) of bars.

A notable feature of research on drinking establishments is the tendency to study facilities located in dense urban environments. To the contrary, resort-style casinos can be larger than a city block and situated on an expansive campus, located on a remote parcel of land in a rural area; it is not uncommon for several bars and nightclubs to be housed within a single facility; and, since patrons are likely to drive or be bussed to a property, an impact radius that is set a 'driving scale' may be warranted. For these reasons, we suggest using a 2-mile impact zone, as opposed to two blocks as is commonly used in dense urban environments, to begin investigating the immediate spillover effects of casinos that are not located on a walkable strip. While the studies reviewed here helped us to think about the criminogenic capacity of some casinos, they do not provide a framework for explaining the correlations observed. To explain why high activity nodes are linked to crime we turn to crime pattern theory and the risky facilities perspective.

High activity nodes and crime

Crime pattern theory

Crime pattern theory (CPT), as argued by Brantingham and Brantingham (2008), stipulates that crime does not occur randomly; instead, incidents are patterned in time and space, occurring where the activity of the offender and victim (or target) intersect. Though originally described as happening in physical space, the intersection of targets and offenders also occurs in the digital domain, through the internet and various electronic media (Brantingham & Brantingham, 2015). Since an individual's activity is shaped by daily routines, routine behavior contributes to the development of an awareness space, including knowledge of the activity nodes and their surroundings (Brantingham & Brantingham, 1981, 2008). Home, work, school, shopping areas, and recreation areas are often listed as primary activity nodes, but activity nodes may also include e-commerce websites, gaming sites, and various electronic forums, such as social media. When activity nodes are common to many people, they function as hubs, where the lives of different people intersect e.g., a local bar or Tinder® could function equally well as recreational dating hubs.

Arguing that most people are situated within a network of family, friends and acquaintances who influence their behavior, Brantingham and Brantingham (2008) assert that interactions with others also shape behavioral patterns, thereby exposing offenders to opportunities and placing potential victims at risk. Social networks shape decisions about what activities to participate in and where to conduct those activities because interactions with others provides information. The social network also provides a reason to go to specific places and engage in activities, often with others in the network. Since each person is enmeshed within a dynamic set of family, friends, and acquaintances drawn from work, school, hobbies, and the like, activity spaces will change as these relations evolve (e.g., someone gets a new job).

One of the reasons why crime is not evenly dispersed is that the criminogenic potential of places is not equal. For example, recreational hubs that offer entertainment and activities to their surrounding communities can become local activity hubs linking area residents and the local business community. Over time, successful properties will become regional attractors, drawing people from a larger area, including tourists from a great distance – business success causes the 'hubness' of the facility to expand. When hubs are perceived to be target rich environments, crime problems may develop.

Crime generators and crime attractors are two types of locations where crimes tend to concentrate. *Crime generators* produce high concentrations of people that enable some individuals, who without any predetermined criminal motivation, act on crime opportunities they encounter while on site. *Crime attractors*, on the other hand, are sites that draw in motivated offenders because of the location's already well-known criminal opportunities; as a result, they become activity nodes for repeat offenders. For instance, casino patrons often carry cash, and many casinos serve free alcohol, so patrons may be less alert than usual: these interacting conditions could produce a target rich environment (Pontell, Fang, & Geis, 2014; Walker, 2008). The property would be classed as a crime attractor if pickpockets and other predators frequent the location looking to take advantage of the patrons who are intoxicated. Between the two, crime attractors are the most criminogenic – as their reputation grows, they may evolve into a regional crime problem, attracting even more motivated offenders from a larger area. Fortunately, not all activity hubs become crime attractors or generators.

Risky facilities

Research shows that even among a single type of facility, crime concentrates at a small number of properties (Eck, Clarke, & Guerette, 2007; Weisburd, 2015) and studies show that aiming problem-solving initiatives at the subset of high-crime places stands to generate the greatest reductions in crime (e.g., Braga, Papachristos, & Hureau, 2014). For example, examining crime problems occurring at motels in Chula Vista, CA, Schmerler and colleagues discovered that only five of 27 properties exhibited high crime levels and the high-crime properties were often located near low-crime properties (2009). An evaluation of the Chula Vista Budget Motel Project showed that crime reduction strategies were more effective when aimed at properties hosting the most extreme problems (Bichler, Schmerler, & Enriquez, 2013).

Efforts to identify the subset of facilities generating a disproportionate amount of crime typically look for distributions approximating the 80–20 rule, targeting properties (about 20%) associated with most of the crime, at times as much as 80 percent of the problem behavior (Clarke & Eck, 2007; Eck et al., 2007). The question facing criminologists is not whether crime concentrates among a class of facility, rather, the question is why certain facilities host more crime than others. High traffic facilities tend to be associated with more crime, thus the volume of use can be a contributing factor to the emergence of a problematic area (Wilcox & Eck, 2011). However, volume of patrons is not the only factor contributing to high crime levels. Arguably, some of the observed variation in criminogenic capacity of a set of properties is related to management and property characteristics.

Extrapolating on the role of place managers, emerging evidence suggests that differing facility characteristics, many of which exist due to decisions made by managers and owners, play a role in the uneven distribution of crime (e.g., Eck, 1995; Felson, 2006; Madensen, 2007; Madensen & Eck, 2008; Madensen & Sousa, 2008). Criminal opportunities can be influenced by everything from the physical layout of the internal and external areas, to the presence of staff and security. For instance, with respect to casinos this would include management decisions about the design and surveillance of parking lots, the density and type of greenery used in landscaping, security presence at the entrance and throughout the facility, as well as the layout and staffing of the gambling floor. Thus, two casinos offering the same amenities and drawing similar crowds, may have significantly different crime potential. A well-designed and managed property should not experience the same degree of crime problems as a property overseen by management that promotes illicit activities or permits crime problems to manifest: a casino will become a crime attractor when management encourages, incorporates, or tolerates illicit enterprises within their domain (Pontell et al., 2014). Individuals can learn about management tendencies through direct experience, and indirectly, through their contacts and media sources. Returning to the Brantinghams' (2015) suggestion that we need to better understand online activity and the role that interaction in this domain plays in crime, we argue that an important source of information about business characteristics is social media, specifically Yelp.com.

Yelping about a good time

Modern communication systems provide mechanisms for understanding how information from personal networks formed by linkages with family, friends, and acquaintances, intertwines with social media. Individuals select places to visit based on their own experience, as well as on recommendations from others. With the advent of Web 2.0 and the introduction of public websites with web-based search engines that allow users to interact and communicate directly, i.e., Wikipedia, Facebook, etc., the experiences and opinions of individuals well removed from our social network influence our behavior. For example, a group of friends living in different communities select a city, equidistant from each person, at which to meet for dinner. Someone nominates a restaurant recommended by a third party. Not knowing anyone in the city, and having no personal experience, the rest consult Yelp.com. Based on anonymous reviews, the suggested restaurant is approved and the group convenes. In this scenario, the final decision is contingent upon information flowing through an electronic communications network, not a personal network. This marks a shift toward electronic word-of-mouth information exchange.

Word-of-mouth (WOM) communication refers to the 'informal communications directed at other consumers about the ownership, usage or characteristics of particular goods or their seller,' (Westbrook, 1987). The digitization of WOM communication through internet channels provides public information about business operations, such as statements about a product or company, transmitted via the internet that are made by potential, actual, or former customers (Dellarocas, 2003; Hennig-Thurau, Gwinner, Walsh, & Gremler, 2004). Of relevance to the present study, consumers have come to rely more heavily on eWOM communication from strangers than purchased advertisements (Hennig-Thurau et al., 2004; Steffes & Burgee, 2009).

Founded in 2004, Yelp.com is a prime example of eWOM communication. This forum permits anyone to freely access reviews of businesses; however, to rate businesses on a scale from 1 to 5, with 5 being the highest, individuals must register for a free account. While Yelp allows members to rate an unlimited number of businesses, it restricts review comments to a maximum of 5,000 characters (Tucker, 2011). Some information about the reviewer is posted with the review, including pseudonym and city of residence (as described by the reviewer).

Yelp prides itself in the validity of the reviews by claiming that no business can pay any amount of money to change, alter, rearrange, or remove any unwanted reviews that appear on their page. Notably, reviewers are not all equal. Termed 'opinion leaders', some consumers have more influence on others' decision-making (Lyons & Henderson, 2005). In 2012, Yelp developers introduced a mechanism to establish the caliber of each review posted. To achieve *Elite status*, a person must frequently provide good quality reviews. Good quality reviews are those that are rated as useful by other consumers. Individuals who are actively posting good quality reviews can submit an application to the Elite Council; otherwise, another member of the Yelp community could nominate them. Preliminary research confirms that Elite status is shown to be an indicator of an opinion leader. For example, Tucker (2011) examined 106 reviews to explore the correlation between the characteristics of reviews and star ratings, concluding that fellow consumers ranked the validity of Yelp reviews based on reviewers' Yelp status.

To ensure information is current, algorithms inspect millions of reviews submitted each day. The algorithms decipher which reviews to post with a formula that considers the overall review quality, and reliability of the post, as well as the reviewer's activity and status in the Yelp community. As a result, Yelp only posts about three-quarters of the reviews they receive which are predominantly selected from the more active users (Yelp.com, n.d.). With increased accessibility through smartphone technology, it is not surprising that by the end of the third quarter in 2018 'yelpers' had written more than 171 million reviews (Yelp.com, n.d.).

With so many members of the public visiting and writing these reviews, Franquez, Hagala, Lim, and Bichler (2013) investigated the utility of Yelp.com and showed that comments could be used to gauge the criminogenic capacity of facilities. As will be discussed shortly, we extend this argument by suggesting that since reviewers report a city of residence, it is possible to calibrate the magnetism or attractiveness of a property with metrics available through social network analysis (Bichler, Malm, & Enriquez, 2014).

Current study

The current study advances casino crime research in two ways. First, while it is important to capture the local impact of criminogenic properties, current social trends and the expanding influence of eWOM highlight the importance of online communities. Drawing upon Brantingham and Brantingham's argument, we must rethink how we conceptualize routine activities, and the factors influencing offender and victim behavior (2015). Extending the work of Franquez et al. (2013), we use Yelp.com to obtain information about facility management and site characteristics. Online communities have the capacity to overcome geographic boundaries, by sharing information with a much broader user base. As a consequence, star ratings and comments about site characteristics generate a wealth of public information about properties. Harvesting from Yelp.com provides an opportunity to study site characteristics in a new way. *It is hypothesized that property magnetism, Yelp ratings, and site characteristics will be significantly related to Yelp posts about onsite crime and deviance.*

Second, we seek to build on the work of Barthe and Stitt (2007, 2009) and Belanger et al. (2012), by continuing to examine the local crime impact of risky-facilities, rather than the broader social and economic impact of gaming. Using a radius of 2 miles, this study investigates which property characteristics are most associated with high-crime casinos. In addition, by linking reviewers' home city to the property site, it is possible to develop a standardized metric gauging property magnetism which could be used to examine the hubness of facilities in relation to crime. Extending the work of Bichler et al. (2014) we use social network metrics to calibrate the draw of an activity node. In doing so, we advance inquiry into the utility of a tenet of crime pattern theory: investigating casinos through a CPT/risky facilities framework provides a theoretically-driven argument for exploring the distribution in criminogenic capacity of properties and classification of activity nodes. *It is hypothesized that facility magnetism will be a significant predictor of observed crime in the vicinity of the casino.*

Methods

Sample

Currently, there are 29 operational casinos within the five-county study region – Los Angeles, Riverside, San Bernardino, San Diego, and Ventura counties.[1] The majority of the casinos are located on reservation land and are owned or operated by local tribes (see Table 2). The facilities vary greatly with regard to amenities and services offered to patrons. Properties range from small gaming sites to those offering a complete resort experience.

Table 2. Casinos characteristics.

	Study Population (N = 29)		Multivariate Model Sample (N = 19)	
Facility Characteristics	Frequency	Percent	Frequency	Percent
Tribal Ownership or Management	20	69%	10	53%
Age Requirement				
18 & Over	5	17%	4	21%
21 & Over	24	83%	15	79%
Property Amenities				
Concert Music Venue	17	59%	9	47%
At least 1 Nightclub	8	28%	2	11%
At least 1 Bar	28	97%	18	95%
Hotel	15	52%	10	53%
Pool	11	38%	7	37%
Parking Structure	15	52%	10	53%

Many properties offer multifaceted entertainment: 59% of the casinos have their own music venue; 28% have at least one nightclub; and 97% have a bar. Of interest, 52% of the properties include onsite hotels and 52% have a multilevel parking structure. Missing data reduced the sample used in the multivariate models to 19 casinos. While we will elaborate on this point later, the final two columns of Table 2 suggest that sample attrition did not compromise the representativeness of the properties examined.

Variables

Observed crime

Since properties were located in different cities distributed across five counties, we used the most viable, publicly available crime data – Crimemapping.com.[2] Using a search radius of 2 miles, we extracted all listed incidents occurring at or near each property from 08/10/2015 to 11/15/2015. We used a 2-mile buffer to ensure that the catchment included all areas under the facility's control, as well as adjacent land. For instance, 37.9% of the casinos are located in rural areas, and while the average size of these buildings was small, only 185,866 square feet, some properties had golf courses and other large amenities. Adding parking, landscaped areas, and access roads, significantly extends the facility size. Admittedly, this is a limitation of the study, as there was a lot of variation within the sample. Properties were also located in urban areas (24.1%), industrial zones (24.1%), and residential neighborhoods (13.8%).

While 6 months of data were available, we set the boundaries of the observation period to three months to avoid season fluctuations caused by summer and winter holidays. We classified crime into two categories: violent crime and non-violent crime. Violent crimes included: assault, homicide, robbery, and sex crimes including rape. Non-violent crimes included 11 types of crime – arson, disturbing the peace, drugs and/or alcohol, driving under the influence, motor vehicle theft, theft/larceny, vandalism, vehicle break in, and other. On average, the impact zones around casinos hosted 42 violent crimes (SD 75) and 139 non-violent crimes (SD 261) during the three months observed (see Table 3). We converted all crime counts to z-scores to explore the effects of being above the mean level of observed crime.

Table 3. Descriptive statistics for study variables.

Variables	N	Mean	SD	Min. – Max.
Observed Crime in the Vicinity				
Violent Crime[a]	19	41.70	74.68	0–307
Non-violent Crime[a]	19	139.13	260.98	0–1,206
Facility Characteristics				
Magnetism	29	966.52	1,037.72	0–3,433
Amenities				
Hotel	29	0.52	0.51	0–1
Nightclub	29	0.28	0.45	0–1
Slot Machines	29	0.69	0.47	0–1
Resort Property	29	0.41	0.50	0–1
YELP Variables				
Star Rating	29	3.05	.50	2.00–4.50
Reported Onsite Crime and Deviance Problems[b]	29	13.99	19.70	0–87.50
Gambling Comments[b]	29	45.61	24.85	8.57–83.64
Food Comments[b]	29	43.88	19.80	8.57–83.33
Bar Comments[b]	29	10.73	7.27	0–28.85
Rudeness of Staff[b]	29	13.28	8.96	0–41.67
Friendliness of Staff[b]	29	22.99	17.14	4.17–100.00

[a] Violent Crime Z scores range from −0.56 to 3.55; Non-violent crime Z scores range from −0.53 to 4.09.
[b] All comments rates are calculated per 100 reviewers.

Facility characteristics

Magnetism. One way to gauge the degree to which a property is a crime generator or attractor is to assess its drawing power or magnetism. Coding magnetism involved a two-step process. First, we captured information about the home or residential city listed by reviewers posting on Yelp. For each review, we generated the Euclidean distance in miles between the location of the casino and the centroid of the reviewers' residential city, and then, we recoded distances to reduce the extreme variability: 1 = lives in the city where the casino is located, 2 = lives in a city located up to 10 miles away from the casino, 3 = 11--20 miles, …, 16 = 141 miles and farther. Since tourists from abroad or other states would unduly inflate the magnetic pull of properties, reviews from people living outside of Southern California were absorbed in the final category. We discovered that the 29 casinos were visited by residents of 523 different cities.

The second step involved using the distance codes to weight the calculation of indegree centrality. To begin, we generated networks for each property by linking each casino to the residential city of each reviewer, weighting the link by the distance scale described above. Linking residential city to casinos generated 1,632 unique ties (3,334 total ties). The network was a single component as people from the same residential city frequented different casinos. Then, we calculated indegree centrality for each casino.[3]

Indegree centrality is a conventional social network metric that indicates how many connections one node or actor receives from other nodes or actors in the network. The basic idea is that casinos that receive Yelp reviews from people living in a greater variety of cities are characterized as being more attractive. Meaning, a casino drawing reviewers from five cities is more attractive than a casino with reviews from residents of 2 cities. In our study, however, we used a valued score, which adds a bit of a complication. We valued each link by a scaled distance. This means that an indegree centrality score of 26 could mean that at least 26 locals yelped about a casino located in their residential city, or 13 yelpers traveled up to 10 miles to get to the casino, and so on. There are different permutations which could sum to 26.

Considering the distance weighting, not only are high scoring properties more attractive but they draw from a wider geographic area, suggesting they are more magnetic (Bichler et al., 2014). As expected, not all casinos were equal – some had greater magnetism than others. For example, people from 96 cities posted comments about their visit to Barona Casino, the highest scoring facility (as a point of reference the least magnetic property had a score of 8). San Diego residents contributed the most to Barona's overall indegree centrality score of 2,309. Drilling down to the strongest city-casino link, a score of 508, tells us that, 127 reviewers traveled from San Diego to enjoy themselves at Barona – a distance of less than 30 miles, centroid to centroid. Of note, the average indegree centrality score was 966.52 (SD 1,037.72).

Amenities. Casinos offer patrons a range of gambling and entertainment services, such as nightclubs, event centers, and hotels; and the presence of specific *amenities* may contribute to, or mitigate, crime and public safety issues. Information about four amenities – hotel onsite, nightclub, slot machines, and resort-style facility – was obtained from casino websites (coded in November 2015). If the website indicated that any of the previously mentioned amenities were present, we assigned a value of 1, otherwise a value of 0 was used. Two amenities were common among casinos: 52% of the casinos had a hotel onsite and 69% had slot machines.

Yelp Variables. As discussed earlier, Yelp.com is a public website developed to enable consumers to share their reviews of businesses. With few prior studies to guide our use of Yelp ratings, we generated two sets of variables. First, reviewers rank properties with a 5 star-rating system (5 being the highest possible score) and provide a brief description or comment of why that business earned the star rating. To measure *star rating*, we averaged ratings for each property. Second, we captured information about *site conditions* with eight dichotomous variables from the comments about: crime and deviance problems (this is a measure of onsite reported crime and deviance), food quality or availability, the main gambling floor, onsite hotel, resort property, alcohol outlets (bars, nightclubs, event venues, etc.), and instances of good and rude customer service. If the reviewer commented on any of the above, we assigned a value of 1, else 0. In total, we extracted information from 3,336 Yelp reviews submitted from 1 January 2013 to 11 November 2015. Since reviews were not distributed evenly among properties, we converted sums for each condition into a rate per 100 posts. Reviewers more frequently commented about three issues – gambling, food, and friendliness of staff.

Results and discussion

Reported crime – bivariate analysis

Modernizing our conceptualization of CPT and the risky facilities debate to include eWOM, we asserted that property magnetism, Yelp star ratings, and site characteristics would be significantly related to onsite crime and deviance issues. Facilities garnering high rates of Yelp posts commenting on instances of crime or deviance are

Table 4. Pearson correlation coefficients of facility characteristics and crime.

	Reported Crime/Deviance (onsite) (N = 29)	Observed Crime Problems (2-mile impact zone) (N = 19)	
Facility Characteristics	Problems p/100 Yelp posts	Violent Crime	Non-violent Crime
Magnetism	−.355*	−.269	−.258
Amenities			
Hotel	−.284^	−.347*	−.329*
Nightclub	−.090	−.190	−.161
Slot Machines	−.462**	−.663**	−.581**
Resort Property	−.445**	−.458**	−.432*
Yelp Variables			
Star Rating	−.629**	−.164	.157
Gambling Yelps p/100 posting	.253^	.300	.176
Food Yelps p/100 posting	−.353*	−.093	.068
Bar Yelps p/100 posting	.035	.279	.402*
Staff Rudeness p/100 posting	.828**	.431**	.092
Staff Friendliness p/100 posting	−.287^	.311*	.609**

Note: Significance levels for the 1-tailed tests are as follows: ^ indicates p < .10; * indicates p < .05; and ** indicates p < .01.

defined for the purposes of this study as having bad reputations that may attract more crime – crime attractors. Table 4 reports the results of the exploration into the viability of using Yelp reports of crime and deviance to study the criminogenic characteristics of risky facilities. In addition, to validate this investigation we explored whether Yelp posts about onsite problems performed similarly to crime observed within a 2-mile impact zone: these correlations are also reported in the table. Three sets of correlations are reported because the Pearson Correlation Coefficients between reported crime and deviance (Yelp posts indicating a bad reputation) and observed crime in the impact zone were less than perfect (Pearson with violent crime = .476; p <.01; Pearson with non-violent crime = .219; n.s.), indicating each measure captured unique phenomena.[4]

Several findings are noteworthy. First, higher property magnetism was significantly associated with fewer reported crime and deviance problems: meaning that properties attracting more Yelpers from a greater distance (larger hubness) were associated with fewer posts about onsite problems. In other words, higher magnetism is associated with better reputations. Second, two amenities stood out as being significantly associated with lower reported problems – having slot machines and being a resort property. This means that generally speaking, larger Class III gaming facilities draw less negative social media attention regarding crime and deviance problems. Third, with one exception, all Yelp variables were significantly associated with crime and deviance posts. Of note, star ratings were significantly lower when problems were reported (Pearson = −.629; p <.01); and, perceived staff rudeness was strongly correlated with reported problems (Pearson = .828; p <.01).

Finally, despite the lack of strong correlations between reported onsite crime and deviance (Yelp comments) and observed crime occurring within 2 miles of facilities (observed crime recorded by law enforcement), all three crime measures preformed similarly in terms of the overall strength and direction of correlations, with one exception. Higher Yelp star ratings were strongly associated with lower reported crime; whereas ratings were only weakly related to observed crime (not significant) and in unexpected directions – the association was positive for non-violent crime. Based on these results we tentatively assert that Yelp may be a viable public source of information about the differential characteristics of crime-prone risky facilities.

Observed crime – multivariate analysis

To further explore the casino-crime nexus, three sets of OLS regression models are reported in Table 5. [5] Each set includes a model to account for observed violent crime occurring at or in the vicinity of casinos and a separate model investigating non-violent crime. The first set of models examines the explanatory influence of amenities controlling for property magnetism. Variables were entered as a block. Model set 2, the Yelp models, investigate the relative importance of star ratings and the nature of comments when accounting for violent and non-violent crime. Again, variables were entered as a block. Significant or substantively important variables (since we have a small sample size and significance is elusive) from model sets 1 and 2 were retained for the final, parsimonious models.

Adjusted R^2 values are reported because missing data reduced the sample to 19 properties, thereby reducing our power and restricting the number of explanatory variables we could enter into each model. Given this limitation, we tested each block of variables with magnetism included to account for property attractiveness. The final set of results present the most parsimonious models which included the best performing variables from each block.

The amenities models revealed that three of the four types of amenities were significantly related to lower crime near casinos. Notably, the presence of slot machines was the most influential factor associated with lower violent and non-violent crime, with a standardized beta coefficient that was more than double that of having a hotel onsite for violent crime and more than triple that of being a resort property for both crime types.

Examining the Yelp models, we found that the variation in violent and non-violent crime was significantly related to reviews commenting about staff friendliness and comments about crime and deviance problems. Comparatively, staff friendliness was a more important predictor of higher violent and non-violent crime. Of note, a high star rating was associated with a reduction in both violent and non-violent crime, but this association failed to reach significance with the small sample.

The parsimonious models perform the best, accounting for about 53% of the variation found in violent crime (adjusted $R^2 = .533$, $F (6, 18) = 6.333$, $p <.001$) and nearly 55% of the variance in non-violent crime (adjusted $R^2 = .548$, $F (6, 18) = 6.661$, $p <.000$). These models include the best performing variables found in each of the other models – the small sample size limited the number of explanatory variables that could be included in each analysis. Overall, holding all other factors constant, three variables best account for varying crime levels at or within the vicinity of casinos in Southern California – (1) comments about friendly staff are associated with higher crime, (2) the presence of slot machines dampens crime problems, and (3) property magnetism is linked to higher violence.

Table 5. Three sets of OLS regression models.

	Amenities Model		Yelp Model		Parsimonious Model	
	Violent Crime	Non-violent Crime	Violent Crime	Non-violent Crime	Violent Crime	Non-violent Crime
Facility Characteristics	STD Beta (S.E.)	STD Beta (S.E.)	STD Beta (S.E.)	STD Beta (S.E.)	STD Beta (S.E.)	STD Beta (S.E.)
Magnetism (indegree centrality valued by distance)	.283 (.000)	.229 (.000)	.191 (.000)	.183 (.000)	.331^ (.000)	.278 (.000)
Amenities						
Hotel	–.326^ (.366)	–.301 (.406)			–.207 (.341)	–.163 (.336)
Nightclub	.042 (.377)	.051 (.418)				
Slot Machines	–.662** (.405)	–.556** (.449)			–.497** (.387)	–.368* (.381)
Resort Property	–.143 (.404)	–.158 (.448)				
Yelp Variables						
Star Rating			–.407 (.610)	–.347 (.564)	–.377 (.486)	–.271 (.478)
Gambling Yelps (p/100 posting)			.143 (.008)	.029 (.007)		
Food Yelps (p/100 posting)			.091 (.010)	.080 (.009)		
Bar Yelps (p/100 posting)			.074 (.029)	.167 (.026)		
Crime & Deviance Problems Noted (p/100 posting)			.491* (.011)	.341^ (.010)	.220 (.010)	.152 (.010)
Staff Friendliness (p/100 posting)			.729** (.015)	.903** (.014)	.528* (.013)	.767** (.013)
Model Fit						
R^2/Adjusted R^2	.528/.425	.419/.293	.522/.363	.592/.456	.633/.533	.645/.548
F	5.147	3.316	3.283	4.348	6.333	6.661
Significance	.003	.021	.016	.004	.001	.000

Notes: These models have an N = 19 and ^ $p < .10$, *$p < .05$; **$p < .01$

Discussion

Yelp ratings

Results for the parsimonious models indicate that patron experiences recorded on public forums (eWOM), used in tandem with information about amenities, contribute to our ability to understand patterns of violent and non-violent crime occurring at or in the vicinity of casinos. The performance of variables created from Yelp comments was interesting. As expected, higher star ratings were generally associated with less crime. Although not significant in the final model, the effects were large enough to be noteworthy. At first glance, our findings support our hypothesis, but they do not concur with prior research. For instance, Franquez et al. (2013) found that highly rated bars had significantly *more* problems. Our study found the opposite, higher casino ratings were associated with *less* crime. We argue that this discrepancy is actually evidence of the discriminant validity of the star rating. Despite the fact that both types of commercial properties cater to the recreational needs of adults, the star ratings for bars and night-clubs might tap into something different than casino ratings. For instance, the objectives of the clientele may vary by facility type, and this may be reflected in how people rate properties. When going to a bar, excessive pouring may constitute exceptional service warranting a high rating, but this 'star quality' might lead to greater intoxication and associated crime issues; whereas high casino ratings may be linked to the overall patron experience based on value for money of the entertainment and facility services. As such, we argue that Yelp ratings may be useful for facility-based research, but not for mixed-facility research. In addition, the richness of comments may also provide a viable source of publicly available information about the management of commercial facilities.

Place management

While Yelp reviews commenting on crime and deviance problems performed as expected, albeit poorly, casino staff friendliness was the most significant and perplexing factor associated with higher crime. Reexamining the original text associated with a 'friendly' rating we found two potential explanations. (1) Reviewers were more inclined to comment on the friendliness of staff when they were experiencing something good, such as winning, cheap or strong drinks served quickly, excellent food, or a short line at check-in. (2) 'Friendly' ratings were also associated with how the staff made guests feel through various actions, such as having immediate contact with the guest upon arrival or entry into a room, being approachable, acknowledging and remembering the patron, and having a sense of humor. Given the link with higher crime, it is possible that within the context of a gambling facility, we tentatively speculate that overly friendly staff/patron interactions may lead patrons to feel so comfortable that they let their guard down to potential offenders. Future research is needed to determine whether the finding is robust and whether our speculation is sound. Meanwhile, this finding is of great interest as many of the site conditions captured by this measure represent aspects of good place management, prompting us to ask whether it is more useful to think of place management as a continuous phenomenon, as opposed to something that can be measured as a categorical variable.

Madensen and colleagues (Madensen, 2007; Madensen & Eck, 2008; Madensen & Sousa, 2008) argue that management style is a critical facet of the criminogenic capacity of places. Management makes decisions about the use of space, maintenance, and choice of activities permitted on the property; they establish behavioral norms, set goals and policies; and, they control access to the facility and direct the use of resources. Using a two-by-two matrix, these authors suggest a typology of four management styles, each with varying criminogenic capacity. Active, engaged managers with a proclivity to proactively eliminate crime opportunities are classified as suppressors, in contrast, promoters are managers who recognize and exploit crime opportunities for personal or business advantages. Passive managers who modify behavior or the environment following crime incidents are referred to as reactors, whereas enablers describe place managers who fail to recognize or respond to problems (Madensen & Sousa, 2008).

Management has many facets. Given all of the elements that constitute effective place management, maybe the management styles can be operationalized with a set of indices. At a minimum, casino-crime studies should use an indices to rate cleanliness and facility appearance, entry and exit screening practices, alcohol and drug controls, and patron/staff engagement. Using several indices would permit greater exploration of the association between management styles and crime. For instance, considering patron/staff engagement, which seems to be the root of what our measure captures, there may be a threshold, beyond which increasing the number of friendly, positive interactions becomes counter-productive. There may be a point at which patrons become overly comfortable and relax their use of routine crime precautions, i.e., leaving valuables unattended, being overly friendly with strangers, and drinking and gambling alone after friends or family go to bed.

Turning to the amenities that management supports onsite, slot machines were associated with significantly less violent and non-violent crime. It is plausible that this can be explained by the legal and practical requirements of managing a Class III gaming floor. The gaming floor becomes more complex with slot machines due to their size and floor pattern layout – slot machines necessitate increased security measures, such as the number of casino employees required to monitor the floor. Slot machine attendants work in close proximity to machine users, providing a high level of surveillance that may deter victimization of patrons, while fulfilling other non-crime related management functions (Austrin & West, 2005). Greater supervision may play a role in reducing crime in the vicinity of casinos as the stronger management presence may disrupt precursor conditions, e.g., alcohol consumption can be better monitored to prevent over intoxication and people playing slots might win smaller amounts thereby reducing the number of people leaving the property with large sums of money. Where facilities lack the resources to heavily staff the casino floor, highly visible security cameras placed throughout the property may offer dual-functions – deterring crime and satisfying the stipulations of regulatory oversight (Kruegle, 2007). Camera systems can be placed indoors and outdoors, thereby increasing surveillance in the areas immediately adjacent to the facility where vehicles are parked and significantly extending the monitoring capacity of security personnel.

Property attractiveness

The findings pertaining to casino magnetism suggest that we may have developed a way of differentiating between crime generators and attractors. Magnetism varied widely, and when used in tandem with a criminogenic Yelp reputation, it may be possible to differentiate properties likely to draw more motivated offenders. Our findings support this supposition. At the bivariate level, magnetic properties were associated with significantly fewer problems – as measured by reports of onsite crime and deviance. However, holding all other factors constant, including reported onsite issues, greater magnetism was significantly associated with higher crime rates in the vicinity of the property. Meaning, that casinos attracting more patrons from a greater distance expose the surrounding community to higher levels of opportunistic crime, specifically, violent crime. Where magnetism is high, and there is a high reporting of onsite crime and deviance, the surrounding community is expected to experience even higher levels of violent and non-violent crimes – such a property would be classed a crime attractor. Exploring our findings further, facilities with high magnetism, but low reported onsite crime problems, may constitute crime generators – theses properties have good reputations but a high level of hubness. These findings are consistent with tenets of CPT. Crimes can concentrate where a greater number of offenders and victims interact in the same target rich environments; however, overlapping activity space is a necessary precursor to crime, but is not sufficient to account for differential crime levels. Instead, it may be possible to differentiate crime attractors or crime generators incorporating information about the public reputation of the property.

Why is this important? Because crime control responses should differ depending on property classification. Crime generators have many unprotected targets, so property management would need to invoke strategies that increase the likelihood that people would engage in routine precautions (Felson & Clarke, 2010). To determine the best preventative solutions future research is needed to identify the circumstances that make targets vulnerable, i.e., time of day, location, etc., known as spatio-temporal characteristics of hotspots (Ratcliffe, 2004). Regarding crime attractors, since facilities draw offenders, crime control might focus more on discouraging offenders from going to the location (Clarke & Eck, 2005). Offender interviews may be needed to determine why the offenders are attracted to the location and how the situation could be remedied.

Impact zone

Using a 2-mile buffer around casinos to measure the impact zone around facilities, raises the issue of transition zones between land-uses. Edges between different types of areas may experience high crime rates due to the mixture of physical features associated with the connecting land types which may provide ideal criminal opportunities (Brantingham & Brantingham, 1993). The crimes could be in part due to the 24-hour nature of casinos which provide potential offenders access to nearby urban neighborhoods and adjacent businesses at all hours of the day. Jane Jacobs (1961) drew attention to boundaries and divisions separating urban neighborhoods from commercial centers by emphasizing the importance of localities having several functions so that there is a constant influx of diverse people on the streets throughout the day. She alleged that crime will not be a viable option if there are enough watchful people, able to instil a feeling of collective security.

While the 2-mile zone proved useful in this study, advancing this line of inquiry will require exploration of alternate operationalization of impact zones to better capture spillover effects. We argue the type of facility and land use should be used to determine the buffer size best suited to capture appropriate crime data. Businesses located in or near urban centers may not require very large buffers, whereas, properties located on larger tracts of land in suburban and rural environments may require a substantially larger distance buffer (e.g., 2 miles) in order to encapsulate associated crimes. For instance, Ratcliffe's (2012) finding that violence is highest 85 feet from a bar is instrumental for thinking about crime *within* a Las Vegas styled casino, but this operationalization would not work when investigating community impacts. Alternatively, Belanger et al.'s (2012) use of a large community-based impact zone (100 km) is too vast for urban locations. In the future, to better approximate impact zones, studies should consider the type of facility and land use in the immediate vicinity.

Study limitations

Several study limitations must be acknowledged – the quality and quantity of information posted to Crimemapping.com, the use of a 2-mile radius, and the lack of patron information. First, drawing crime data from Crimemapping.com limited the study in two ways. (1) Lack of reporting for casinos located in Riverside County, specifically the Coachella Valley not only reduced our sample size by 10 but also left a region comprised entirely of Indian gaming casinos underrepresented in the final analysis. (2) This source provides few details about the incident (restricted to temporal aspects and general crime type) and limited geographic precision (street block level), thereby prohibiting detailed study of the context of crime incidents. The second limitation of the study is that using a 2-mile radius prohibited us from differentiating between crimes occurring on the casino grounds, as opposed to crimes happening in the neighboring communities. As noted above, all crime occurring at or near each property was lumped together. Future research should investigate the difference by partitioning the data. Finally, a true measure of patronage would be useful to better model target richness/opportunity. For starters, conducting interviews with casino staff would reveal context to better understand activity that is going on from their standpoint. Similarly, patron interviews would provide invaluable insight into their perceptions of what is occurring, and this information would better inform crime prevention and policing efforts (Haberman, Groff, Ratcliffe, & Sorg, 2015).

Conclusion

This study investigated covariates that might account for crime occurring within the vicinity of Southern California casinos using only publicly available resources. Using data extracted from Crimemapping.com and Yelp.com, our study was able to determine that casinos that have slot machines were associated with less crime. Also, casinos with more Yelp.com reviews that included comments about staff friendliness were associated with higher crime; whereas higher star ratings were associated with lower crime. Lastly, property magnetism (measured with indegree centrality calculated on a travel network) proved valuable in detecting high crime facilities and demonstrated how this standardized measure, used in conjunction with public posts about onsite crime and deviance, could be used to differentiate types of crime hotspots – crime generators and attractors. And, while further research is needed to better understand casino-related crime from the perspective of staff and community members, we can also learn a lot about the criminogenic capacity of places from people yelping about a good time.

Notes

1. A list of properties is available upon request.
2. What is the alternative to crimemapping.com? At the time this study was conducted, there were none. Obtaining data from 29 different agencies or divisions, since each casino was located in a different jurisdiction, was untenable in this region. The difficulty associated with getting facilities-based data from law enforcement agencies in Southern California was documented by Marteache, Jimenez, and Lizarraga (2018) – when 50 agencies were asked for crime incidents occurring at and around commuter train stations, only two agencies provided data. One of the most frequent responses from agencies was that the data was posted to crimemapping.com, so the information was already available.
3. Notably, casino size in square feet and indegree centrality were highly correlated (Pearson .840; $p < .01$), suggesting that larger facilities draw more clientele from an expansive area. Notably, the correlation is not perfect suggesting that indegree centrality captures something unique. Since our measure of indegree centrality captures a more complex concept, we retained it for the analysis.
4. Two additional inter-item correlations are reportable. Staff rudeness was inversely correlated with star rating (Pearson = –.710; $p < .01$): fearing multicollinearity staff rudeness was dropped for the multivariate model. Additionally, the presence of onsite hotels was correlated with indegree centrality (Pearson = .609; $p < .01$); meaning that casinos with a hotel attract clientele from greater distances. Both variables were retained because the correlation was not large enough to be prohibitive.
5. With no prior regression-based findings regarding the intersection of casinos-crime in multiple cities, this study sought to begin the investigation with simple OLS models. From this foundation, subsequent research will be able to assess the applicability of Poisson or negative binomial regression.

Acknowledgments

The author(s) presented a version of this manuscript at the annual meeting of the Western Society of Criminology (WSC), February 2018, Long Beach, CA. They would like to thank Melanie Aguayo, Kayla Arroyo, Stephanie Castro, and Andres Serrato for their assistance with data collection and helpful comments on earlier drafts.

Disclosure statement

No potential conflict of interest was reported by the authors.

Funding

The author(s) received no financial support for the research, authorship, and/or publication of this manuscript.

References

Albanese, J.S. (1985). Effect of casino gambling on crime. *Fed. Probation*, *49*, 39.

Austrin, T., & West, J. (2005). Skills and surveillance in casino gaming. *Work, Employment and Society*, *19*(2), 305–326.

Barthe, E., & Stitt, B.G. (2007). Casinos as "hot spots" and the generation of crime. *Journal of Crime and Justice*, *30*(2), 115–140.

Barthe, E., & Stitt, B.G. (2009). Temporal distributions of crime and disorder in casino and non-casino zones. *Journal of Gambling Studies*, *25*(2), 139–152.

Belanger, Y.D., Williams, R.J., & Arthur, J.N. (2012). Assessing the impact of the introduction of casinos in two northern alberta first nation communities. *American Review of Canadian Studies*, *42*(1), 1–19.

Bichler, G., Malm, A., & Enriquez, J. (2014). Magnetic facilities: identifying convergence settings of juvenile delinquents. *Crime & Delinquency*, *60*(7), 971–998.

Bichler, G., Schmerler, K., & Enriquez, J. (2013). Curbing nuisance motels: an evaluation of police as place regulators. *Policing: an International Journal of Police Strategies & Management*, *36*(2), 437–462.

Braga, A.A., Papachristos, A.V., & Hureau, D.M. (2014). The effects of hot spots policing on crime: an updated systematic review and meta-analysis. *Justice Quarterly*, *31*(4), 633–663.

Brantingham, P.J., & Brantingham, P.L. (1981). *Environmental criminology*. Beverly Hills: Sage Publications.

Brantingham, P.J., & Brantingham, P.L. (2008). Crime pattern theory. In R. Wortley & L. Mazerolle (Eds.), *Environmental criminology and crime analysis* (pp. 78–93). UK: Willan.

Brantingham, P.L., & Brantingham, P.J. (1993). Nodes, paths and edges: Considerations on the complexity of crime and the physical environment. *Journal of Environmental Psychology*, *13*(1), 3–28.

Brantingham, P.L., & Brantingham, P.J. (2015). Understanding crime with computational criminology. In M.A. Andresen & G. Farrell (Eds.), *The criminal act: the role and influence of routine activity theory* (pp. 131–145). Basingstoke, UK: Palgrave Macmillan.

CBS News. (2017, June 7). Man leaving gardena casino attacked, shot by robbers [video file]. Retrieved from: https://www.youtube.com/watch?v=eqRABEH8RzY).

Chang, S. (1996). Impact of casinos on crime: The case of Biloxi, Mississippi. *Journal of Criminal Justice*, *24*(5), 431–436.

Clarke, R.V., & Eck, J. (2005). *Crime analysis for problem solvers in 60 small steps*. Washington, DC: Office of Community Oriented Policing Services, United States Department of Justice.

Clarke, R.V., & Eck, J. (2007), *Understanding risky facilities. Problem-Oriented Guides for Police Problem-Solving Tools Series, Guide. No. 6, Office of Community Oriented Policing*, US Department of Justice, Washington, DC.

Contreras, K.S. (2006). Cultivating new opportunities: tribal government gaming on the pechanga reservation. *American Behavioral Scientist*, *50*, 315–352.

De Anda, R., Levine, J.G., Schrader, D., & Thornberg, C., Ph.D. (2014). 2014 California tribal gaming impact study: an updated analysis of tribal gaming economic and social impacts, with expanded study of rstf and charitable effects. *Beacon Economics*. LLC

Dellarocas, C. (2003). The digitization of word of mouth: Promise and challenges of online feedback mechanisms. *Management Science*, *49*(10), 1407–1427.

Dunstan, R. (1997). Gambling in California. *IX. Economic Impacts of Gambling*. Retrieved from https://www.library.ca.gov/crb/97/03/Chapt9.html

Eck, J.E. (1995). A general model of the geography of illicit retail market places. In P.S. Vol. 4., J. E. Eck, & D. Weisburd (Eds.), *Crime and Place, Crime* (pp. 67–94). Monsey, NY: Criminal Justice Press.

Eck, J.E., Clarke, R.V., & Guerette, R.T. (2007). Risky facilities: crime concentration in homogeneous sets of establishments and facilities. *Crime Prevention Studies*, *21*, 225–264.

Evans, W.N., & Topoleski, J.H., (2002). The national bureau of economic research. *The Social and Economic Impact of Native American Casinos*. Retrieved from http://www.nber.org/papers/w9198.pdf

Falls, G.A., & Thompson, P.B. (2014). Casinos, casino size, and crime: A panel data analysis of Michigan counties. *The Quarterly Review of Economics and Finance*, *54*(1), 123–132.

Felson, M. (2006). *Crime and Nature*. Thousand Oaks, CA: Sage.

Felson, M., & Clarke, R.V. (2010). Routine precautions, criminology, and crime prevention. In H. D. Barlow & S. Decker (Eds.), *Criminology and Public Policy* (pp. 106–120). Philadelphia, PA: Temple University Press.

Franquez, J., Hagala, J., Lim, S., & Bichler, G. (2013). We be drinkin': a study of place management and premise notoriety among risky bars and nightclubs. *Western Criminology Review*, *14*(3), 34–52.

Gazel, R.C., Rickman, D.S., & Thompson, W.N. (2001). Casino gambling and crime: A panel study of Wisconsin counties. *Managerial and Decision Economics*, *22*(1–3), 65–75.

Gerstein, D. Murphy, S., Toce, M., Hoffmann, J., Palmer, A., Johnson, R, ... Hill, M. (1999). *Gambling Impact and Behavior Study: Report to the National Gambling Impact Study Commission*. Chicago, IL: National Opinion Research Center at the University of Chicago.

Grinols, E., & Mustard, D. (2006). Casinos, crime, and community costs. *The Review of Economics and Statistics*, *88*(1), 28–45.

Grinols, E.L., Mustard, D.B., & Dilley, C.H. (2000). Casinos, crime and community costs. *SSRN Electronic Journal*. doi:10.2139/ssrn.233792

Groff, E. (2011). Exploring 'near': Characterizing the spatial extent of drinking place influence on crime. *Australian & New Zealand Journal of Criminology*, *44*(2) Retrieved January 17, 2016, 156–179.

Haberman, C.P., Groff, E.R., Ratcliffe, J.H., & Sorg, E.T. (2015). Satisfaction with police in violent crime hot spots: using community surveys as a guide for selecting hot spots policing tactics. *Crime & Delinquency*, *62*(4), 525–557.

Hakim, S., & Buck, A.J. (1989). Do casinos enhance crime? *Journal of Criminal Justice*, *17*(5), 409–416.

Hennig-Thurau, T., Gwinner, K., Walsh, G., & Gremler, D. (2004). Electronic word-of-mouth via consumer-opinions platforms: What motivates consumers to articulate themselves on the Internet? *Journal of Interactive Marketing*, *18*(1), 38–52.

Jacobs, J. (1961). *The death and life of great American cities*. New York: Modern Library.

Kruegle, H. (2007). *CCTV surveillance: Analog and digital video practices and technology*. Amsterdam: Elsevier Butterworth Heinemann.

KTLA5 (7 June 2017). Man Leaving Gardena Casino with Winnings Is Shot 4 Times in Robbery; Assailants at Large. http://ktla.com/2017/06/07/1-shot-in-possible-robbery-near-gardena-casino-lapd/.

Lyons, B., & Henderson, K. (2005). Opinion leadership in a computer-mediated environment. *Journal of Consumer Behavior*, *4*, 319–329.

Madensen, T. (2007). Bar management and crime: Toward a dynamic theory of place management and crime hotspots. PhD. dissertation, University of Cincinnati. Cincinnati, OH.

Madensen, T., & Eck, J.E. (2008). Violence in bars: Exploring the impact of place manager decision-making. *Crime Prevention and Community Safety*, *10*, 111–125.

Madensen, T., & Sousa, W. (2008, July). Integrating place managers and broken windows theory. Presented at the 17th International Symposium on Environmental Criminology and Crime Analysis, Anchorage, AlaskaJuly).

Marteache, N., Jimenez, I., & Lizarraga, M., (2018, February). *Crimemapping.com: The Holy Grail?* Presentation at the 45th annual meeting of the Western Society of Criminology Conference, Long Beach, CA.

Moufakkir, O. (2005). An assessment of crime volume following casino gaming development in the City of Detroit. *UNLV Gaming Research & Review Journal*, *9*(1), 15.

Pontell, H., Fang, Q., & Geis, G. (2014). Economic crime and casinos: China's wager on Macau. *Asian Journal of Criminology*, *9*(1), 1–13.

Ratcliffe, J.H. (2004). The hotspot matrix: a framework for the spatio temporal targeting of crime reduction. *Police Practice and Research*, *5*(1), 5–23.

Ratcliffe, J.H. (2012). The spatial extent of criminogenic places: a changepoint regression of violence around bars. *Geographical Analysis*, *44*(4), 302–320.

Schmerler, K., Hunter, D., Eisenberg, D., & Jones, M. (2009), "Reducing crime and disorder at motels and hotels in Chula Vista, CA", Submission for the Herman Goldstein Award for Excellence in Problem-Oriented Policing, available at: www.popcenter.org/library/awards/goldstein/2009.

Steffes, E., & Burgee, L. (2009). Social ties and online word of mouth. *Internet Research*, *19*, 42–59.

Stitt, B., Nichols, M., & Giacopassi, D. (2003). Does the presence of casinos increase crime? An examination of casino and control communities. *Crime & Delinquency*, *49*(2), 253–284.

Tucker, T. (2011). Online word of mouth: characteristics of yelp.com reviews. Elon University, Communication Science. Retrieved January 16, 2016, from Google Scholar: http://www.elon.edu/docs/eweb/academics/communications/research/vol2no1/04tucker.pdf

Walker, D. (2008). Do casinos really cause crime?. *Econ Journal Watch*, *5*(1), 4–U1.

Walker, D.M. (2010). Casinos and crime in the USA. Chapter 19 of Benson. In L. Bruce & P. Zimmerman (Eds.), *Handbook on the economics of crime* (pp. 488–517). Northampton, MA: Edward Elgar (November).

Weisburd, D. (2015). The Law of Crime Concentration and the Criminology of Place. *Criminology*, *53*(2), 133–157.

Westbrook, R. (1987). Product/consumption-based affective responses and post purchase processes. *Journal of Marketing Research*, *24*, 258–270.

Wilcox, P., & Eck, J.E. (2011). Criminology of the unpopular: implications for policy aimed at payday lending facilities. *Criminology & Public Policy*, *10*(2), 473–482.

Williams, R.J., Rehm, J., & Stevens, R.M.G. (March 11, 2011). The Social and Economic Impacts of Gambling. Final Report prepared for the Canadian Consortium for Gambling Research. http://hdl.handle.net/10133/1286

Yelp.com. (n.d.). About Us. Retrieved January 16, 2016, from Yelp.com: http://www.yelp.com/about

Porch pirates: examining unattended package theft through crime script analysis

Ben Stickle, Melody Hicks, Amy Stickle and Zachary Hutchinson

ABSTRACT

Package theft is an emerging crime type due to the tremendous growth in online shopping and the delivery of goods directly to a home. Unattended delivery creates an opportunity for thieves to steal packages after delivery and before the resident collects them. It is believed that these types of incidents are increasing dramatically, and media attention has amplified awareness and concern of 'porch pirates.' Currently, little is known about unattended package theft and the present study represents the first known scholarly examination of this crime. Using Video Data Analysis to examine 67 YouTube videos of porch pirates engaged in criminal activity, the authors develop a Crime Script Analysis and identify Situational Crime Prevention (SCP) practices that can interrupt porch piracy. Findings indicate porch piracy occurs during daylight hours, at homes closer to a roadway, and most often with packages that can be easily seen from the roadway which are of medium size and usually have brand names on the box. Further, traditional SCP techniques such as fences, cameras, and guardians appear to have little impact on the thieves. Prevention techniques are discussed with the most promising including: increasing the risks, concealing packages, and removing packages. Additional findings, prevention techniques, and limitations are discussed.

Introduction

In recent years, retailers have increasingly relied on unattended home deliveries to meet the consumer demand for products, as well as to make the package delivery process convenient. This trend has inadvertently added a new twist to the typical residential theft; it has resulted in a crime colloquially known as 'porch piracy.' This unusual term is used to describe when a package is stolen from a residential property after it has been delivered; it can also be referred to by a variety of other names, including package theft and delivery theft. Not only is package theft a problematic crime for consumers because of the associated cost and accompanying frustration it entails, but it is also a concern for retailers because the crime is a by-product of current delivery practices. Unfortunately, there is very little information about package theft, in general, and even less information is available concerning how it is committed. Therefore, to understand how porch pirates steal packages, we conducted a Video Data Analysis (VDA) of recorded package thefts to study criminal actions. Next, we identified a Crime Script Analysis (CSA), allowing us to classify the steps involved in stealing a package. Finally, from a Situational Crime Prevention (SCP) perspective, we identify the most likely ways to interrupt the script and reduce package theft. This present research is useful to consumers, retailers, and police leaders to prevent or mitigate package theft losses potentially.

Porch piracy

Due to its relative infancy, package theft has not been researched in-depth by scholars. However, a review of the available industry research reveals pertinent information regarding home delivery trends, the estimated number of victims, and the approximate cost of the crime for the consumer, where package theft is likely to occur, the criminal charges that offenders may face, and existing preventative technologies.

In 2017, consumers around the world spent over 2.3 trillion dollars on online retail goods (eMarketer, 2018). Because of the immense volume of packages that must be delivered, online retail and delivery companies have readily embraced a package delivery method that is called 'unattended home delivery,' meaning delivery companies drop off the package(s) at the consumers' property regardless if they are home. Companies have adopted this method because it can cut delivery costs by an estimated fifty percent as opposed to attended deliveries where the purchaser must be at the drop-off location to receive packages (Punakivi, Yrjölä, & Holmström, 2001).

Unfortunately, unattended deliveries offer little protection against theft. One consumer survey by August Home indicated that in 2016, an estimated eleven million individuals in the United States were victims of package theft. Victims had to pay, on average, approximately $200 to replace stolen items (Business Wire, 2016). This cost to consumers is likely to increase as the average value of each package is also increasing (McKinnon & Tallam, 2003; Ogonowski, 2019). This represents a growing concern as the number of packages being delivered unattended is increasing, and so are the values of these packages.

The financial aspect of package theft is also a cause for concern for retailers. A 2017 survey by the Shorr Packing Corporation, reported that forty-one percent of the respondents avoided buying certain items for fear that they may get stolen, and sixty-one percent felt that online retailers are not currently doing enough to deter thefts. A more recent report by C + R Market Research (2019) also found that fear about package theft is substantially influencing consumers to avoid making purchases online.

There are conflicting results among consumer surveys and studies about where package theft occurs. One study found that rural areas have more problems with package theft on a per capita basis (Campo, 2017). However, package theft is also an issue in urban areas. For example, according to a recent analysis by SafeWise, California has the worst package theft problem in the U.S., with San Francisco being the U.S. city most affected by it (Edwards, 2019). Moreover, a recent analysis by the *New York Times* indicated that the city of New York attributes the loss of around 90,000 packages per day to a combination of package theft and other unknown reasons (Hu & Haag, 2019).

As package theft becomes more common, the question arises as to who the legal victim is and how they should be compensated. The criminal cases thus far have generally seen offenders charged with theft and place the consumer as the victim, instead of the retailer. Although the majority of states consider package theft to be a misdemeanor offense, some states, such as Texas, are making it a felony (Fischer, 2019). However, a criminal charge does not necessarily result in the return of the victim's package. Therefore, victims are attempting to cover their loss by insurance claims, paying out of pocket, or turning to the supplier. Some major online retailers are footing the bill for these thefts. One such example is Amazon's 'A-to-Z Guarantee,' which guarantees delivery or else a full replacement/refund will be given.

Companies are also taking more pro-active initiatives in an attempt to thwart package thieves. Amazon has started a service known as 'AMZL Photo on Delivery,' which has package couriers take a photo of the package once it has been dropped off on the purchaser's property and notifies the customer. Additionally, Amazon has also initiated a service known as 'Amazon Key,' which gives delivery employees one-time access into a consumer's home to deliver packages inside. Similarly, companies like Phrame give shoppers the option to have packages delivered to the trunk of their car (Phrame, 2018).

For some customers, services like Amazon Key and Phrame may be cost-prohibitive, costing around $200 each. For those in the market for cheaper alternatives, there are several versions of lockboxes and package bags that let users share a lock combination with their known delivery workers. Consumers also have the option of having their items delivered to an alternate address, which is a relatively low-cost solution but could be inconvenient.

While any of these theft prevention options may serve as a good starting point to deter and prevent porch piracy, no known research has examined how porch pirates steal packages. In the present study, we use Video Data Analysis and Crime Script Analysis to identify Situational Crime Prevention techniques that can be used by scholars, consumers, retailers, and police to interrupt and prevent porch piracy.

Video Data Analysis (VDA)

Video Data Analysis provides unique analytic potential that enables researches to study crime by 'capturing events frame by frame, observe them in slow-motion, focus on different actors at different replays, examine behavior and emotion expression that only last very briefly, and focus meticulously on temporal dynamic events' (Legewie & Nassauer, 2018, p. 8). VDA provides the opportunity to evaluate 'crime in action' as Wright and Decker (1994), Wright & Decker (1997)) and others (see Jacobs, 1999; Stickle, 2017) have demonstrated is highly valuable to criminology. VDA also creates an 'incomparably richer record' (Jordan & Henderson, 1995, p. 52) of situational details that occur during dynamic criminal events while reducing researcher bias and enhancing accuracy and validity (Nassauer & Legewie, 2018). VDA has been successfully applied to a variety of crime situations, including violent protests (Bramsen, 2018; Nassaure, 2016; Nassauer, 2018b), robberies (Mosselman, Weenink, Lindegaard, 2018; Nassauer, 2018a), police use of force (Willits & Makin, 2018), drug sales (Moeller, 2018; Sytsma & Piza, 2018), and shoplifting (Dabney, Hollinger, & Dugan, 2004). Combining VDA with other analytic tools is encouraged by Nassauer and Legewie (2018), which will create a robust analysis for understanding criminal behavior.

Crime Script Analysis (CSA)

Crime Script Analysis is a method for outlining the consequential steps and actions that occur to prepare for, undertake, and complete a crime. CSA gained popularity in criminology after Derek Cornish (1994) adapted it from the cognitive sciences. As criminals make decisions based on their knowledge, the environment, witnesses, victims, and so forth, they develop 'scripts' they tend to follow during the next crime unless there are 'inhibitory factors present' (Tedeschi & Felson, 1994, p. 181). Identifying these scripts is beneficial because it enhances the understanding of a crime by viewing criminal acts as a process rather than a singular event. CSA is a versatile tool and has been applied to a variety of crimes including mass shootings (Osborne, Capellan, 2017), drug markets (Chiu, Leclerc & Townseley, 2011; Jacques & Bernasco, 2013), sex offenses (Brayley, Cockbain, Laycock, 2011; Leclerc, Wortley, & Smallbone, 2011), illegal waste dumping (Thompson & Chainey, 2011), stalking (Leclerc, 2013; Yanowitz & Yanowitz, 2012), online crimes (Willison & Siponen, 2009), and money laundering (Gilmour, 2014). CSA is an especially suitable technique for ascertaining how a 'new or complex crime' is committed (Braley et al. 2011, p. 133) which, positions it well for use in the present study of an emerging and unstudied crime, porch piracy.

Situational Crime Prevention (SCP)

The combination of VDA and CSA lends naturally to the Situational Crime Prevention techniques developed by Clarke (1997). SCP, 'seeks to identify changes in the design and management of the environment that have the potential to reduce crime with the fewest economic and social costs possible' (Clarke, 2010, as cited in Mayhew & Hough, 2012, p. 18–19) and provides an established structure to develop methods to prevent package theft. The application of SCP techniques is only successful when it is focused on a specific category of crime (Clarke, 2017), such as porch piracy rather than 'theft' (broadly speaking). For example, SCP has been used to examine the use of gas poisoning to complete suicide in the UK (Clarke & Mayhew, 1988), residential burglary in a particular town (Poyner & Webb, 1991), occupational corruption (Tunley, Button, Shepherd, & Blackbourn, 2018), public transportation crime in El Salvador (Natarajan et al., 2015), wildlife poaching in Uganda (Moreto, 2019), and more (see Guerett, 2009 for a review of 206 SCP projects).

Method

Data

We searched for videos available on YouTube.com from February to March 2018 using the following terms: 'porch piracy,' 'package theft,' and 'package thieves.' When selecting videos, we applied the working definition of optimal capture, 'visual data must enable researchers to establish a seamless sequence of relevant lower-level action and provide compelling empirical evidence for systematic links between those actions' (Nassauer & Legewie, 2018, p. 21). In other words, inclusion in this study required, (1) a video of at least one individual removing a package(s), (2) from a residential property, (3) and captured the majority of the suspects' entry onto the property, the theft, and the exit. We excluded videos that showed the same location being targeted multiple times, the theft of only non-packaged items (e.g. letters, bicycles), videos of poor quality, and those that did not capture the suspects' approach, theft, and exit. Sixty-seven videos (n = 67) met the criterion and were incorporated into the analysis.

Variables

After an initial screening of many of the videos and review of the crime scripting literature, we identified three unique stages of porch piracy; (1) entry: how the criminals approached the property, (2) execution: how they executed the theft and (3) exit: how they exited the property. In addition to collecting data in these areas, we also collect information about the offenders and packages. Table #1 displays the variables recorded in the present study.

Analysis

Two of the authors used an iterative process of inductive coding by viewing dozens of videos together while discussing, interpreting, and identifying the possible coding schemes. Once the initial codes were established, a third researcher tested the coding scheme and

Table 1. Variable table.

Variables	Categories
Perpetrator Characteristics	
Number of perpetrators who committed theft	1, 2, 3, 4+
Number of accomplices	1, 2, 3, 4+
Did the accomplice(s) stay in the vehicle	yes/no
Sex of perpetrators involved	male/female
Race of perpetrators involved	Black, Hispanic, White, Asian, other
Blatant attempt to disguise appearance	sunglasses, hoodie/coat, hat, other
Transportation Characteristics	
Means of Transportation	car, truck, van, SUV, motorcycle, bicycle, skateboard, by foot
Vehicle Parking/Idling Location	in the street, in driveway, other
Vehicle Orientation in Driveway	pulled in, backed-in the driveway
Was a vehicle door left open to facilitate escape	yes/no
Place Characteristics	
Distance from theft location to road	close (0–25 ft.), intermediate (26-50ft.), far (51+ ft.)
Time of Day	day/night
Gate Presence	yes/no
Was the gate closed	yes/no
Fence presence	yes/no
Property owner's vehicle	vehicle was on the property/was not on the property
Stolen Package Characteristics	
Number of packages/items	1, 2, 3, 4+
Size of packages/items	small, medium, large
Is the package visible from the street	yes/no
The package marked by a specific retailer	yes/no
Approach Characteristics	
The approach of the property	walk/run
Vehicle cased the neighborhood	yes/no
Theft Characteristics	
Attempted to see if anyone was home	doorbell, knocked, looked through windows, looked around
Return for multiple packages (same theft incident)	returned 1 time, 2 times, 3+ times
Exit Characteristics	
The exit of the property	walk/run

provided feedback. After this iteration, adjustments were made to the coding scheme (see Table #1), and data collected with each video was reviewed independently by three coders. This deductively driven process, as encouraged by Lindegaard and Bernasco (2018) and demonstrated by Liebst, Heinsku, and Ejbye-Ernst (2018), resulted in a standard coding scheme that was adopted by all researchers and enhanced consistency, reliability, and validity.Acknowledging a call to incorporate inter-coder reliability in VDA (Lindgaard & Bernasco, 2018) and enhance specification, verification, and validation in CSA (Borrion, 2013), the authors independently coded each video. Next, we used the resulting data and Kleiss's Kappa value for each variable to measure observer agreement. Values of Kappa close to 1 show perfect agreement, while values closer to 0 imply agreement expected by chance. In the present study, the Kappa values ranged from 0.307 to 0.981, with an average of 0.642. Using the scale developed by Landis and Koch (1977), the average Kappa value suggests substantial agreement among coders. Some aspects of interpreting visual data are more difficult to be precise, such as distances and the way they exited the property. Therefore, if two out of three agreed, that code was chosen. However, if no agreement was reached, the data was coded not applicable or unknown.

Findings

Offender analysis

This study is the result of a purposive sample, and therefore, findings should not be considered representative of the general population. Further, identifying demographics such as age, gender, race, and other offender features from short videos is difficult to be precise and resulted in the lowest inter-coder reliability. However, because this is the first known study of this emerging crime type, the information may be valuable for future research and is presented.

The study revealed a nearly even split of offender sex with 34 men (49%), and 35 women (51%). Due to the difficulty in determining age, we opted to define those who appeared under 45 years of age (94%), those who appeared over 45 (3%), and persons upon whom there was no coder agreement (3%). Evaluation of the suspects' race resulted in identifying 36 white individuals (54%), ten black individuals (15%), 6 Hispanic persons (9%), 2 Asian individuals (3%), and 13 persons (19%) who agreement could not be reached. We also sought to examine socioeconomic status by evaluating the offender's appearance, clothing, and transportation. Based on this information, we identified 20 people (30%) as lower status, 45 individuals (67%) as middle status, one person (1.5%) as upper status, and only one person (1.5%) could not be identified, or coders could not agree.

Package analysis

Understanding the type, size, number, visibility, and distance of the packages from the street is vital to understanding how package theft occurs and identifying prevention efforts. We set three distance ranges between the porch and roadway finding 41 thefts (61%) occurred at 25 feet or closer, 20 thefts (30%) occurred between 26 and 50 feet, no

(0%) recorded thefts took place at more than 51 feet, and in 6 incidents (9%) there was no agreement or an unknown distance.

There were 98 packages stolen within the data. In four instances, the thief was interrupted during the crime and left the packages as they fled; these packages are not included in the count of total stolen packages. Therefore, of completed thefts ($n = 63$), the averaging number of packages stolen is just over 1.5 per incident. However, the most frequent theft was of a single package (39%), followed by two packages (18%), three packages (6%), and six packages (1%).

The stolen item size was evaluated based on the largest package. Findings reveal small packages described as being 12 inches or less in all dimensions accounted for 26 (40%) of thefts, medium packages identified as between 13 and 36 inches in measurement had the highest number of thefts contributing to 32 (48%) of thefts, and large packages of greater than 36 inches in diameter accounted for 8 (12%) of thefts. Regardless of what size the packages were in 62 incidents (93%), they appeared to the researchers to be visible from the street. Lastly, 31 thefts (46%) of packages had a brand name displayed on the package (e.g. Amazon), while 33 (49%) had no identifying brand, and three (5%) were undetermined.

Crime script analysis

According to Borrion, 'crime scripts should be rich enough to include the range of information needed by designers to devise physical control measures' (2013, p. 6). However, because most videos of crimes on YouTube only include the actual crime event and perhaps a few seconds of footage before and after, the analysis was limited to the data available. Under these constraints and following previous CSA research examples, we identified three unique stages of package theft; approach, execution, exit. Each stage is explained and described below.

Approach

There were few fences to block the approach of offenders observed in the videos ($n = 5$), accounting for about 7% of all incidents. In each case, a gate was present, and in only one incident was the gate locked. In 21% of cases ($n = 14$), a resident's vehicle was clearly seen parked on the victims' property. In contrast, in the remaining cases, a vehicle was absent (48%), or it was unclear based on the video (31%). Very few of the offenders (12%, $n = 8$) appeared to 'case' the residence before the theft. We classified casing as making several trips past the residence and looking around the area. This may be an artifact of short video clips edited to show the 'theft' and not capture details before or after. Those who did case the property tended to walk or drive by several times or park in front of the property for some time observing the surroundings.

While only a few 'cased' the property, a significant portion (60%, $n = 40$) looked around the surroundings while walking to the porch. In other words, as they approached the property, they could be observed visually scanning the area around the home more than a person would typically do, resulting in what could be described as suspicious behavior. As the offenders approached, 72% ($n = 48$) walked in what appeared to be a leisurely manner, 24% ($n = 16$) walk or ran quickly, and in 4% ($n = 3$), the researchers had no agreement. In only seven incidents (10%), was there any attempt by the thief to disguise themselves. Of those who did the most common method was a coat or hoodie (60%,

$n = 6$) or holding a hand to block a camera's view or wearing large sunglasses (40%, $n = 4$). None of these efforts appeared to be particularly useful.

Upon arriving at the porch, five individuals (7%) appeared to knock on the door or ring the doorbell before taking the packages. It was not always clear from the video if the suspects actually knocked and rang, and in a few cases, these efforts appeared to be a deception while looking around the property. While not explicitly coded for, the researchers noticed several cases where suspects would approach the home with something in their hands. In a few cases, this appeared to be some paperwork. During one theft, a suspect brought the empty garbage can from the street back to the house before stealing a package. In three instances, a suspect had a small package with them when they approached. In each of these cases, it seemed the item was to be used as an available ruse if interrupted; for example, a fake delivery attempt to reduce suspicion or a homeowner appearing to be returning a garbage can.

Execution

The execution stage is when the actual 'theft,' which occurs, i.e. possessing a package with the intent to deprive the owner. For the present study, we classified this as the moment the offender took the package. The following provides a description of these features as well as offender actions during the execution of the theft. All of the thefts occurred during daylight hours. It is difficult to say if this was because residential camera footage is clearer during the day, if porch pirates rely on daylight to see if packages are present, or if more residents are home in the evening, thereby reducing opportunity.

Generally, (96%), there was only one offender who approached the residence and took a package. However, in three instances, two individuals worked together to accomplish the theft. Conversely, in 25 incidents (37%), there was an accomplice. These accomplices were identified because they took some 'active' part in completing the crime, such as serving as a lookout or, most commonly (80%), serving as an escape driver.

During the actual theft, most thieves ($n = 49$, 73%) did not make any explicit attempt to determine if a resident was home. While in 13 incidents (19%), it was unclear if an attempt was made. In five incidents (8%), the thieves made a distinct effort to determine if someone was home before the theft included ringing the doorbell (2 incidents) and knocking (3 incidents). In only two cases (3%) did the thieves opened the package before exiting the property.

Exit

Most often (90%), the thieves took the item from the porch area and exited the property. However, in seven cases (10%), the offender made multiple trips between the street area and the porch to retrieve multiple items. In these instances, the multiple return trip was to continue taking packages that could not be carried in a single trip. Similar to the approach, the manner they left the property was recorded as either leisurely or quickly. Generally, (60%) of offenders exited the property quickly, either running or moving fast to exit the property.

After the package had been taken, the highest portion of offenders used a vehicle to exit the scene (61%). In 22 incidents, a car was used, 13 thefts used an SUV or van, and in six incidents, a truck was used. Unusually, in two cases, a U-Haul rental vehicle was used. In 50% of incidents ($n = 34$), the vehicle was left parked on the street in front of the residence, and in seven incidents (10%), the thief pulled the vehicle onto the victims' driveway. When the suspects' vehicle was parked in the driveway about half the time (42%), they backed the vehicle in. Further, regardless of where the vehicle was parked, a high number of suspects left a door or trunk open (54%, $n = 23$) while they approached the porch and then used the open the door to quickly place the package inside the vehicle upon return. Of the incidents that did not use a vehicle, the majority were on foot ($n = 20$), and the remainder ($n = 5$) used a skateboard or bicycle.

Discussion

Package theft is an emerging crime trend, and little is known about how often it occurs, who engages in the theft, and how the theft is accomplished. Using Video Data Analysis of actual thefts, we examined the incidents using a Crime Script Analysis and identified three stages of the theft; entry, execution, and exit. Next, we will discuss important aspects of this crime type and identify Situational Crime Prevention techniques that can be used by victims, police, and package delivery organizations to block opportunities to commit package theft.

Situational prevention of porch piracy: some proposals

Due to the purposive sample used to analyze porch piracy, these proposals for intervention are speculative. Drawing on SCP techniques described by Cornish and Clarke (2003), we have identified several techniques that appear particularly applicable to porch piracy. Specifically, we concentrate on increasing the effort, inducing the risk, and reducing the rewards.

Reduce the rewards

Reducing the rewards or benefits the offender expects to obtain from the crime is an essential step in disrupting crime. However, because offenders do not know what is inside the package, reducing the rewards must be addressed in a general sense. With porch piracy, part of the reward is likely the hunt, discovery, and successful theft of the package, with the contents being the secondary reward. Therefore, to reduce the known rewards, two efforts are practical: concealing the target and removing the target.

Concealment involves efforts to disguise, camouflage, or hide a package. This is important as the crime script analysis revealed that 98% of packages were visible from the street, with 61% estimated to be within 25 feet of the roadway. These packages tended to be of medium size (e.g. between 13 and 36 inches), and 46% had clear branding (e.g. Amazon) on the package. High visibility from roadways and easily recognized brands are likely a critical factor in package theft; therefore, concealing delivered packages should be considered. Methods to conceal unattended package delivery include placing packages inside a storm door or behind a plant, column, furniture, or another object on the porch. For areas particularly prone to porch piracy, placing an empty storage container on the porch to conceal packages could offer protection as it is unlikely that thieves would break the crime script by walking up to the house to see if a package had been delivered. Alternatively, delivering packages to a side or rear door may conceal many packages from direct street views. Retail and delivery companies may consider removing the branding from their packages, so they are less identifiable and enticing. Finally, delivery to established United States Postal Service boxes at the roadway or through mail slots installed in a residential home, when size permits, also reduce the visibility of packages and may reduce theft.

Removing targets can be accomplished in many ways. The first is by the homeowner as soon as a package is delivered. To reduce unattended package delivery, shipping organizations may consider shifting delivery hours during the afternoon or the evening to coincide with when more people are at home. Further, when leaving a package, a knock on the door or ring of the doorbell is an inexpensive and quick way to notify the resident of the arrival of a package. For organizations with the technology in place, electronic notification of delivery may also reduce the amount of time a package is untended on the porch. Expanding on this concept Amazon has developed Amazon Key, which allows a delivery drive onetime access to a home to place the package inside. Another technique developed by Package Guard is a small object that is secured to the porch that senses when a package is delivered and notifies the resident. Although less convenient for many persons, delivery at an alternative location such as a nearby convenience store, postal store (e.g. USPS, UPS, FedEx, Amazon Locker), or community neighbor is likely to affect rates of theft. All of these efforts either remove the package or reduce the time packages are left unattended.

Increasing the effort

All things being equal, offenders tend to select targets that require the least effort and fewest changes from their routine activities (Cohen & Felson, 1979). Increasing the effort involves making the offenders' activities more difficult or inconvenient. While the present study did not reveal that the presence of a fence inhibited thefts, prior research indicates fences are useful tools to increase the effort required to enter the property for other crimes (Wortley & McFarlane, 2011), and should be considered among other methods to increase the effort for criminals. Additionally, the present study observed no theft when the distance from the porch to the roadway was over 50 feet. Therefore, the position of houses with the roadway appears to have an impact on theft and may be related to the effort needed to walk or drive the distance from the road to the porch.

Another method for increasing the effort involves target hardening, which encompasses obstructing offenders, usually with locks, barriers, and other techniques to protect the object from crime. Several target hardening methods could be applied to block opportunities for package theft. These include methods that both conceal and secure a package such as allowing delivery companies to deliver inside a home (e.g. Amazon Key), directly to a vehicle truck (e.g. Phrame), or a lockable box on a private porch.

Other alternatives include bags (e.g. Porch Pirate Bag) made of reinforced ballistic nylon with instructions for delivery companies to insert packages into them and secure them with a lock to the door. Some residents may consider using bars and gates to block porch areas to all but residents and delivery personal. However, these alternatives may not be ideal, as the items are not concealed. Thieves may still put forth the effort to complete the theft since the item is observable.

Increase the risks

The risk of detection is generally thought of as an essential part of an offender's decision-making process. Increasing risks involves making it more likely that the offender will be observed. Therefore, increasing risk includes extending guardianship, strengthening formal surveillance, increasing natural surveillance, reducing anonymity, and utilizing place managers (Cornish & Clarke, 2003). One popular method is the installation of home video surveillance, which is thought to extend guardianship. However, the deterrence impact by cameras is unknown as the present study only included video of criminal acts. Another technique could be to post signs indicating the home is under surveillance. However, the CSA in this study did not find thieves were concerned about cameras, as only 8% took any effort to conceal their identity – even when several observed the camera.

Because most package thefts are occurring during daylight hours, traditional motion lights and other techniques to increase the risk of identification of the thief may not be effective. However, a unique item mentioned before, Package Guard, not only automatically notifies homeowners when a package arrives, but also set off an audible alarm if the package is removed before the homeowner disables the alarm. While this product provides no physical prevention, the alarm may increase the risk of a thief being observed or captured and thus prevent the theft. Formal surveillance can be increased by forming neighborhood watch groups and notifying neighborhood residences as soon as theft occurs. Other forms of formal surveillance and guardianship include training delivery drivers to observe for suspicious behavior, and notifying police when and where these crimes occur so additional patrols can be implemented.

Many SCP techniques involve increasing natural surveillance; that is, the ability for others to see a home and for those in the home to see out. However, with porch piracy, careful consideration should be made when increasing natural surveillance as some efforts to increase surveillance may expose the unattended package to all who pass by on the street. A careful balance should maintain the ability for surveillance while allowing areas to conceal a delivered package.

Reducing the anonymity of delivery drivers may be an essential step to increase the risks. While difficult to determine in the present study, several criminals appeared to be masquerading as delivery drivers (i.e. in one case wearing a FedEx jacket), carrying 'dummy' packages, holding papers, and a clipboard, or driving a U-Haul were concerning. Delivery companies are encouraged to establish uniforms and clear ID to reduce anonymity and confusion among the community about who should be approaching homes.

Crime script analysis of porch piracy: some proposals

Crime Script Analysis is the process of breaking down a criminal act into stages to identify the best points to disrupt criminal activity. Due to limited video data before and after the crime, the present study was only able to approach from the roadway to the home, the execution of the theft, and the exit from the porch to the roadway.

Approach

The approach to a residence lasts only as long as it takes the offender to walk or run from the property edge to the porch – which in most cases is only a few seconds. Therefore, this is a problematic area to offer prevention techniques. The present study revealed that a fence, gate, visible cameras, residents' cars on the property, and other environmental factors did not appear to deter any thieves from approaching a residence. Therefore, the most precise way to interrupt the approach is for the package to be hidden from view of the street. Without a visible package, the thief will likely never approach the home.

Execution

Here again, the execution of the theft takes only seconds as no tools or specialized skills are needed to acquire a package. Warning signs, cameras, and similar efforts may dissuade a thief after arriving at the porch. However, no evidence of this was observed in the present study. Moreover, a motion sensor that triggers an audible alarm or voice message acknowledging the presence of a person on the porch may increase the perception of risk and guardianship enough to discourage the theft at the point of execution. Lastly, increasing the effort at this point may reduce theft. For example, if a thief must break into a locked delivery box or cut though a cut-resistant package bag, the execution may be interrupted.

Exit

The final observable script for a porch pirate is the exit from the property. Here too, this is done quickly with few interruption points. However, neighbors, delivery personnel, and police should be observant for individuals who are walking or running from homes with packages in their hands. The present study observed only two instances of thieves who attempted to conceal the items upon exit. Similarly, in four instances, a thief was interrupted by the homeowner, and in each of these cases, the thieves were exiting the property. Therefore, the exit stage may provide the most overt circumstances that are readily identifiable to others and thus be an essential area to focus on interrupting the script.

Limitations and future directions

During a review of current VDA research and reflection on their research, Lindgaard and Bernasco (2018) described lessons learned when conducting VDA, several of which are presented here as limitations to the present study. First, there is a video selection bias when utilizing surveillance videos uploaded to YouTube, such as an overrepresentation of criminal failures or humorous events. Secondly, and related, cameras do not always capture other aspects of the crime, such as what occurs before or after the crime, or when a suspect walks out of view of the camera.

Thirdly, many of the features of VDA and SCA are difficult to be precise. For instance, deciding on the distance to the roadway, age of the offender, size of a package, if the offender ran or walk. To address this concern, we measured inter-coder reliability and had an average Kappa score indicating Substantial Agreement across the variables; however, we struggled for inter-coder reliability in imprecise areas (e.g. distance to the roadway). Therefore, the results should be interpreted cautiously. Lastly, similar caution should be taken when examining demographics and other aspects of the results as this study uses a purposive sample of YouTube videos and cannot be broadly applied in all situations.

Due to the limited nature of this research, we call for future studies to triangulate these findings with other sources. Specifically, we believe that focusing on victim surveys, offender interviews, and official police data (when it becomes available) will provide continued insights into this unique problem. We also recommend police agencies encourage victims to report thefts and begin keeping records of package theft as most agencies include package theft within a general code of 'theft' or 'larceny.' Without adequate and specific data on this crime, additional efforts to reduce it will be hampered.

Conclusion

Online shopping is exploding in growth in the United States, and along with that is a dramatic increase in shipping and unattended package delivery. As a result, package theft is a growing concern, as indicated in a survey of 2,000 consumers finding 36% have experienced a package theft (C + R, 2019). This present study is the first known scholarly research addressing this emerging crime trend. It provides valuable insights into the techniques thieves use to steal packages along with methods to prevent this crime.

The present study reveals important and unique features of this crime, the offenders, the environment, and criminal methods. The offenders were split evenly between women and men, racially mirrored the general population, and most (67%) appeared to be middle class. In this study, there were 98 packages stolen during 67 theft incidents. Thefts all occurred during daylight and more frequently when the home was closer to the roadway, with 61% occurring within 25 feet and the remaining between 26 and 50 feet. In 93% of cases, the packages were visible from the roadway, and 46% had some brand clearly on the package. Medium-sized packages (between 13 and 26 inches) were stolen more frequently (48%), followed by smaller packages (12 inches) at 40%.

A Crime Script was developed to allow for close examination of package theft and to enable Situational Crime Prevention techniques to be applied at different stages. These stages were identified as the approach to the residence, the execution of the theft, and the exit of the property. During the approach, gates, cameras, and resident vehicles on the property did not appear to interrupt the crime. Further, few thieves were observed 'casing' the area or taking any precautions to conceal their identity. During the execution of the theft, generally, only a single thief (96%) took the packages; however, in 37% of cases, an accomplice was serving as a lookout or escape driver. Few thieves, 8%, made any effort to determine if anyone was at home during the theft. During the exit from the property, only 10% returned for additional packages, most (60%) exited the property quickly (running or walking fast), and 60% used a vehicle to exit.

The most useful Situational Crime Prevention techniques that can be used to interrupt the crime script involve reducing the rewards, increasing effort, and increasing the risk. Within these techniques, concealing packages and removing packages are likely the most effective. These efforts can occur in many ways, including concealing packages behind items on the porch or inside non-locking boxes so they cannot be seen from the roadway. Additionally, notifying residents of package arrival, delivering later in the day, or delivering directly to stores, neighbors, package delivery points, inside the home or vehicle, or within a locked box on the porch will likely be effective. Finally, increasing the risk via formal surveillance, including monitored cameras (e.g. Amazon Ring), neighborhood watches, police patrols, training on suspicious behavior to delivery drivers, alarms and more, may also interrupt the crime.

Unfortunately, with limited information on how often package theft occurs, where it most frequently occurs, who commits the crime, likely victims, and other vital factors, this crime will likely continue to grow in popularity. This present study has taken the first step in understanding how package theft occurs and offered suggestions to prevent and interrupt the crime. Additional data and research into this emerging crime must be undertaken to have a full understanding of prevention methods. What does seem clear is that any efforts of increasing risks, reducing the rewards, or increasing the risk at any point in the crime script will need the cooperation of residents, delivery companies, researchers, innovative private companies, and police. We, therefore, encourage collaborative efforts to address this crime by collecting and sharing data and continued evaluation of Situational Crime Prevention and Crime Script Analysis to identify methods to prevent this emerging crime type.

Disclosure statement

No potential conflict of interest was reported by the authors.

Funding

No funding was received for this project

References

Borrion, H. (2013). Quality assurance in crime scripting. *Crime Science*, *2*(1), 6–11.

Bramsen, I. (2018). How violence happens (or not): Situational conditions of violence and nonviolence in Bahrain, Tunisia, and Syria. *Psychology of Violence*, *8*(3), 305–315.

Brayley, H., Cockbain, E., & Laycock, G. (2011). The value of crime scripting: Deconstructing internal child sex trafficking. *Policing*, *5*(2), 132–143.

Business Wire. (2016, October). *11 Million U.S. Homeowners Experienced Package Theft Within the Last Year, August Home Study Reveals*. Retrieved from https://www.businesswire.com/news/home/20161025005648/en/11-Million-U.S.-Homeowners-Experienced-Package-Theft

C+R Market Research. (2019, November). *2019 Package Theft Statistics Report*. Retrieved from https://www.crresearch.com/blog/2019-package-theft-statistics-report

Campo, C. (2017). *Watch out for 'porch pirates' who want to steal your holiday gift packages*. Retrieved from https://www.cnbc.com/2017/11/21/package-theft-is-a-big-risk-especially-during-the-holiday-shopping-season.html

Chiu, Y.N., Leclerc, B., & Townsley, M. (2011). Crime script analysis of drug manufacturing in clandestine laboratories: Implications for prevention. *The British Journal of Criminology, 51*(2), 355–374.

Clarke, R.V. (1997). Introduction. In R.V. Clarke (Ed.), *Situational crime prevention. Successful case studies* (pp. 1–44). New York: Harroe and Heston.

Clarke, R.V. (2017). Situational crime prevention. In R. Wortley & M. Townsley (Eds.), *Environmental criminology and crime analysis* (pp. 286–303). London: Taylor & Francis.

Clarke, R.V., & Mayhew, P. (1988). The British gas suicide story and its criminological implications. *Crime and Justice, 10*, 79–116.

Cohen, L.E., & Felson, M. (1979). Social change and crime rate trends: A routine activity approach. *American Sociological Review, 44*(4), 588–608.

Cornish, D.B. (1994). The procedural analysis of offending and its relevance for situational prevention. In R.V. Clarke (Ed.), *Crime prevention studies, Volume 3* (pp. 151–196). Monsey, NY: Criminal Justice Press.

Cornish, D.B., & Clarke, R.V. (2003). Opportunities, precipitators and criminal dispositions: A reply to Wortley's critique of situational crime prevention. In M.J. Smith & D.B. Cornish (Eds.), *Theory and practice in situational crime prevention volume 16* (pp. 111–124). Monsey, NJ: Criminal Justice Press.

Dabney, D.A., Hollinger, R.C., & Dugan, L. (2004). Who actually steals? A study of covertly observed shoplifters. *Justice Quarterly, 21*(4), 693–728.

Edwards, R. (2019, November 27). *These are the top ten major metros for package theft*. Retrieved from https://www.safewise.com/resources/smart-doorbell-buyers-guide/#top-metros-package-theft

eMarketer. (2018). E-commerce share of total global retail sales from 2015 to 2021. Statista. Retrieved from https://www.statista.com/statistics/534123/e-commerce-share-of-retail-sales-worldwide/

Fischer, C. (2019, June 19). *New Texas law makes stealing packages off porches a felony*. Retrieved from https://abc13.com/stealing-packages-you-could-go-to-jail-thanks-to-texas-law/5352898/

Gilmour, N. (2014). Understanding money laundering. A crime script approach. *The European Review of Organized Crime, 1*(2), 35–56.

Guerette, R.T. (2009). The pull, push, and expansion of situational crime prevention evaluation: An appraisal of thirty-seven years of research. In J. Kuntsson & N. Tilley (Eds.), *Evaluating crime reduction initiatives, volume 24* (pp. 29–58) Boulder CO: Lynne Rienner Publishers.

Hu, W., & Haag, M. (2019, December). *90,000 packages disappear daily in N.Y.C. Is help on the way?* Retrieved from https://www.nytimes.com/2019/12/02/nyregion/online-shopping-package-theft.html

Jacobs, B.A. (1999). *Dealing crack: The social world of streetcorner selling*. Lebanon, NH: UPNE.

Jacques, S., & Bernasco, W. (2013). Drug dealing: Amsterdam's red light district. In B. Leclerc & R. Wortley (Eds.), *Cognition and crime: Offender decision-making and script analysis. crime science*. London, UK: Routledge.

Jordan, B., & Henderson, A. (1995). Interaction analysis: Foundations and practice. *The Journal of the Learning Sciences, 4*(1), 39–103.

Landis, J.R., & Koch, G.G. (1977). The measurement of observer agreement for categorical data. *Biometrics, 33*(1), 159–174.

Leclerc, B., Wortley, R., & Smallbone, S. (2011). Getting into the script of adult child sex offenders and mapping out situational prevention measures. *Journal of Research in Crime and Delinquency, 48* (2), 209–237.

Leclerc, C. (2013). New developments in script analysis for situational crime prevention: Moving beyond offender scripts. In B. Leclerc & R. Wortley (Eds.), *Cognition and crime: Offender decision-making and script analysis. crime science* (pp. 221–236). London: Routledge.

Legewie, N., & Nassauer, A. (2018). YouTube, Google, Facebook: 21st-century online video research and research ethics. *Forum Qualitative Sozialforschung/Forum: Qualitative Social Research*, *19*(3), 21–28.

Liebst, L.S., Heinskou, M.B., & Ejbye-Ernst, P. (2018). On the actual risk of bystander intervention: A statistical study based on naturally occurring violent emergencies. *Journal of Research in Crime and Delinquency*, *55*(1), 27–50.

Lindegaard, M.R., & Bernasco, W. (2018). Lessons learned from crime caught on camera. *Journal of Research in Crime and Delinquency*, *55*(1), 155–186.

Mayhew, P., & Hough, M. (2012). Situational crime prevention. The home office origins. In N. Tilley & G. Farrell (Eds.), *The reasoning criminologist: Essays in honor of Ronald V. Clarke* (pp. 15–29). Abingdon, Oxon: Routledge.

McKinnon, A.C., & Tallam, D. (2003). Unattended delivery to the home: An assessment of the security implications. *International Journal of Retail & Distribution Management*, *31*(1), 30–41.

Moeller, K. (2018). Video-recorded retail cannabis trades in a low-risk marketplace: Trade Value and temporal patterns. *Journal of Research in Crime and Delinquency*, *55*(1), 103–124.

Moreto, W.D. (2019). Provoked poachers? Applying a situational precipitator framework to examine the nexus between human-wildlife conflict, retaliatory killings, and poaching. *Criminal Justice Studies*, *32*(2), 63–80.

Mosselman, F., Weenink, D., & Lindegaard, M.R. (2018). Weapons, body postures, and the quest for dominance in robberies: A qualitative analysis of video footage. *Journal of Research in Crime and Delinquency*, *55*(1), 3–26.

Nassauer, A. (2016). From peaceful marches to violent clashes: A micro-situational analysis. *Social Movement Studies*, *15*(5), 515–530.

Nassauer, A. (2018a). How robberies succeed or fail: Analyzing crime caught on CCTV. *Journal of Research in Crime and Delinquency*, *55*(1), 125–154.

Nassauer, A. (2018b). Situational dynamics and the emergence of violence in protests. *Psychology of Violence*, *8*(3), 293–304.

Nassauer, A., & Legewie, N.M. (2018). Video Data Analysis: A methodological frame for a novel research trend. *Sociological Methods & Research*, *X*(X), 1–40.

Natarajan, M., Clarke, R.C., Carcach, C., Ponce, C., de Sanfeliú, M., Escobar Polanco, D., ... Shi, M. (2015). Situational prevention and public transport crime in El Salvador. *Crime Science*, *4*(1), 1–15.

Ogonowski, P. (2019, December). *10 ecommerce average order value statistics* [Updated 2019]. Retrieved from https://www.growcode.com/blog/average-order-value/

Osborne, J.R., & Capellan, J.A. (2017). Examining active shooter events through the rational choice perspective and crime script analysis. *Security Journal*, *30*(3), 880–902.

Phrame. (2018). How it works. Phrame. Retrieved from https://www.phrame.com/how-it-works

Poyner, B., & Webb, B. (1991). *Crime free housing*. Oxford: Butterworth-Architecture.

Punakivi, M., Yrjölä, H., & Holmström, J. (2001). Solving the last mile issue: Reception box or delivery box? *International Journal of Physical Distribution & Logistics Management*, *31*(6), 427–439.

The Shorr Corporation. (2017). The 2017 package theft report: Porch pirates, purchase habits, and privacy. Retrieved from https://www.shorr.com/packaging-news/2017-05/2017-package-theft-report-porch-pirates-purchase-habits-and-privacy

Stickle, B.F. (2017). *Metal scrappers and thieves: Scavenging for survival and profit*. New York, NY: Springer.

Sytsma, V.A., & Piza, E.L. (2018). Script analysis of open-air drug selling: A systematic social observation of CCTV footage. *Journal of Research in Crime and Delinquency*, *55*(1), 78–102.

Tedeschi, J.T., & Felson, R.B. (1994). *Violence, aggression, and coercive actions*. Washington, DC: American Psychological Association.

Tompson, L., & Chainey, S. (2011). Profiling illegal waste activity: Using crime scripts as a data collection and analytical strategy. *European Journal on Criminal Policy and Research*, *17*(3), 179–201.

Tunley, M., Button, M., Shepherd, D., & Blackbourn, D. (2018). Preventing occupational corruption: Utilizing situational crime prevention techniques and theory to enhance organisational resilience. *Security Journal*, *31*(1), 21–52.

Willison, R., & Siponen, M. (2009). Overcoming the insider: Reducing employee computer crime through Situational Crime Prevention. *Communications of the ACM, 52*(9), 133–137.

Willits, D.W., & Makin, D.A. (2018). Show me what happened: Analyzing use of force through analysis of body-worn camera footage. *Journal of Research in Crime and Delinquency, 55*(1), 51–77.

Wortley, R., & McFarlane, M. (2011). The role of territoriality in crime prevention: A field experiment. *Security Journal, 24*(2), 149–156.

Wright, R., & Decker, S.H. (1997). *Armed robbers in action: Stickups and street culture*. Lebanon, NH: UPNE.

Wright, R.T., & Decker, S.H. (1994). *Burglars on the job: Streetlife and residential break-ins*. Lebanon, NH: UPNE.

Yanowitz, K.L., & Yanowitz, J.L. (2012). The role of gender in the generation of stalking scripts. *Sex Roles, 66*(5–6), 366–377.

OPEN ACCESS

Fieldwork protocol as a safety inventory tool in public places

Vania Ceccato

ABSTRACT
This study reports on experiences using fieldwork protocols (FPs) in guiding the inventory of safety conditions in public places. Relying on theories of environmental criminology, situational crime prevention, and crime prevention through environmental design (CPTED), FPs are used to collect data on-site for three different types of public places: subway stations, shopping centers and parks. The fieldwork data are compared with other data sources and mapped using geographical information system (GIS) technology or building information modeling (BIM). Based on criteria of validity, reliability, and generalizability of evidence collected on-site, the study shows that FPs are better suited for environments that follow some uniform structure (subway stations) than other types of public places (urban parks). The article concludes with lessons for using FPs in guiding data collection for safety inventories and recommendations for future research.

Introduction

There is no novelty in stating that crime and fear of crime vary over time and space. To tackle problems of safety, researchers have long been developing tools in an attempt to capture the situational conditions that could lead to crime and/or trigger fear of crime. Some researchers have focused on capturing the quantitative character of the urban landscape and how that affects crime levels and/or fear (Ceccato, Haining, & Signoretta, 2002; de Melo, Matias, & Andresen, 2015; Weisburd, Morris, & Groff, 2009). Others have devoted attention to finding ways of qualitatively assessing links between safety and features of the urban landscape (Armitage, 2013; Bamzar, 2019; Cozens, Saville, & Hillier, 2005; Ekblom, 2019; Grönlund, 2012). Among these quantitative and qualitative approaches, fieldwork protocols (FPs) stand out as a popular tool for data collection. Creswell (2013, p. 168) defines FP as 'a predesigned form used to record information collected during an observation or interview.' Despite the vast use of FP in other research fields (e.g. Creswell, 2013) and also in criminology, there is a lack of studies assessing their potentialities to collect in-depth data.

The aim of this study is to report on experiences using FPs in guiding the inventory of safety conditions in public places based on environmental criminology theories and approaches. By using validity, reliability, and generalizability criteria, we assess how well

FPs work for inspecting and collecting data through observation in subway stations, parks, and shopping centers. We submit that a well-designed FP enhances the quality of the data obtained on-site, which is fundamental for further analysis, either qualitative or quantitative. Principles of environmental criminology such as situational crime prevention and crime prevention through environmental design (CPTED) and routine activity work as a theoretical reference in the elaboration of these protocols.

The novelty of this article is that the evaluation of FPs done here combines interdisciplinary knowledge of architecture, urban planning, and environmental criminology. The article is also novel because it systematizes robust evidence in a methodological comparison of studies applied to public places of the same municipality (Stockholm, Sweden) and one in a northern European capital city (Vilnius, Lithuania), stretching over a period of more than 10 years.

The article starts with a discussion of the main environmental criminology theories that underlie the search for safety clues in the physical environment of the city. Fieldwork protocols are evaluated using principles of validity, reliability, and generalizability. The current study is framed later with a presentation of the study areas, methodology, and results. Conclusions and recommendations are finally presented, followed by some relevant background materials presented in the Appendix.

Theoretical background

Safety in public places

A public place can take a variety of forms and shapes. It can be a *public park*, open for all, a *station*, where many people pass by but may be restricted at certain hours of the day, or a hermetic *shopping center* that is public but not publicly owned, which means that not all parts are accessible by all. Social interactions and their results in these public places, such as being a victim of crime, are affected by differences in accessibility to these environments both temporally and spatially (Brantingham & Brantingham, 1995; Felson, 2002; Rhodes & Conly, 1981). This constitutes a reason for reflecting about the concept of public place. Public place can be defined as a space legally open and accessible to all without permission of anyone else, like a common (Németh, 2012). Most public places are conditionally free because actions allowed in these spaces fall under the laws of the locality in which these spaces are located.

Public place is more than an accessible place. It may bear a morality, which defines which behaviors are welcome, allowed, wanted, or enforced (Ceccato, 2016). Crime is dependent on a place's morality. The moral norms and the efficacy of their enforcement largely 'depend on what kinds of activities take place within them and what kinds of people tend to be present, both of which are likely to vary by time of day, week and/or year' (Wikström & Treiber, 2017, p. 82). The routine activity approach establishes that crime only occurs where and when the 'basic conditions' for crime are present (Cohen & Felson, 1979) and only when a crime-prone person spends enough time in a criminogenic setting (Wikström, Mann, & Hardie, 2018). A public place 'may become criminogenic when their activities and users encourage (or do not discourage) behavioral norms that conflict with the law, and/or they are ineffective at enforcing the law' (Wikström & Treiber, 2017, p. 82). This criminogenic setting depends on how its microenvironments are designed, how it is used through the day by residents and visitors, and how well it is interlinked to the rest of the neighborhood and city.

Urban environments and crime prevention through environmental design

The type of building, its function and architectural design influence what occurs in the building, including in places surrounding it. According to situational crime theory (Clarke, 1983, 1997), this implies that environments can be planned following principles that reduce the opportunities for crime. Situational crime theory focuses on opportunity-reducing processes that are aimed at particular forms of crime; entail the management, creation or manipulation of the immediate environment in an organized and permanent manner as possible; and result in crime being more difficult and risky or less rewarding and justifiable (Clarke, 1997). In an environment, this can be done by stimulating surveillance, fostering territoriality, and reducing areas of conflict by controlling access and improving overall perceived safety (Armitage, 2013; Cozens et al., 2005; Ekblom, 2011, 2019; Iqbal & Ceccato, 2016; Jeffery, 1977; Newman, 1972; Saville, 2013). These principles underlie what is called crime prevention through environmental design (CPTED). CPTED is defined by Crowe (2000, p. 46) as 'the proper design and effective use of the built environment which can lead to a reduction in the fear of crime and the incidence of crime, and to an improvement in the quality of life.' The most traditional principles of CPTED are natural surveillance, access control, territorial reinforcement, and space management, but since the 1960s other principles (Jacobs, 1961; Newman, 1972; Reynald & Elffers, 2009) have been incorporated to include the social dimensions of neighborhoods (Armitage, 2013; Cozens et al., 2005; Saville, 2013; Saville & Clear, 2000). The international literature has shown evidence that incorporating some of these principles of CPTED can help to create a safe and secure environment that encourages social interaction, promoting safety (for a review, see Cozens & Love, 2015).

According to Ceccato, Falk, Parsanezhad, and Tarandi (2018), most CPTED interventions have been implemented together with other situational crime prevention techniques (Clarke, 2012) with reference to housing developments and neighborhoods (e.g. Armitage, 2013; Ceccato & Bamzar, 2016; Clarke, 1983; DeKeseredy, Donnermeyer, & Schwartz, 2009), transportation systems (Ceccato & Paz, 2017; Loukaitou-Sideris, 2012), parks (Iqbal & Ceccato, 2016), and commercial properties and shopping centers (Ceccato & Tcacencu, 2018; Ceccato et al., 2018; Lindblom & Kajalo, 2011).

Observers are the ones that collect the information through inspection of the environment. They have a central role implementing CPTED because they 'inspect' a particular environment, its design (internal and external), how it relates to the rest of the area, and how all these aspects affect crime opportunities and/or perceived safety. Although not free from criticism (Armitage, Monchuk and Rogerson 2011; Pain, 2000; Shaftoe & Read, 2005; Sutton, Cherney, & White, 2008) and showing contradictory evidence (Cozens et al., 2005), CPTED is valuable. This approach aims at gaining a better understanding of the effect of micro-spaces on individual behavior, either as a potential target or an offender seeking opportunities.

The most widely known CPTED principle relies on the notion of natural surveillance, which can be implemented in many ways. Open lines of sight in parks by guardians, handlers, and park managers can help to enhance natural surveillance (Felson, 1995), as can the implementation of closed-circuit television (CCTV). Another important dimension refers to *territoriality* and indicates how the physical design can develop a sense of ownership in specific areas (Reynald & Elffers, 2009). Saville (2013) states that *sense of ownership* can help to create the idea of shared standards among different user groups (including gender perspective and people with special needs). *Access control* refers to property control using barriers, enclosures, and entry portals as well as pedestrian-friendly urban streetscapes or the installation of safety information signs through wireless network transmissions (audio/video) in smart cities. This can be combined with *activity support* that encourages interactions between residents and other users, thereby discouraging crime. *Target hardening* is about how the design of a space can make it difficult for people to steal or damage private and/or public property. *Image of the place/maintenance* informs how pleasant esthetics keep potential criminals away because well-kept environments show that people are in control of the area. These principles have been called in the north American literature, the first generation of CPTED. According to Saville (2018), the second-generation CPTED includes principles that attempt to combine place's physical features with the social dimension of the environment and promote safety as part of sustainable development through social cohesion, connectivity, and community participation. There is also a third-generation CPTED, that relies on the potential of technology solutions to improve safety while adopting a green approach (Saville, 2018). In Scandinavia, CPTED principles have been implemented in the last three decades as a mix of first, second, and third generation in both new and existent residential areas much more as synonym of situational crime prevention than linked to the acronym CPTED.

In principle, CPTED can be implemented in FPs to inspect a particular feature of the environment in relation to safety, be that a park, a building, or a whole neighborhood. These protocols allow data to be gathered on-site after visual inspection or counting of items in the environment by the observer. Data are organized in an analog and/or digital form (through templates, structured questionnaires, checklists, diaries, or notes, for example). However, few studies have spent time assessing the adequacy of these protocols in criminology. Since there is no standard method for comparing the performance of these FPs as safety inventory tools, one way forward is to check whether and how the data coming from them satisfy some of the basic criteria of research, such as validity, reliability, and generalizability.

Fieldwork protocols: validity, reliability, and generalizability

Previous research has shown that fieldwork protocols are able to capture what is most important in the environment to explain why crime (or fear) happens at that particular place and time (Ceccato et al., 2018; Iqbal & Ceccato, 2016). What should one expect from a safety inventory tool such as an FP?

First, it is expected that FPs can work effectively in collecting unbiased data (see issues of the validity and reliability criteria, for example). Second, FPs should provide stable measurements across items in the protocol (see issues of internal validity). Third, FPs can be created in a uniform way but can still be flexible and 'be translated' into different types of public places and contexts (see issues of criterion generalizability, for example). In summary, Table 1 offers a list of the basic conditions for protocols expected

Table 1. Basic conditions of fieldwork protocols in safety inventory.

Fundamental elements of FPs	Characterization of FPs for research
Validity – how successfully the fieldwork protocol has actually achieved what it set out to do.	*Content validity* means that if the protocol is created to assess the presence of four CPTED principles (natural surveillance, access control, territorial reinforcement, and space management) in an area, then these principles should be the backbone of the fieldwork protocol. *Criterion validity* is the extent to which records collected using the protocol correlate (at a particular time or in the feature) with other pre-existing records, as initially hypothesized.
Reliability – the consistency of a measure in the fieldwork protocol, over time, internally and across observers. It depends on how measurable the hypotheses/ relationships are.	*Reliability over time* is the extent to which data collected are consistent over time, e.g. data collected at rush hour compared with data recorded at the same time of the day. *Internal consistency* is dependent on the stability of the measurements across items in the protocol, typically a measure based on the correlations between different items on the same test. A fieldwork protocol should promote *inter-observer reliability*, i.e. different observers should show a capacity to identify 'the same reality' or similar evidence when assessing CPTED principles in a particular place.
Generalizability – whether the fieldwork protocol (or findings) can be applicable in other research contexts or situations.	Potential causal links between crime and types of environment (obtained by fieldwork protocols) should be tested and, whenever possible, applied to other environments of the same type, to other contexts and to other types of events in similar environments.

to be satisfied when designing protocols for data collection and/or on-site analysis for safety inventory.

Validity refers to the extent to which the FPs capture and measure the 'right' (expected) elements that need to be measured (Kelley, 1972). *Content validity* is the extent to which an FP includes all the constructs of interest, while *criterion validity* is the extent to which an observer's responses to variables in the protocol are correlated with other variables that one would expect them to be correlated with (not necessarily from the FPs). Examples of validity in data collection and on-site analysis using FPs are shown in Table 1.

Equally important when designing the FP is to consider the *reliability* of the tool which, according to Leung (2015), refers to exact replicability of the processes and the results coming from the protocols. This assumes that the use of FPs can be repeated (in different points in time or space) and/or that two or more observers can reach similar interpretations of 'a reality' by using the same questions, categories, and procedures. Measurements and observations on-site are expected to be accurate and consistent across places and across observers. In order to ensure that, time must be dedicated to thorough planning of the fieldwork, data-gathering procedures, sampling size of observers and on-site techniques. Table 1 shows that *reliability* can be assessed in three ways: across time, across items, and across different observers.

If one is interested in using FPs in other contexts or other situations, then one should be checking the *generalizability* of the data and analysis on-site. In the case of safety inventories, testing *generalizability* is a challenge and, sometimes, not even desirable, because case studies are often bound to a single framework applied to one or more phenomena (e.g. sexual harassment) in a certain public place (e.g. a park), in a particular context (e.g. city center), hence generalizability of qualitative research findings is usually not a required attribute of quality. However, as demand for knowledge synthesis from qualitative research has grown, evaluation of generalizability has lately increased via qualitative meta-synthesis, by summarizing qualitative findings from disparate studies into a single framework, so that the findings can be used more often in practice and policy (Finfgeld-Connett, 2010; Leung, 2015).

Drawing from the current body of knowledge, we submit that the performance of FPs can be compared using case studies as it is going to be reported in this study.

The current study

Study areas

Fieldwork protocols (FPs) are used for data collection in three different types of public place: subway stations, parks, and shopping centers in Sweden's capital, Stockholm, and a park in the capital of Lithuania, Vilnius. The municipality of Stockholm (*Stockholms stad*) has a population of 960,031 inhabitants (2019), spread over 188 square kilometers, the largest in Sweden and in Scandinavia. As a municipality, the City of Stockholm is subdivided into district councils or boroughs, which carry the responsibility for primary schools and social, leisure, and cultural services within their respective areas. The implementation of CPTED principles started voluntarily in the late 1990s in Sweden. It was not until 2005 that the National Housing Board incorporated some CPTED principles in its policies (Grönlund, 2012). However, even today these principles are not mandatory in new housing developments or commercial buildings.

Stockholm's *subway system* is the 20th longest in the world, with a track length of 110 kilometers divided among three lines: green, red, and blue. The Central Station (*T-Centralen* subway station) has the largest number of passengers per day, in a system composed of 100 stations, of which 47 are underground and 53 above ground (Ceccato, 2013). The *shopping center used here as study area* is a mall located adjacent to a metro line on the outskirts of Stockholm, in an area with relatively high crime levels. When built in the late 1970s, and even when later refurbished, the shopping center was not planned with CPTED principles in mind. Finally, evidence from *parks* is based on two case studies, one from Stockholm, Sweden, and the other from Vilnius, Lithuania. For details about the parks, see Ceccato and Lukyte (2011) and Iqbal and Ceccato (2016).

Data and methods

Figure 1 illustrates data collection process and the four steps taken to assess FPs as tools for inspecting the physical and social environment of three types of public place. In this article, we concentrate on reporting activities under step 4. **Step 1** describes the data collection used in study cases. Note that each case study was developed independently over a course of about 10 years. As step 1 illustrates, rather than adopting a single perspective, this research makes use of both qualitative and quantitative perspectives – a mixed method approach – to allow a better understanding of the problems being

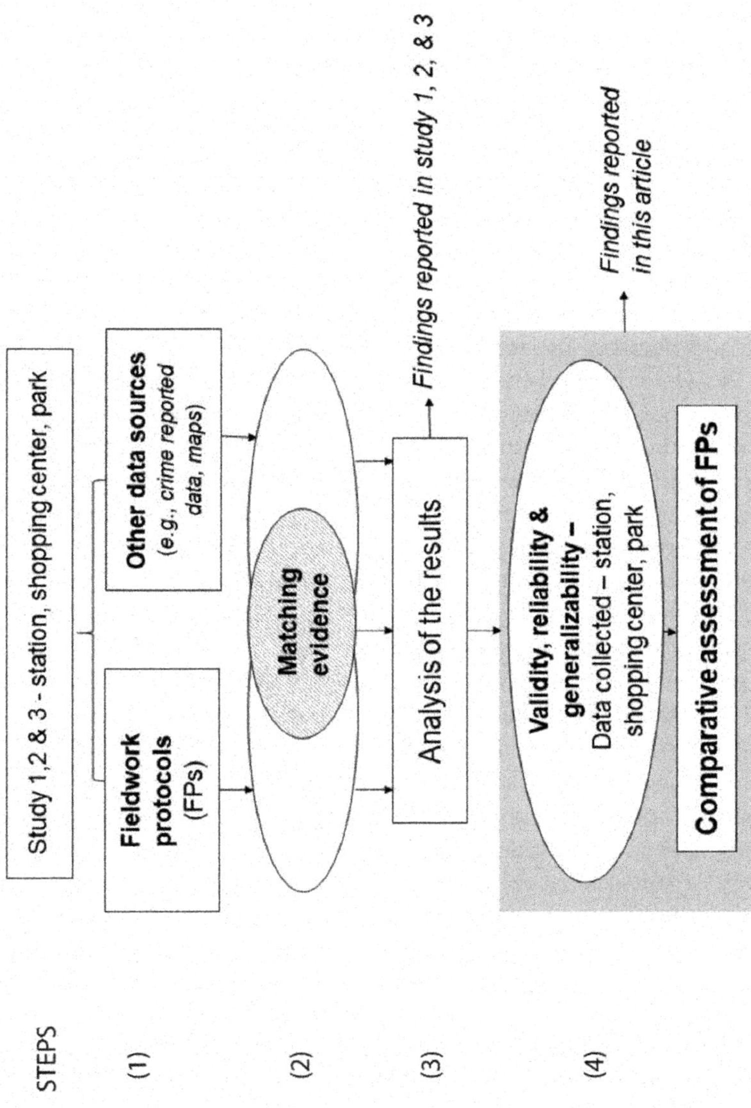

Figure 1. The methodological steps of this study.

researched (Clark & Creswell, 2011). This means we combined data from maps, crime police data, photographs and observations with FPs described in detail in each study. **Step 2** describes the processes of combining data from different sources and finding common patterns as well as aspects and issues that showed different patterns when these different data sources were put together. In **step 3**, findings were reported in four different studies as described below.

Steps 1, 2 and 3 – Data collection and analysis

For the case study of the *subway stations*, FPs were composed of checklists, such as the one presented in Appendix, combined with photographs, and later analyzed with secondary data sources using georelational databases, spatial statistical techniques, and geographical information systems (GIS). Although the internal environments of subway stations follow some common standards (e.g. illumination, platform/lobby structures), they are not exactly the same, which can impact on the stations' vulnerability to crime and perception of safety. To capture these environmental differences, a systematic and detailed inspection using FPs was used in all stations of the subway system. The FPs were detailed checklists implemented in spreadsheets divided into five different parts following the station's parts: the platform, the transition area, the lobby, the exits, and the immediate surrounding area (see Appendix). The station *platform* is where the trains arrive and passengers wait. The *transition area* is the area between the platform and the gates/ticket booths and commonly includes stairs and elevators to the platform. The *lobby* is the area between the gates/ticket booths and the exits or tunnels. The *exits* are areas limited to entering the lobby area, either directly from the street or via a tunnel. The surroundings include the *immediate surroundings* around each exit, i.e. the field of view from a station exit (Figure 2).

In each part, different aspects of the station's environment were collected and measured. For instance, visibility, surveillance capacity, crowdedness, and smell in the elevators were assessed using a low-medium-high scale. Visibility was a function of how much one could see from the location, thereby giving an inside-outside perspective, 'you' in relation to others, while surveillance was defined as how well others can see 'you,' providing the outside-inside perspective. For instance, for all stations the visibility and possibility of surveillance were assessed; any dark places or vandalism was noted and registered using the protocols. Likewise, the presence of security cameras and guards, drunken people, overall crowdedness, and area-specific features such as types

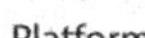

Figure 2. The five sections of subway stations: platform, transition, hall, exit/entrance and immediate surroundings. Photographs by Adriaan C. Uittenbogaard, Roya Bamzar and Vania Ceccato, 2011-2018.

of entrance gates, cash machines, and types of wall were noted. For instance, crowdedness was classified as low for 0–5 people, medium for 6–10 people, and high for more than 11 people in each section of the station. Unlike pure quantitative research which deals primarily with numerical data and quantifiable interpretations of reality, this type of data collection and on-site analysis also involves qualitative research dealing with non-numerical information and its phenomenological interpretation, which directly relates to the human senses and subjectivity (Leung, 2015), in other words, the way we use and perceive the environment. Thus, smell was subjectively categorized (as low, medium or high) by its strength from, for instance, urine. The features that characterize the stations' surroundings (e.g. the presence of shops, bus stops, parking, ATMs, bars, motorways, parks, litter, drunken people) were checked using these FPs, including in which type of immediate surrounding the station was embedded, such as residential, commercial, or mixed. All subway stations were inspected on a weekday, between 10 am and 4 pm, thus avoiding atypical hours (peak hours and busy weekends) in the summertime. Using crime and perceived safety as dependent variables, we used the data collected at the stations in the FPs as covariates in regression models. (Details see Ceccato & Uittenbogaard, 2014; Ceccato, Uittenbogaard, & Bamzar, 2013)

For the case study of the *shopping center*, on-site data collection was performed using checklists. Results were later compared with secondary data and complemented with questions from a digital safety survey (Google forms) and photographs. Both results were later mapped using a 3-D model implemented in building information modeling (BIM). Drawing on CPTED principles, a conceptual framework for assessing spaces and times that are criminologically relevant to crime and perceived safety was proposed. How much visitors are exposed to crime depends on their location at a particular time in the mall as well as internal and external features such as good lighting, design and position of doors, windows and staircases, and entrances. The analysis was carried out looking at *functional spaces*, those spaces which have a defined function in the shopping mall, such as stores, restaurants, banks or toilets. *Open public spaces* in a shopping mall have a key role in terms of safety, as they are settings of convergence at all times. Shopping centers also have *transitional areas*, such as corridors, stairs, and paths. Length and width, location, types of materials, enclosure and design all affect how safe these transitional areas are. The *entrances/exits* carry the identity of the shopping center. They can be of many types, for pedestrians and for cars, giving access to the parking lot, for example. In any case, well-functioning entrances allow the flow of people (or cars), under normal and emergency conditions. The shopping center's *immediate surroundings* are also an important criminogenic factor for what happens inside the mall. Data were collected through fieldwork inspection using protocols in a spreadsheet completed during a series of visits to the shopping center in particular environments most targeted by crime and incidents of public disturbance. Spots showing high crime areas were inspected using FPs. Fieldwork information was later combined with reports of occurrences of crime (secondary data) over a period of 17 months (from January 2015 to May 2016) and a perceived safety survey applied using mobile telephones and photographs of the shopping center (for details, Kajalo and Lindblom, 2010); Ceccato et al., 2018; Ceccato, 2018). The crime records constituted by police recorded data collected from three sets of coordinates covering the location of the shopping center, and cartographic maps were later digitalized using either AutoCad or GIS. Figure 3 illustrates the results of the secondary data mapped using BIM, which served as

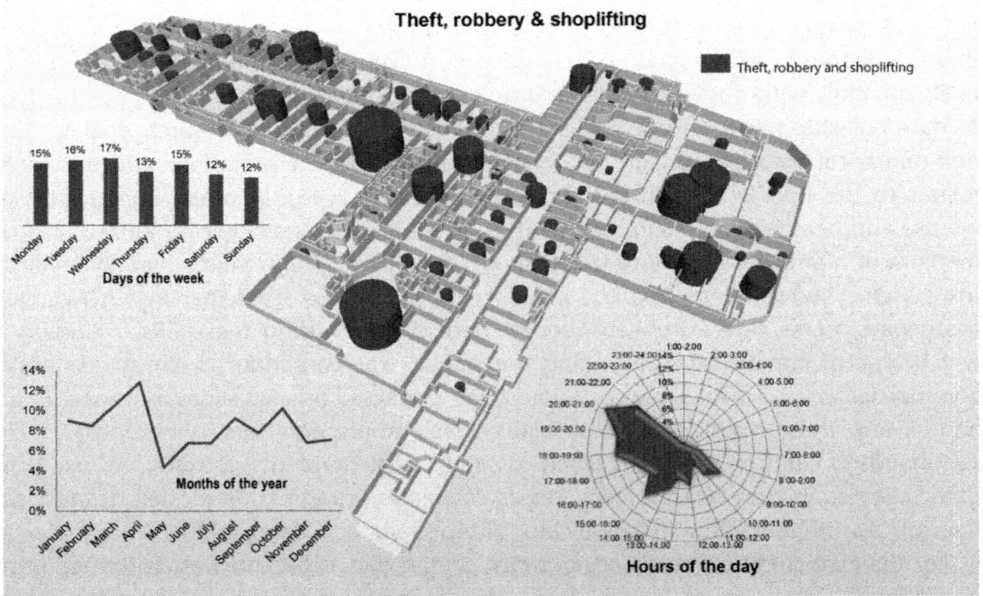

Figure 3. Secondary data mapped using building information modeling as background information for working with fieldwork protocols in shopping centers.

background information for defining fieldwork strategies using the protocols. For instance, using these BIM (Building Information Modelling) maps, we were able to visualize the spots with major safety problems in space and time.

For the case study of the *parks*, FPs were used on a 'safety walk' (Vilnius case), and a park inspection (case studies in Stockholm) allowing the visual inspection of the park through observations. In Vilnius, the safety walk (or audit) is an inventory of the features of an area (or a park) that affect individuals' perceptions of safety. Safety walks help individuals to look at a space that feels unsafe and determine why it feels unsafe, applying CPTED principles, routine activity theory and situational crime prevention as guidance. Safety walks can be used to demonstrate how daily fears translate into concerns about the physical environment, which is useful information for planners (Ceccato & Hansson, 2013). During the walk, participants decided when and where to stop if they felt they had something to tell. Twenty-five individuals participated in the safety walk, which took about one-and-a-half hours on a weekday in the spring of 2011.

The protocol (Figure 4) allowed for each participant to indicate wherein the park problems occur, descriptions of the problems, and some basic participant information, such as age and gender. In the example of the park by Iqbal and Ceccato (2016), FPs were also used as a safety inventory tool with safety walks in combination with maps of police-recorded data as well as safety questionnaires as alternative sources of information. Observers using FPs in the park varied their observations over time in an effort to collect data that reflect the park at all times (Details see Ceccato & Hanson, 2013; Iqbal & Ceccato, 2016).

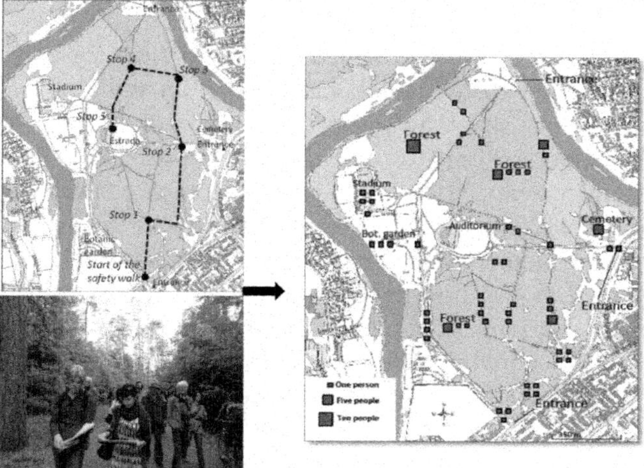

Use of protocols in safety walks

1. Preparation

Invite participants (strive as far as possible to gather people of different backgrounds and interests) that reflect the people who reside and/or work in that particular place. Define time & place for a preparation meeting.

2. Meeting the participants

Explain the aim of the walk. Show how the area to be visited and how they may be split into groups to cover the area. Produce maps of the area where the walk will be held. Show the protocol to be used and how it can be filled in. One aim of the walk is to strengthen the feeling of the area. Discuss with participants the history of the park and changes that have occurred. Encourage participants to bring mobile phones to record the safety walk by taking photographs and recording comments along the way.

3. Introduction to the walk & protocol

Meet at the designated place and time. Propose a route to participants and immediate actions to participants (what to see, what to make notes about, as previously discussed in 2). The leader can plan 1–2 locations as examples and help participants fill in the protocols.

4. Actions along the walk

Ask participants to find places/times that tend to concentrate visitors and whether they can be improved. Ask them to express how it feels (or how they imagine it feels) to be alone at different locations at different times of the day, as well as in different seasons. Stop along the route and keep the conversation open so everyone gets their say. Make sure they keep their eyes open for things that pop up along the way. What does the entrance look like? Is better illumination needed? Are there environmental features that create barriers to access for visitors? Highlight that different groups think of different things when they think of "safety" (be prepared for conflicting views).

5. Actions along the walk

Compile all completed protocols from the participants into a single database. Summarize the experiences and identify problematic locations and any meaningful differences and points of conflict between participants' views. Inform the next steps in the study (using data collected on-site). Provide your contact details to participants so they can get in touch and add information or further thoughts and can get feedback from the fieldwork organizer.

Figure 4. Fieldwork protocol used in a safety walk through Vingis Park, Vilnius, Lithuania. The route of the safety walk (upper-left corner), participants, and the output map with identification of places described as unsafe. Based on Ceccato and Hansson (2013)

Step 4 – Comparative assessment of FPs and scores

Step 4 illustrates how FPs were assessed based on how well FPs performed in 'inspecting and collecting data through observation' in terms of validity, reliability and generalizability. Since different scales of analysis were used in each study, 'the original data' were not appropriate to indicate how well FPs performed as a data collection/inspection tool. In order to be able to compare the data collected from these studies, 'data' were transformed into 'a qualitative assessment' and 'scores' varying from high, to medium and low in terms of validity, reliability and generalizability, as illustrated in the next section. For example, FPs from parks got much more discrepant evaluations from observers than stations did. This means that stations got a higher score in *generalizability*, for example, than FPs applied to parks did, assuming constant potential differences in the profile of inspectors, such as age and gender.

The final comparative assessment (**Step 4**) was systematically performed for all three public places using three subjective scores – *high, medium* and *low* – linked to the criteria of *validity, reliability*, and *generalizability* of FPs. This means that the public place that imposed 'less of a challenge' for FPs as a data collection tool in terms of *validity, reliability*, and *generalizability* earned the highest score (*high*). Conversely, FPs from parks got much more discrepant evaluations in terms of *validity, reliability*, and *generalizability* than FPs applied to stations did, so FPs from parks scored *medium/low* in all assessment criteria. If moderate challenges in the application of an FP were found during the fieldwork in a particular environment, a score of *medium* was associated with the FP. For example, the internal reliability was *medium/low* for parks (because of heterogeneous differences of the park environments, size and location) but *high* for stations (the standardization of the stations facilitates internal reliability).

Results

Reporting findings by type of public place

Subway stations

Findings showed that safety conditions in transport nodes depend on "multi-scale conditions that act at various levels in an urban environment. The analysis involved an evaluation of the relationship between events of crime and environmental attributes of subway stations and surrounding areas collected using FPs (an example is illustrated in Appendix), which were later analyzed using regression models and GIS. These conditions are determined by the environmental attributes of the station, the characteristics of the immediate environment, the type of neighborhood in which the station is located, and the relative position of both the station and the neighborhood in the city (Ceccato, 2013). The temporal dimension (peak/off-peak, day of the week, and season) was considered an important dimension of the study. The results are summarized in three articles (Ceccato, 2013; Ceccato & Uittenbogaard, 2014; Ceccato et al., 2013) that independently report the importance of FP as a data collection tool. They highlight some of the challenges of validity (content and criterion), in other words, the adequacy of CPTED principles applied to transit environments as well as among the different measures.

Shopping centers

The study showed that violent and property crimes and acts of public disturbance in shopping environments are spatially and temporally clustered in three-dimensional space. In order to assess the environments where crime is most concentrated, a systematic and detailed inspection of the crime locations in the shopping center (including photographic documentation) using FPs was conducted together with an assessment of the surrounding area of the shopping center.

Results from the visualization combined with the fieldwork inspection provided the basis for making suggestions for improvement of the most targeted settings and/or areas in the shopping center. The results are illustrated in Table 2. This analysis was also combined with perception of safety by visitors and published in two publications (Ceccato, 2018; Ceccato et al., 2018) reporting the adequacy and challenges of using FPs when different data sourses do not match each other (criterion validity) and when FPs are used in public places that are privately owned.

Parks

The inspection of these two parks brought out a range of issues often found in previous women's safety audits: broken lights, places where it is difficult to get one's bearings (lack of signs), bushes growing in places which would make individuals feel unsafe, graffiti, trash, dogs running around freely, slippery pavement in the winter, prohibited parking areas, and bikers riding on walking paths. These two studies indicate that the most important methodological challenge was to translate CPTED principles into features that could be identified in the parks using FPs to serve as an inventory tool to pinpoint safety problems. Features of territoriality, activity support and target hardening were visible, as was park maintenance. Also, the size of the park made it difficult to control the whole area, and in some places, the design made it permeable for cars. As expected, the problem of poor inter-observer reliability was much more evident in the safety survey in Vilnius park than in the Stockholm case study. However, FPs were regarded as useful tools of data collection and fieldwork analysis (Details see Ceccato & Hanson, 2013; Iqbal & Ceccato, 2016). Some of the most important challenges are discussed in detail in the next section.

Assessment of fieldwork protocols

Table 3 summarizes how well FPs perform in terms of validity, reliability, and generalizability of the evidence captured by one or more observers in the environment of subway stations, shopping centers, and parks. By comparing the evidence from FPs among themselves as a safety inventory tool (stations, a shopping center, and parks) and with other data sources, one can assess how well this evidence can establish links with these environments. Below we provide a few examples.

Table 3 shows that when using FPs for all three types of public places it is easier for the observer (the one inspecting the environment) to ensure content validity (how successfully the FP has actually achieved what it set out to do by covering all dimensions under CPTED principles) than criterion validity (e.g. the extent to which observer measures are correlated with other, pre-captured measures). Example: High robbery rates are often validated against measures of poor surveillance or other environmental features of places that

Table 2. Examples of places most in need of intervention along CPTED principles.

Types of environment	Main safety issues
(a) **Functional spaces**  	*permeable spaces *poor territoriality markers *lack of access control *easy escape *unintended use of premises
(a)  	*poor natural surveillance (blocked view, hidden spots) *access control & permeable spaces *image/poor management
(a)  	*tight corridors *disruption by physical barriers * poor natural surveillance – stalls affect visibility *products easy to steal
(a) **Entrances/Exits**  	*illumination *easy escape *lack of access control

(*Continued*)

Table 2. (Continued).

Types of environment		Main safety issues
(a) 		*illumination *easy escape *alcohol/drug use *rowdy youngsters *unintended use of premises

Source: Ceccato et al. (2018, p. 201).

promote anonymity (the criterion). Content validity is dependent on the theoretical preparedness and experience of the observer: how well they can transfer their knowledge into the protocol. The observer can ensure that by making sure that all dimensions of the FPs cover the theoretical principles that are being tested. Different types of public place pose challenges to the performance of FPs in terms of validity. They perform better in subway stations (albeit depending on the part of the station) than they do in shopping centers and parks. High validity is found, for instance, in built-up areas of the parks, but low validity in open, forested, or the most remote areas.

Reliability over time is the extent to which data collected are consistent over time, e.g. data collected at rush hour compared with data recorded at the same time of the day. Example: Noise levels in decibels at a subway station's platform at early rush hour should be similar to noise levels recorded on other days at about the same time. Concerning *reliability* of the measures *over time*, the protocol also scores higher in subway stations than in other environments. Open spaces, such as parks, impose the biggest challenge to the use of FPs, because they vary over time, even more so for a park (unpredicted flow of visitors) than for an indoor shopping mall (predicted flow of visitors).

Internal consistency is dependent on the stability of the measurements across items in the protocol, typically a measure based on the correlations between different items on the same test. In our case studies, we have seen examples when high scores of poorly maintained place correlated with high scores of 'poorly lighted,' broken lamps, damage illustrating a high score for internal consistency.

It is expected that an FP should promote *inter-observer reliability*, i.e. different observers should show a capacity to identify 'the same reality' or similar evidence when assessing CPTED principles in a particular place. This means that an experienced researcher identifies evidence of territoriality (e.g. detects the presence of a wall between private and public space) in a way similar to how a novice student would, guided by the same FP. This is because the use of FPs assumes that observers share a similar theoretical template to be able to identify similar 'things' in the environment that indicate a problem with safety, or 'environmental weakness' (Ekblom, 2011).

Table 3. Validity, reliability, and generalizability of evidence from fieldwork protocols by type of environment.

		Environmental features – safety inventory		
		Subway stations	Shopping center	Parks
Validity	Content	**High** – depends on the parts of the station, e.g. high validity in the platform but low in transition or surrounding areas. CPTED theory fits well for micro-spaces, but not all elements of it.	**Medium** – depends on the parts and size of the shopping center, e.g. high validity in functional spaces such as stores but low in transition areas and entrances. Theory – as for subways.	**Medium/Low** – not all CPTED principles can be tested in parks (e.g. territoriality). Park size and city location impose limitations to fieldwork protocols. High validity in built-up areas of the park, low in open areas.
	Criterion	**Medium** – factors collected by the protocol do not always automatically indicate causal links with pre-existent measures, e.g. the evidence of presence of CCTVs in a station by the protocol does not automatically validate good levels of surveillance at the station at a particular time and/or in the future.	**Medium** – fieldwork protocols suggest that high levels of luminance in a store (or other functional places) do not automatically validate good levels of illumination or high declared levels of perceived safety, at a particular time or in the future (predictive validity).	**Medium** – as in stations and shopping environments, it is not easy to ascertain the extent to which a measure is related to an outcome using the fieldwork protocol, because causality also depends on pre-existent measures as well as the knowledge and experience of the observer/researcher.
Reliability	Time	**High/medium** – based on the assumption that the use of fieldwork protocols (with the same questions, categories and procedures) can be repeated over time. It is crucial to identify beforehand temporal patterns before comparisons are made, e.g. peak and off-peak hours at subway.	**High/medium** – fieldwork protocols produce stable and consistent results as an inventory safety tool. As in stations, knowledge about potential temporal variations of a phenomenon in the shopping center over time is fundamental, such as the number of visitors to the center by hours of the day, days of the week and season.	**Medium/low** – a park's environment is bound to change with daily, weekly, and seasonal variations (in particular in contexts where winters include cold temperatures), which limits the degree to which fieldwork protocols as an inventory safety tool produce stable and consistent results.
	Internal	**High** – fieldwork protocols used in stations measure whether several items (that propose to measure the same general construct) produce similar scores.	**High** – as in stations, standardized entrance halls facilitate comparisons between different items (e.g. indoor illumination) on the same test using dummy or numerical scales.	**Medium/low** – fieldwork protocols might impose limitations when used for parks because of heterogeneous differences of the park environments, size and location.
	Observer	**High** – passengers at particular times share commonalities (they are all in transit, going somewhere), which facilitates the use of fieldwork protocols and comparisons within and between groups at particular times.	**Medium** – visitors to a shopping center are far from being homogeneous, looking for different products and/or services. Fieldwork protocols and comparisons within and between groups can be facilitated by grading and Likert scales but also by photographs and notes from different observers.	**Medium** – as in shopping centers, park visitors are far from being homogeneous (passing through to school, sitting on benches, drinking), but they all share a commonality: they are spending time at the park. Fieldwork protocols allow for a variety of different park users in urban planning to increase validity of the tool.

(*Continued*)

Table 3. (Continued).

	Environmental features – safety inventory		
	Subway stations	Shopping center	Parks
Generalizability	**High/medium** – fieldwork protocols using CPTED principles when applied to stations can easily be generalized throughout the transit system, although differences in contexts (inner city, end stations) impose limitations to the degree of generalization.	**Medium** – potential causal links between crime and types of environments in a shopping center obtained using a fieldwork protocol can be generalizable to other types of shopping centers. However, shopping centers vary highly in size, complexity of services, and location.	**Medium** – as in shopping centers, parks vary highly in size and function (urban forests, neighborhood parks, water parks) as well as location, limiting the generalizability of findings coming from fieldwork protocols, either from inventory of crime location and/or perception of safety.

However, it is not always easy to impose this 'common template' from the start, since we may all come together with 'different cognitive templates' regardless how many years of experience as observers we have. This is well illustrated by Ekblom (2011) in his attempt to define 'territoriality' in CPTED. The author points out the difficulty of choosing indicators of territoriality in the field, between the 'real and obvious' hinders and 'the symbolic and subtle' barriers:

> In practical terms (territoriality) is realized often through barriers both symbolic (such as signage or changes in road surface), and real (such as fences defining particular spaces). (Ekblom, 2011)

The difficulty of keeping a high *inter-observer reliability* can be remediated if observers are always well-trained based on the same visual cues before they set off for the fieldwork. From the example above, this means that observers should discuss thoroughly 'the visual cues and boundaries' of CPTED definitions before they go to fieldwork.

A high inter-observer reliability becomes a challenge when CPTED principles are imposed in different country/cultural contexts (Armitage, 2013; Ekblom, 2011). Ekblom (2011) suggests that the concepts and the practical definitions of territoriality – for instance, public, semi-public, and private space as suggested by Newman (1972) – are likely to be individually and culturally determined, particularly with regard to the balance of the individual versus the collective dimensions. The author states that 'territoriality also requires particular roles to be understood: owner, occupier, visitor, intruder and so forth' (Ekblom, 2011, p. 23).

We argue here that poor *inter-observer reliability* promoted by FPs (resulting, say, from observers varying widely on how they assess a particular reality) is not necessarily a limitation of the tool for practical purposes. This is because these differences in perceptions and opinions indicated by observers can be a desirable feature in participatory planning schemes, reflecting perhaps a more interdisciplinary take on a problem.

Overall, when all these criteria were assessed together, FPs scored higher in transit environments than they did in those environments found in shopping centers or parks with regards to generalizability (Tables 3 and 4).

This means that conclusions about a station (drawn from the evidence in these protocols) can more easily be generalized throughout the transit system than it can be done for information collected for a shopping center or a park. The standardization of transit systems is the reason for this outcome. While 100 subway stations have some similar elements in their design, structure and size, shopping centers vary greatly, from a strip mall with a limited number of stores, to a large grouping of establishments with a number of eclectic services and functions, including sports, culture, and entertainment. In summary, Table 4 indicates that FPs applied to subway stations scored 'high' in all three aspects of evaluation (validity, reliability, and generalizability), while parks did not score 'high' in any of them.

Discussion of the results

Drawing from section 4.1, results show that safety inventories in subway stations, a shopping center, and parks indicate the adequacy of FPs as a tool for data collection through observation. Using different methods of analysis, each individual study illustrates environmental features were captured using FPs. However, FPs as a safety inventory tool for data collection are not free of problems. Some of the challenges relate to validity (content and criterion), in other words, the adequacy of CPTED principles applied to transit environments as well as among the different measures. Others are related to reliability or generalizability.

Overall, FPs are better suited for collecting on-site information for subway stations than for shopping centers or parks. Note, however, that these conclusions are dependent on the following three assumptions.

(1) The observer starts from similar theoretical principles of CPTED/environmental criminology and fear of crime when employing this protocol, which is not always the case. There might be variations in knowledge and experience with the tool or theories that are bound to affect what one sees in reality. On top of that, cultural differences in the way observers approach CPTED are bound to affect the use of

Table 4. Overall assessment of validity, reliability and generalizability of FPs applied to subway stations, shopping center and parks.

	Environmental features collected using FPs*		
	Subway stations	Shopping center	Parks
Validity	*High*	*Medium*	*Medium/Low*
	Medium	*Medium*	*Medium*
Reliability	*High/Medium*	*High/Medium*	*Medium/Low*
	High	*High*	*Medium/Low*
	High	*Medium*	*Medium*
Generalizability	*High/medium*	*Medium*	*Medium*
	3 High	**4 Medium**	**3 Medium**
	1 Medium/High	**1 High**	**3 Medium/Low**
	1 Medium	**1 High/Medium**	

[a]For example, because of differences of the park environments, size and location, the internal reliability of FPs for parks was classified as *medium/low* while for FPs for stations, where the standardization of the stations facilitates internal reliability, the score assigned was *high*.

FPs (as reference, see the previous discussion about *territoriality*, pointed out by Ekblom (2011)) and how the data collected on-site are interpreted as evidence.

(2) The evidence from the protocols is compared with other data sources, and among types of environment, as done in this study. This ensures a certain degree of validity of the evidence collected in the field.

(3) The relationship between safety and environment captured by the observer is dependent on city-country contexts as well as temporal variations at the time of data collection. Issues of *generalizability* have to be considered for each particular case. As previously discussed, *generalizability* is not always a desirable or relevant feature of research and should not be considered as the 'only' measure of the quality of FPs for data collection. Qualitative meta-synthesis (summarized qualitative findings from disparate studies into a single framework) should be encouraged (Finfgeld-Connett, 2010; Leung, 2015), since the search for *generalizability* from different types of studies and frameworks is fundamental to create a common base for practice and policy.

Conclusions and recommendations

The aim of this study was to report on the experiences of FPs as a guide for taking inventory of safety conditions in public places. By using validity, reliability, and generalizability criteria, we assessed how well these FPs worked for collecting data in subway stations, parks, and shopping centers. The article summarizes more than 10 years of the research in this field in Sweden and Lithuania, involving different observers using similar FPs. These protocols varied in the way they were employed in the field, from well-structured checklists in subway stations, to a loose itinerary template employed in safety walks in parks. Although the inspection of an environment using protocols is not conclusive with regards as to whether the environment is the main cause of crime, this article provides some evidence as to how data gathered by these tools can help elucidate the links between crime and environment in a more systematic way. This also applies to the use of protocols to capture the relationship between environment and people's perceived safety.

This study also makes an important theoretical contribution to CPTED frameworks. It shows that in conjunction with data mapped using BIM diagrams and GIS, CPTED principles implemented in these FPs can provide a solid toolkit for inspecting safety conditions in public places. Further hypothesis testing with data from FPs can be executed using more structured ways of collecting data, as illustrated in Appendix. Data permitting, future research should devote time to test, in a more rigorous manner, the potential of FPs for data collection by better controlling content validity and reliability parameters (time and inter-user). This route of development requires improvements in this analytical model, as suggested by Ekblom (2011), improvements that demand an in-depth discussion of the basic constructs behind each element of CPTED before any fieldwork starts.

In particular, future research should devote time to improving *inter-observer reliability* of the data collected using the FPs. This means that different observers should show a capacity to identify (or perceive) similar evidence when assessing CPTED principles in a particular place. Issues of 'minimum agreeable knowledge' of the theoretical concepts among observers before starting the fieldwork would be desirable in future studies, not only related to crime (e.g. CPTED, situational crime prevention, routine activity) but also perceived safety (e.g. basic notions about environmental and personal triggers of fear).

This also involves a discussion of 'a minimum sample of observers' and 'group representativeness' (number of participants by type inspecting an area) taking part in the fieldwork before drawing conclusions about 'types of observer' and 'perceptions of safety' for a particular environment. For detection of problems with both crime and perception of safety, the use of grading and Likert scales as well as photographs and notes can facilitate and guide comparability between measures from different observers. Internet, mobile phones, and apps of all sorts should be further explored to facilitate data collection. Regardless of the method, pre-tests such as pilot studies using principles of research validity, reliability, and generalizability are encouraged before applying FPs in full as an inventory tool in a particular study.

Future studies using FPs should reflect upon the importance of conclusions drawn based on specific urban and rural contexts. The difference in nature and magnitude of security problems faced by cities of the Global South also demands a consideration of whether the available planning tools and theories are adequate for interpreting their critical problems. For instance, one wonders what CPTED means for architects and urban planners engaged in planning refugee camps, where women and children are often victims of sexual abuse. Similarly, practical challenges are also faced by safety experts performing fieldwork inspection in residential areas where walls are made of cardboard and streets lack asphalt and illumination.

This study shows evidence that FPs can be a valuable tool in planning because they can be used by a wide variety of groups of experts and in different circumstances and offer a wide range of benefits to participants from different backgrounds. However, as any other tool, they are not problem-free. Based on current evidence, FPs perform better in subway stations (albeit depending on the part of the station) than they do in shopping centers and parks. FPs, as part of safety walks in particular, have potential as suggested by Dymén and Ceccato (2012) to be a supportive tool for urban planners and safety experts to engage individuals to take action and 'correct' safety problems while contributing to citizens' empowerment.

Disclosure statement

No potential conflict of interest was reported by the author.

Funding

This work was supported by the Boverket National Board of Housing, Building and Planning [8061/2018].

References

Armitage, R. (2013). *Crime prevention through housing design: policy and practice*. Basingstoke, UK: Palgrave Macmillan.

Armitage, R., Monchuk, L., & Rogerson, M. (2011). It looks good, but what is it like to live there? Exploring the impact of innovative housing design on crime. *European Journal on Criminal Policy and Research, 17*, 29–54.

Bamzar, R. (2019). Assessing the quality of the indoor environment of senior housing for a better mobility: A Swedish case study. *Journal of Housing and the Built Environment, 34*(1), 23–60. doi:10.1007/s10901-018-9623-4.

Brantingham, P., & Brantingham, P. (1995). Criminality of place: Crime generators and crime attractors. *European Journal on Criminal Policy and Research, 3*, 1–26.

Ceccato, V. (2013). *Moving safely: Crime and perceived safety in Stockholm's subway stations*. Plymouth: Lexington.

Ceccato, V. (2016). Public space and the situational conditions of crime and fear. *International Criminal Justice Review, 26*, 69–79.

Ceccato, V., Falk, Ö., Parsanezhad, P., & Tarandi, V. (2018). Crime in a Scandinavian shopping centre. In A.R. Ceccato V. (Ed.), *Retail crime: International evidence and prevention* (pp. 179–213). Cham: Palgrave Macmillan.

Ceccato, V., & Bamzar, R. (2016). Elderly victimization and fear of crime in public spaces. *International Criminal Justice Review, 26*, 115–133.

Ceccato, V., Haining, R., & Signoretta, P. (2002). Exploring crime statistics in Stockholm using spatial analysis tools. *Annals of the Association of American Geographers, 22*, 29–51.

Ceccato, V., & Lukyte, N. (2011). Safety and sustainability in a city in transition: The case of Vilnius, Lithuania. *Cities, 28*(1), 83–94. doi:10.1016/j.cities.2010.10.001

Ceccato, V., & Hansson, M. (2013). Experiences from assessing safety in Vingis park, Vilnius, Lithuania. *Review of European Studies, 5*(5), 1–16.

Ceccato, V., & Paz, Y. (2017). Crime in São Paulo's metro system: Sexual crimes against women. *Crime Prevention and Community Safety, 19*, 211–226.

Ceccato, V., & Uittenbogaard, A.C. (2014). Space–time dynamics of crime in transport nodes. *Annals of the Association of American Geographers, 104*, 131–150.

Ceccato, V., Uittenbogaard, A.C., & Bamzar, R. (2013). Safety in Stockholm's underground stations: The importance of environmental attributes and context. *Security Journal, 26*, 33–59.

Ceccato, V., Tcacencu, S. (2018). Perceived safety in a shopping centre: A Swedish case study. In V. C. A & R. Armitage (Eds.), *Retail crime* (pp. 215–242). Cham: Palgrave Macmillan.

Clark, V., & Creswell, J.W. (2011). *Designing and conducting mixed methods research*. Thou-sand Oaks, CA: Sage.

Clarke, R.V. (1983). Situational crime prevention: Its theoretical basis and practical scope. In M. M. Tonry, N (Ed.), *Crime and justice: An annual review* (pp. 225–256). Chicago: University of Chicago Press.

Clarke, R.V. (1997). *Situational crime prevention: Successful case studies*. New York, NY: Harrow & Heston.

Clarke, R.V. (2012). *The theory of crime prevention through environmental design*. Rutgers University, NJ: CPTED.

Cohen, L.E., & Felson, M. (1979). Social change and crime rate trends: A routine activity approach. *American Sociological Review, 44*, 588–608.

Cozens, P., & Love, T. (2015). A review and current status of crime prevention through environmental design (CPTED). *Journal of Planning Literature, 30*, 393–412.

Cozens, P.M., Saville, G., & Hillier, D. (2005). Crime prevention through environmental design (CPTED): A review and modern bibliography. *Property Management, 23*, 328–356.

Creswell, J.W. (2013). *Qualitative inquiry & research design: Choosing among five approaches*. Thousand Oaks, CA: Sage.

Crowe, T. (2000). *Crime prevention through environmental design: Applications of architectural design and space management concepts*. Oxford: Butterworth-Heinemann.

de Melo, S.N., Matias, L.F., & Andresen, M.A. (2015). Crime concentrations and similarities in spatial crime patterns in a Brazilian context. *Applied Geography*, *62*, 314–324.

DeKeseredy, W.S., Donnermeyer, J.F., & Schwartz, M.D. (2009). Toward a gendered second generation CPTED for preventing woman abuse in rural communities. *Security Journal*, *22*, 178–189.

Dymén, C., & Ceccato, V. (2012). An international perspective of the gender dimension in planning for urban safety. In V. Ceccato (Ed.), *The urban fabric of crime and fear* (pp. 311–339). Netherlands: Springer.

Ekblom, P. (2011). Deconstructing CPTED... and reconstructing it for practice, knowledge management and research. *European Journal on Criminal Policy and Research*, *17*, 7–28.

Ekblom, P. (2019). Sharpening up CPTED – Towards an ontology based on crime science and ecology. In P. Ekblom & R. Armitage (Eds.), *Rebuilding crime prevention through environmental design: Strengthening the links with crime science*. (pp. 266). Abingdon, Oxon: Routledge.

Felson, M. (1995). Those who desincourage crime. In (Eds.), *Crime and place* (pp. 53-66). Monsey, NY: Criminal Justice Press.

Felson, M. (2002). *Crime and everyday life*. Thousand Oaks: Sage.

Finfgeld-Connett, D. (2010). Generalizability and transferability of meta-synthesis research findings. *Journal of Advanced Nursing*, *66*, 246–254.

Grönlund, B. (2012). Is hammarby sjöstad a model case? Crime prevention through environmental design in Stockholm, Sweden. In V. Ceccato (Ed.), *The urban fabric of crime and fear* (pp. 283–310). Netherlands: Springer.

Iqbal, A., & Ceccato, V. (2016). Is CPTED useful to guide the inventory of safety in parks? A study case in Stockholm, Sweden. *International Criminal Justice Review*, *26*, 150–168.

Jacobs, J. (1961). *The death and life of great American cities*. New York: Vintage Books.

Jeffery, C.R. (1977). *Crime prevention through environmental design*. Beverly Hills: Sage.

Kajalo, S., & Lindblom, A. (2010). The perceived effectiveness of surveillance in reducing crime at shopping centers in Finland. *Property Management*, *28*, 47–59.

Kelley, T.L. (1972). *Interpretation of educational measurements*. New York: Macmillan.

Leung, L. (2015). Validity, reliability, and generalizability in qualitative research. *Journal of Family Medicine and Primary Care*, *4*, 324–327.

Lindblom, A., & Kajalo, S. (2011). The use and effectiveness of formal and informal surveillance in reducing shoplifting: A survey in Sweden, Norway and Finland. *The International Review of Retail, Distribution and Consumer Research*, *21*, 111–128.

Loukaitou-Sideris, A. (2012). Safe on the move: The importance of the built environment. In V. Ceccato (Ed.), *The urban fabric of crime and fear* (pp. 85–110). Netherlands: Springer.

Németh, J. (2012) Controlling the commons: How public is public space? *Urban Affairs Review*.

Newman, O. (1972). *Defensible space – Crime prevention through urban design*. New York: Collier Books.

Pain, R. (2000). Place, social relations and the fear of crime: A review. *Progress in Human Geography*, *24*, 365–387.

Reynald, D.M., & Elffers, H. (2009). The future of Newman's defensible space theory: Linking defensible space and the routine activities of place. *European Journal of Criminology*, *6*, 25–46.

Rhodes, W., & Conly, C. (1981). Crime and mobility: An empirical study. In P.J. Brantingham & P. L. Brantingham (Eds.), *Environmental criminology* (pp. 167–188). Beverly Hills; Canada: Sage.

Saville, G. 2013. Third generation of CPTED. www.alternation.ca.

Saville, G. (2018). *SafeGrowth: Building neighborhoods of safety & livability 230*. Charleston: CreateSpace.

Saville, G., & Clear, T. (2000). Community renaissance with community justice. *The Neighborworks Journal*, *18*, 18–24.

Shaftoe, H., & Read, T. (2005). Planning out crime: The appliance of science or an act of faith?. In N. Tilley (Ed.), *Handbook of crime prevention and community safety* (pp. 245–265). Devon, UK: Willan Publishing.

Sutton, A., Cherney, A., & White, R. (2008). *Evaluating crime prevention*. Melbourne: Cambridge University Press.

Weisburd, D., Morris, N., & Groff, E. (2009). Hot spots of juvenile crime: A longitudinal study of arrest incidents at street segments in Seattle, Washington. *Journal of Quantitative Criminology, 25*, 443–467.

Wikström, P.-O.H., & Treiber, K. (2017). Beyond risk factors: an analytical approach to crime prevention. In B. Teasdale & M.S. Bradley (Eds.), *Preventing crime and violence* (pp. 73–87). Cham: Springer International Publishing.

Wikström, P.-O.H., Mann, R.P., & Hardie, B. (2018). Young people's differential vulnerability to criminogenic exposure: Bridging the gap between people- and place-oriented approaches in the study of crime causation. *European Journal of Criminology, 15*, 10–31.

Appendix – Example of fieldwork protocol: Stockholm's subway stations

Idstation = Station's ID, Station name, Station code, Characteristics of the station's platform (horizontal) and Selection of stations by line Red, Blue and Green (vertical).

Example of variables*

Idstation	Station name	Station code	PVis	Pillu	Pcorn	Phide	Psun	Ploun	PSur
1	T Centralen	T_1	M	y	n	y	n	n	M
2	T Centralen	T_2	H	y	n	n	n	n	H
3	T Centralen	T_3	H	y	y	n	n	n	M
4	Slussen	Slu	M	y	n	y	n	n	L
5	Gamla Stan	GaS	M	y	n	y	n	n	L
6	Fridhemsplan	F_B	M	y	y	y	n	n	M
7	Fridhemsplan	F_G	M	y	y	y	n	n	L
8	Hjulsta	Hju	H	y	n	y	n	n	H
9	Akalla	Aka	H	y	n	y	n	n	M
10	Tensta	Ten	M	y	n	y	n	n	M
11	Husby	Hub	H	y	n	y	n	n	M
12	Rinkeby	Rib	M	y	y	y	n	n	M
13	Kista	Kis	M	y	n	y	y	y	M
14	Rissne	Ris	H	y	n	n	n	n	H
15	Hallonbergen	Hab	H	y	n	y	n	n	M
16	Duvbo	Duv	H	y	n	n	n	n	H
17	Näckrosen	När	H	y	n	y	n	n	M
18	Sundbyberg Centrum	Sbg	M	y	y	y	n	n	L
19	Vreten	Vre	M	y	n	y	n	n	M
20	Huvudsta	Huv	H	y	n	n	n	n	H
21	Solna Centrum	SoC	H	y	n	y	n	n	M
22	Västra Skogen	VäS	M	y	y	y	n	n	M
23	Stadshagen	Sha	H	y	y	y	n	n	M
24	Rådhuset	Råd	H	y	y	y	n	n	L
25	Kungsträdgården	Ktg	M	y	y	y	n	n	L
26	Hässelby Strand	HäS	M	y	n	n	y	n	H
27	Hässelby Gård	HäG	H	y	n	y	y	n	H
28	Johannelund	Jol	H	y	n	n	y	n	L
29	Vällingby	Vby	M	n	y	n	n	n	M
30	Råcksta	Råc	H	y	n	y	y	n	M

PVis	Platform – high visibility	H/M/L
Pillu	Platform – sufficient/effective illumination	Y/N
Pcorn	Platform – dark corners	Y/N
Phide	Platform – hiding places	Y/N
Psun	Platform – sun light easily illumantes the covered places	Y/N
Ploun	Platform – lounge is easily visible	Y/N
PSur	Platform -high potential surveillance	H/M/L

a*Note that variables were whenever possible collected for all sections of the stations: platform, lounges, transition area, exits and immediate surroundings.*

Example of variables – Pvis = Visibility at platform; Pillu = Illumination conditions at platform; Pcorn = Presence of dark corners at platforms; Phide = Hiding places at platform; PSun = Sunlight easily illuminates platform; PLoun = Platform visibility towards lounge area; PSur = Possibility of surveillance by others at platform.

Index

Note: Page numbers in **bold** indicate tables; those in *italics* indicate figures.